Passport To The Best Of

CAPE TOWN

SOUTH AFRICA

PASSPORT PUBLICATIONS (SA) CC
CAPE TOWN · SOUTH AFRICA

Photo Credits (a-z):

Airport Company of South Africa, Aquila Private Game Reserve, Artscape Theatre, Aubergine Restaurant, Bantry Bay Luxury Apartments, Billie Boutique, Blowfish Restaurant, Boulders Beach Lodge, Cape Capers, Cape Town City Ballet, Carrie Hampton, Club Mykonos, Cape Town International Convention Centre, Diamond House, Drive Africa, Eco Tours SA, Ferryman's, Gold Dust, Gold Of Africa, Grand West Casino, Grassroute Tours, JB Rivers, Jewel of Africa, Kopanong, Mama Africa, Marimba, Mediscapes, Milnerton Golf Club, Nac Makana, Pan African Market, Paulaner Brauhaus, Peddlars on The Bend, Presidential Shirt, Robben Island Museum, Sanctuary Spa, Simonstown Penguin Festival, Societi Bistro, Sutra, Table Mountain National Park, The Cape Milner Hotel, The Clipper Restaurant, The Commodore Hotel, The Metropole Hotel, The Place on The Bay, The Safari Club, Theatre On The Bay, Thunder City, Touchline Media, Two Oceans Aquarium, V & A Waterfront, White Shark Projects, Winchester Mansions, Wine Village, Zevenwacht Restaurant.

Special thanks for the provision of photographs to South African Tourism.

Addtional maps provided by:
Canal Walk and V&A Waterfront

Special thanks:
We would like to thank the following people for their generous support and contributions in compiling this travel guide:

Carrie Hampton, Greta Wilson, Ingrid Lomas of Surgical Attractions, Ashley Lillie, Faizal Gangat of Cape Capers, Michael Carney of V&A Waterfront, Vernon Vlok, Janine Van De Venter, Karmen Flemming, Keith De Wet.

Last but not least, a very special thanks to Kathi Luxton for her incredible dedication, all the hard work and patience, without whom this publication would not have been possible.

ISBN 0-620-31698-5

This edition was first published in November 2004 by Passport Publications (SA) CC, Cape Town, South Africa

Executive Publisher:
Frank Riester
Project Manager:
Kathi Luxton
Proof Reader:
Jenny Gove
International Sales & Distribution:
Vernon Vlok
Advertising:
Janine Van De Venter
Design, Illustration & DTP:
Karmen Flemming & Keith De Wet
Pre-Press:
Robbie Frey, Resolution
Maps:
Patrick Labrosse, Paperkey
Printing:
Sino Publishing House, Hong Kong

© 2004 Passport Publications (SA) CC

Contact us:
We invite all readers to notify us of any errors, changes or outdated information. Please write to the following address:

Passport Publications (SA) CC
P.O. Box 415
Constantia 7848
South Africa
Fax: (27) 21.794.0658
Email: info@gopassport.com
www.gopassport.com

AUTHOR - CARRIE HAMPTON

As I arrived to review a guest house in Knysna, a little girl came racing up to me and asked without hesitation, *"Are you the trouble maker?"*

Since I hadn't been there for more than a moment I wondered how she knew. Then she blurted out, *"my Daddy told me a trouble maker was coming to see us."* Travel Writer..... Trouble maker - easily confused, but out of the mouth of babes.......

Small moments can be as memorable as greater occasions, and inspire me in my job as a travel writer. So does sharing my acquired knowledge about Cape Town - the place in the world I have chosen to put down roots. Over ten years ago this London-born world traveller, also arrived as a visitor to Cape Town, and the strange feeling that I had finally 'arrived' just wouldn't go away. It was so strong that however hard I tried to leave I just couldn't, so I stayed! As a result, I have been able to write this guide book from the point of view of a visitor as well as a resident, and to address the needs of both.

I have endeavoured to show you Cape Town as it really is, without glossing over the less palatable parts. I feel it is important that visitors to Cape Town have access to the full picture, which can be a source of enrichment from angles you hadn't previously considered. I feel so privileged to live here in Cape Town and hope this guide enlightens you to the many wonderful aspects of my adopted home.

Best wishes,

Carrie Hampton

Carrie Hampton has had her work published all over the world in a variety of publications. These include top UK, USA and African magazines and newspapers. 'Passport to the Best of Cape Town' is the latest in a number of African guide books written by Carrie, which include; On Safari, Adventure Traveller Southern Africa and Essential Kenya. If you do a search for "Carrie Hampton" on the internet, you will find the many websites she has written and over 50 on which her travel articles and accommodation reviews appear.

Carrie Hampton meeting Nelson Mandela

A NOTE FROM THE PUBLISHERS...

Writing a foreword on a book about Cape Town without stringing together a host of clichés has become a challenge. If you speak with someone who has visited this beautiful city, they cannot help but describe it in overused but entirely appropriate accolades such as; "Majestic Table Mountain, two oceans thundering together at Cape Point, blonde beautiful beaches, serene winelands and historically moving Robben Island."

While compiling this travel guide, it has been our goal to produce a publication offering visitors the most comprehensive information on every possible aspect of Cape Town's tourism industry. And to introduce visitors to all the best known, as well as the more unusual 'off the beaten track' sights and activities. To this end we have incorporated several categories and chapters on many unpublicised, yet incredible places to visit, sights to see, and things to do, which are not always covered in other guide books.

The categories 'Introducing Cape Town', 'General Information' and 'Travel Preparations' will arm any visitor to the Cape shores with all the information you need to plan and prepare for your time in and around the City.

All businesses and service providers in this publication were nominated following our proven quality selection criteria and present the reader with some of the finest establishments in the Western Cape. Additional details and comprehensive travel information can be found on our multi-award winning website www.gopassport.com.

We have included 40 discount vouchers and invite you to make liberal use of these during your stay. Every tourist also needs maps and for this reason we included them as an added bonus, together with some complimentary postcards to send home.

Cape Town's blend of sport and leisure activities, cultural attractions and shopping malls, combined with breathtaking scenery and landscapes, make Cape Town a tourism Mecca at the foot of "darkest Africa"…

We invite you to come and see it for yourself.

Frank Riester
Executive Publisher

Kathi Luxton
Project Manager

CITY OF CAPE TOWN | ISIXEKO SASEKAPA | STAD KAAPSTAD

**CITY OF CAPE TOWN - OFFICE OF THE MAYOR
ISIXEKO SASEKAPA - I OFISI KASODOLOPHU
STAD KAAPSTAD - KANTOOR VAN DIE BURGEMEESTER**

Cape Town has been rated as one of the most beautiful cities in the world and was voted 5th by BBC viewers as their choice of "50 places to see before you die". Tourism is a vital source of income to the City's economy and the job opportunities created by companies in this sector plays a very important role. With her rugged mountains, two oceans, gracious wine lands and magnificent skyline, combined with the friendly hospitality and international standards it offers, it is not hard to understand why visitors from all four corners of the Earth make their way towards Cape Town for their holidays and why it is one of the fastest growing cities in the world.

Over the last few years the world has seen Cape Town grow from strength to strength on many levels. Positive international attitudes and perceptions have resulted in companies investing in her economy and visitors snapping up prime property. The CBD is being transformed into a bustling metropolitan residential area and the Waterfront almost becoming a mini-city on its own. The opening of the Cape Town International Convention Centre has also attracted large numbers of foreign visitors to our shores.

It gives me great pleasure, as Mayor of Cape Town, to once again put my name to a Passport publication. 'Passport To The Best Of Cape Town' has for the past 6 years been one of Cape Town's top reference guides and have consistently produced guides of the highest quality featuring the best of what Cape Town has to offer, not only serving as a vital travel accessory to tourists visiting the City, but as an informative reference guide to locals and travel professionals as well.

The increase in size of the publication, together with the enormous effort put into the collation of the editorial, is certainly an indication of the growth not only Passport to the Best of Cape Town as a publication, but also of Cape Town as a destination. The foresight of the Publisher into the information required by a visitor is evident in the categories covered and the comprehensiveness of its content.

It therefore goes without saying that I fully endorse this prestigious and informative guide and wish Passport Publications all success with this and their future endeavours.

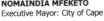

NOMAINDIA MFEKETO
Executive Mayor: City of Cape

HOW TO USE THIS GUIDE

Passport to the Best of Cape Town is designed to be entertaining as well as factually informative, and will prove to be an invaluable resource for anyone visiting this beautiful city. Our Author, Carrie Hampton, has purposely kept the style light-hearted, yet has not glossed over the less savoury aspects of an emerging city.

She has tried to give the reader a good balance of how life really is in Cape Town, which for the visitor and more fortunate resident is absolutely fantastic. Life for the poor is of course difficult and an important part of any visit to Africa, is to acknowledge all aspects of life - which ultimately gives you a more balanced perspective on your own place in the world.

COLOUR CODED SECTIONS

To make this guide as user friendly as possible, we have colour coded each of the categories which will enable readers to easily access the information they seek. A table of these colour codes has been placed on the inside front cover flap for easy reference. We have also colour coded the contents page accordingly.

Leading into each set of listings, is a double page colour photograph followed by editorial pages containing factual and fascinating local information, plus stories and anecdotes, to add extra depth to your enjoyment of Cape Town.

TELEPHONE NUMBERS

All telkom phone numbers quoted in this book include the local code, i.e. Cape Town code is 021. When dialling Cape Town from anywhere else in South Africa, you need to use this code, but it can be left out if dialling within the city. If calling South Africa from abroad, you need to use the country code: 00 27, plus the local code without the zero, i.e. for Cape Town you would dial 00 27 21, plus the local number.

PRICES

The local currency is South African Rand (ZAR). All rates and entry fees are correct at time of going to press (late 2004), but expect prices to go up annually - normally before the summer tourist season. The strength of the Rand will determine your perceived value for money, but even at its strongest, you are still likely to find South Africa good value for high quality.

We hope that by using this guide, you will have the best holiday possible in this most exquisite of cities - Cape Town.

CONTENTS - PAGE 1

CONTENTS - PAGE 2

CONTENTS - PAGE 3

The juxtaposition of worldly sophistication with African simplicity, makes Cape Town a city full of surprises. It appears more Mediterranean in style than African, until you look further than the elegant surroundings of your hotel or restaurant. Cape Town has plenty of these, plus opera, ballet, theatre, chic shopping malls, health clubs and fast cars. But the contrast to this wealth is very apparent, and you only have to drive from the airport to the city to see how the poor live.

Rich and poor are a fact of life, regardless of who is running the country, and 10 years of democracy is still a short time in which to enrich the less fortunate. The process goes on and the overwhelming success of the ANC in the 2004 elections, shows that the people still support the government, even if they haven't always felt the financial benefits personally. They are at least free, with the prospect that things will get better.

PROUDLY SOUTH AFRICAN

South Africa's citizens are proud of their country and its peaceful progress into a mature democratic state. But the country did have an enormous advantage by having the world's most revered individual as their leader - Nelson Mandela. Other heads of state pale when placed against the attributes

and spirit of this great man. His energy is instrumental in forging new pride in South Africa, which can be seen in the many burgeoning empowerment companies and uplifting township projects throughout the country. There is even a Proudly South African endorsement for any service or product who adheres to a code to promote South Africa and create jobs and economic growth. This book holds the Proudly South African stamp of approval.

CAPE TOWN QUIRKS

Capetonians are particularly proud to be so and hold dear the sights and sounds, customs and culture of their city. They hardly raise an eyebrow as the noon day gun explodes over the city, while visitors fear an attack. They hear the muezzin calling the faithful to prayer and listen to the bells of St George's Cathedral, and accept each to their own. Their easy going nature and benevolent spirit has given the city a reputation for being one of the world's least xenophobic and most tolerant.

POLYGLOT OF LANGUAGES

The variety of languages spoken in Cape Town, might lead you to believe that you will not understand anything other than English - and even then you will have to cope with some Cape lingo (for some examples see the section on Learning English under African skies). But you might understand more than you think in the streets of Cape Town. Afrikaans is a language taught only in South Africa, but Dutch visitors seem to understand it

quite well. Although perhaps not when the Cape Coloureds speak it, because their strong Cape accent may make that impossible. You may however get some gist from the often raucous and humorous way in which it is delivered. Xhosa is the language spoken by most black residents of Cape Town and is full of interesting clicks and intonations. But you might also hear French or Portuguese from Congolese and Angolans, many of whom fled their country's persistent fighting.

CAPE CLICHÉS

You've heard them all before; Fairest Cape, Mother City, Tavern of the Seas, Rainbow Nation.....but the reason these are such overused clichés, is because they are all true. Cape Town is one of the fairest places in the world, it is a city with a nurturing heart, and is a safe port of call whatever your means of getting here. Don't let these tired accolades speak for themselves, come and see Cape Town for yourself.

SCENIC SPLENDOUR

It is of course impossible to talk about Cape Town without making reference to the city's most dominating feature - Table Mountain. This monumental rock has been a guiding force for centuries and has been instrumental in creating the character of Cape Town and its people. You cannot help but be drawn to it and feel the urge to get to the top of it - not to conquer but to admire. This mountain shall not be mastered, and it if the weather is good, it is advisable not to put off until tomorrow what you could do today (which is the antithesis to most Capetonians attitude). Otherwise you may be greeted with the famous table cloth of cloud at the summit.

TOO MANY THINGS TO DO

It is impossible to be bored in Cape Town. The landscape lends itself to lots of outdoor activities, and lying on the beach in the sun can definitely be included. So can hiking up the hills and abseiling or paragliding down them. Or horse riding, kite flying, fishing, golf and sailing - information for all of these can be obtained from Cape Town Tourism (corner Castle/Burg Streets in the CBD, tel: 021 426 4260).

Culture vultures have plenty to keep them busy too with township tours and formal and informal performances of all kinds like theatre, ballet, opera and contemporary dance.

Shopping is great too, with everything from ethnic crafts to trendy Young Designers clothes in flashy malls, open markets and roadside stalls.

SOCCER WORLD CUP

South Africa won the bid to host the 2010 Soccer World Cup, and some matches will be held at Cape Town's Newlands Stadium.

INDULGING IN FOOD

South African food stores and supermarkets still tend to only stock fruits and vegetables that are in season and therefore naturally ripened. This makes a huge difference to the taste, which you will surely notice. There are so many great restaurants, but not enough time to try them all - so take your cue from this guide, and choose from our recommendations which will satisfy every kind of taste.

ECONOMY

South Africa's economy is doing incredibly well and is a testament to its sound economic policies. The Rand comes and goes in strength, which does affect tourism, but Cape Town remains a good value, high quality destination. Take reliable advice as contained in this book, and your accommodation, restaurant and touring choices will not disappoint you.

There are always a few things to consider and prepare before a holiday, and the information on this page will help smooth the way for an enjoyable visit to Cape Town.

VISAS

Tourism Offices & Embassies

SA Tourism is represented abroad - for details of your nearest SA Tourism office see their website: www.southafrica.net. For a full list of all international South African embassies and consulates, visit www.gov.za/structure/samissions.

Citizens of the United States, Canada, Australia, New Zealand, Japan and the European Union do not require a visa to stay in South Africa for visits of up to 90 days. Other nationalities should check with a travel agent. For detailed information on Relocation & Immigration see the relevant section of this book.

FLIGHT & TRANSPORT

There are direct flights from Europe to Cape Town (and plenty via Johannesburg - which adds another 2 hour flight, plus waiting time to your journey). Public transport in South Africa is limited and not of a great standard, but hire cars are affordable and easy to arrange. For a variety of transport options turn to the 'Getting Around' pages of this guide. Be warned, petrol cannot be purchased with credit cards - you will need cash for this.

DISTANCES

South Africa uses the metric system of kilometres (km): 1 mile = 1,621km

ACCOMMODATION

The range of accommodation is astonishing, with excellent quality in every price range. Check our accommodation listings for suggestions of where to stay. In the off season you don't necessarily need to book in advance, except for the most exclusive establishments, which tend to be in demand all year round.

Electricity

The South African power supply is 220/230 volts AC, with a 15 amp round pin 3-prong plug - which is different from UK, European or American plugs. Many hotels have adapters, but you might like to bring your own or buy one here. Two-pin adapters for mobile phones are widely available. Most hotels have 110 volt outlets for electric shavers.

HEALTH REQUIREMENTS & MEDCAK CARE

There is no national health scheme in South Africa, so it is wise to purchase a good travel insurance. No vaccinations are required for cholera or smallpox, but if arriving from a yellow fever zone, you must have a valid international yellow fever inoculation certificate. There is no malaria in Cape Town. Cape Town tap water is safe to drink.

DISABLED FACILITIES

Most attractions and hotels in Cape Town are wheelchair friendly. The following companies can provide services for disabled travellers: Flamingo Tours, Tel/Fax: 021 5574496, info@flamingotours.co.za, www.flamingotours.co.za and Titch Travel & Tours, Tel: 021 6894151, Fax: 021 6893760, titcheve@iafrica.com, www.harveyworld.co.za

MONEY

International credit cards such as American Express, Diners Club, Mastercard, Visa and their affiliates are very widely accepted in Cape Town and around South Africa. Thomas Cook and American Express traveller cheques are also widely accepted and can be changed at any bank, foreign exchange bureau or at the international airport. Cash can be accessed through many bank machines with your bank card or credit card (as long as you remember the code).

BEST TIME TO COME TO CAPE TOWN

Most tourists visit Cape Town during our spring and summer from October to March - with perhaps February being the best month. South African summer school holidays are usually from the first week in December to mid January, when South Africans descend on Cape Town and the Garden Route coast. Early March and Easter are also peak periods so if you are coming at any of these times it is wise to book ahead.

TEMPERATURE

Temperature is recorded in degrees Celsius (°C):

$50°F = 10°C$
$68°F = 20°C$
$86°F = 30°C$
$95°F = 35°C$

Summertime weather is very Mediterranean with little rain, 11+ hours of sunshine and long light evenings. The only thing to mar this perfect summer weather is the south east wind - which can be extremely forceful. Avoid this if you can, by finding a sheltered spot - see our 'Beaches' pages for wind-free coves.

Spring (September/October) and **Autumn** (April) are great times to visit Cape Town as these months are usually balmy in-between seasons when nature is at its showiest. If you're into flowers come in August or September, or spot whales from the land between July and October. Vineyards are heavy with fruit in January and February, but their autumn colours are stunning in May and June.

Winter nights are cold but never get to freezing point by the coast, although the further inland you go, the colder it gets, with occasional snow on mountain peaks. There will be stormy days of rain and wind followed by days or weeks of perfect sunny days with a tangy chill in the air. Time it right and winter becomes the perfect 'secret' season, with plentiful accommodation and lower rates.

WHAT TO WEAR

With the possibility of four seasons in one day, it is hard to know exactly what to pack. A jacket is essential (light for summer, thick for winter), so is a hat and sunglasses. Capetonians hardly ever use an umbrella because of the accompanying wind, so don't bother bringing one. Detailed weather forecasts of southern Africa, updated hourly and including the latest satellite image, are available at www.weather.iafrica.com

DUTY FREE

Duty Free allowance for visitors coming into South Africa is 1 litre spirits, 2 litres wine, 400 cigarettes, 50 cigars, 50ml perfume, 250ml eau de toilette and gifts & souvenirs to the value of R500. Wine and spirits are so much cheaper here than in Europe, that you'd be foolish to bring your own.

FIREARMS

Permits are required for firearms and are available at the entry points. A permit is valid for 180 days, after which it can be renewed at any South African police station. For further details contact the Customs Dept Tel: 021 413 5000.

SOUTH AFRICAN PUBLIC HOLIDAYS

South Africa has plentiful public holidays, which pleases workers but not large industry, who lose considerable working days:

1 January New Year's Day

21 March - Human Rights Day

8 April - Good Friday (Friday before Easter Sunday)

21 April - Family Day (Monday after Easter Sunday)

27 April - Freedom Day

1 May - Workers Day

16 June - Youth Day

9 August - National Women's Day

24 September - Heritage Day

16 December - Day of Reconciliation

25 December - Christmas Day

26 December - Day of Goodwill

CURRENCY & CREDIT CARDS

Time Zones

South African time is GMT +2. There are no time zone differences within South Africa and the country has not adopted a daylight time saving system in summer.

The local currency is South African Rand. Forex facilities are available all over the city and there are plenty of banks. You don't need to change money before arrival, as you can do so at the Bureau de Change at Cape Town International Airport. You can also draw money direct from your foreign bank account with your bank card or credit card. South Africa has a modern and sophisticated banking and commercial system, and most shops and hotels accept credit cards.

VAT

South Africa has VAT of 14% on most purchases and services. If you are a foreign visitor to South Africa, you can claim back the VAT on purchases taken out of the country. It is a very easy process, which can be done at Cape Town or Johannesburg International Airport, or to save time, you can attend to the paperwork at the Vat Refund Office in the V& A Waterfront (open 9am - 9pm, tel: 021 4211216 or 021 408 7600). You will bring your airline ticket, passport and receipts. You will still need to show some of the items prior to checking in your luggage at the airport. You are then given a cheque which can be cashed into any currency by the bank teller on the other side of customs.

POSTAL SERVICES & INTERNET CAFÉS

Post from Cape Town is pretty efficient but not cheap. A postcard to Europe or USA costs R3.45. A standard airmail letter up to 50grams is R4.00, but if it is birthday card shaped, it costs R13.25. It has something to do with the shape not the weight! The Post Office also offers registered mail and courier services. Other well known courier services operate from Cape Town to international destinations. Many shops will arrange transportation of large items for a fee. Postnet branches are one stop shops for many business needs like courier services, faxing, photocopying, binding, and internet stations. Independent Internet Cafés can be found all over Cape Town and charges are reasonable.

SHOPPING & BUSINESS HOURS

Telephones

The international dialling code from outside South Africa is 00 27 and the local code for Cape Town is (0)21. If dialling abroad from within South Africa you should dial 09 +country code.

Mobile phones are available for hire at the airport or at Cape Town Tourism Visitors' Centre, tel: 021 426 4260 or from CelluRent tel: (021) 418 5656, www.cellurent.co.za.

Blue public phone booths take coins (20c, 50c and R1), green public phones require Telkom phone cards. These can be purchased in post offices and many shops (some public phones advertise the closest sale point).

Most City Centre and suburburban shops open weekdays 9am - 5pm. They only open until 12.30 or 1pm on Saturdays. Supermarkets often keep longer opening hours. Large shopping malls usually close later than city shops, and stay open late into the evening and all day Saturday, Sunday and most public holidays. Government agencies and businesses keep traditional weekday business hours. Banks close at 3.30pm on weekdays, and are open on Saturday mornings from 9am to 11am. Muslim-owned businesses close between noon and 1pm on Fridays.

TIPPING

Many waiters and waitresses (waitrons) rely on tips to supplement their meagre wages. A 10% tip is acceptable or 15% if the service has been good. Tables of over eight often have an automatic 10% service charge added. A tip of R5 per piece of luggage is standard for hotel and airport porters. Tipping petrol pump attendants, who clean your windscreen and check your oil and water, is optional but R2 is a good figure.

BEGGARS

Street children and beggars at traffic lights may approach you for a handout. Social workers counsel against giving money to children as it often gets used for glue sniffing. If you wish to do something good for these children, give them food or donate to a charitable organisation that helps them. Peddlers at traffic lights, often try selling you things you don't really want, others offer to take your car rubbish or tell you a joke for a tip. Everyone is just trying to make a living.

Parking Attendants

In most shopping areas, uniformed parking attendants mind your car and help you unload your groceries in the hope of a tip. R2 is an acceptable figure. There are also 'unofficial' car guards, often in competition with one another, who whistle and wave their arms around to point out a parking bay. The City of Cape Town is committed to controlling this practice, but a tip is as gratefully received by them as anyone else. Be generous if your car guard has stayed up all night while you are dining in a warm restaurant.

SAFETY IN THE CITY

Cape Town's Central Business District and major malls make considerable efforts to safeguard against crime, and surveillance cameras are situated throughout the CBD. Nonetheless, tourists should take the sensible precautions they would in any major city. Avoid carrying large sums of cash, having cameras loose or leaving belongings unattended. Take advice from locals on where not to go after dark. Take care at lonely lookout points, especially at dusk or after dark.

WALK THE CITY

Cape Town is intent on keeping its City Centre alive and safe for all to enjoy. The Cape Town Partnership has taken this commitment seriously and has created a meaningful infrastructure through business and city council collaboration to ensure a safe and cleaner city. Cape Town is a wonderful city to walk around - go to our section 'Cape Town on Foot', for suggestions of where to go on foot.

Grand Parade and Town Hall

HEALTH MATTERS

No special medical precautions are necessary to visit Cape Town. The tap water is safe to drink - although you might prefer to use bottled water anyway. Cape Town has first-rate medical, dental and cosmetic beauty facilities, and a whole industry has evolved around medical tourism. People arrange their holidays around surgical operations, dental procedures, laser eye surgery and cosmetic surgery. Surgeon and safari holidays are popular, as are post procedure recovery at some of the relaxing spas. (See section on Medical Tourism). Visitors are advised to have travel health insurance which guarantees treatment at private hospitals.

FOOD FACTS - EATING OUT

THE CAPE'S CULINARY MIX

The Dutch established Cape Town to provide fresh produce for spice trading ships between Europe and the Far East. So it's no surprise that today Cape Town's cultural mix finds strong expression in its cuisine. Various European traditions - originally Dutch and English, but increasingly Mediterranean - merge with African ingredients and flavours and Eastern traditions brought by slaves from Malaysia and Java. Cape Town's chefs embrace the latest Asian and Pacific Rim trends, with Thai and North Indian cuisine

Jewel of India

well represented. You can trace your own spice trails across Cape Town, and dine with a different cultural emphasis each night.

WHAT'S NEW IN OUR PANTRY

The competitiveness of local markets and the sophistication of leading international chefs have pushed development of new products towards a wider range of choices. South African wines have moved with increasing stature onto the world market, and the 'local is lekker' philosophy means that chefs prefer to use local products, such as boutique cheeses, olives & olive oils, game meat and birds. In May, the Cape Gourmet Festival is a fortnight long extravaganza of fine food and wine, often starring leading international chefs. The annual September V&A Waterfront-Cape Times Wine Festival has led to a complementary Cheese Festival. (See the section entitled 'Restaurant Guide', for a list of Food & Wine events).

Peddlars On The Bend

AFFORDABLE FINE DINING

The nicest surprise about Cape Town's restaurants is how affordable they are in world terms. Take advice from this guide and SA's Top 100 Restaurant Guide, to help you choose a restaurant offering superb quality with international standards at half the price. Many eateries have superb views and most have an extensive wine list with award-winning South African wines. In Cape Town, you can eat and drink exceptionally well for about R200 per head. But for those on a budget, there are deliciously affordable alternatives and some great health food outlets. Restaurants don't usually include a service charge, so it is customary to leave a tip of 10%-15%.

The Commodore Hotel

LOCAL DELICACIES

FISH

Perlemoen (abalone) are so prized internationally that they are difficult to obtain locally.

Crayfish (Cape rock lobster) are available but expensive.

Local sea fish like kingklip, Cape salmon, and kabeljou rival the best in Japan according to local sushi chefs.

A lekker local dish is Smoorsnoek - a stew of snoek fish potatoes and tomatoes.

Slightly smelly, salted dried mullet known as Bokkoms, take some getting used but are prized by some (read West Coast section).

MEAT

Ostrich, springbok, and even more exotic meats such as zebra, kudu and crocodile are seen on many menus.

Bobotie is a favourite Cape Malay dish of curried and sweetened minced lamb or beef topped with a savoury egg custard.

A tasty Waterblommetjiebredie stew of water lily buds and lamb is something a bit different found in the Cape.

Indian inspired Samoosas of curried meat or vegetables, fried in a pastry pocket are on sale at most corner shops.

Societi Bistro

Biltong is another traditional South African snack of raw beef or game meat spiced and dried, then shaved finely or left in chunks.

TEA & CAKES

Rooibos tea is a locally produced, caffeine-free tea whose fans claim it has major health benefits.

Rusks are twice baked, hard-as-rock, coffee dunking biscuits originally made by the Voortrekkers for long journeys.

Melktert (custard tart) and koeksusters (twisted deep-fried donuts dripping in syrup) are traditional local desserts.

Tea at Mount Nelson Hotel

WELCOME
TO
CAPE TOWN

AIRPORT ARRIVALS & DEPARTURES

Fly Direct

Cape Town International gives you direct access to 21 cities in 14 different countries, and if you take a short 2-hour flight to Johannesburg, the rest of the world is at your doorstep with direct flights to 103 cities.

Parking

Automated pay stations for the public car park accepts coins, notes or credit cards, but you won't need these if you are collecting a hire car. For current parking charges call: 021 934 7698.

Post Office

There is a Post Office Counter facility alongside the Domestic Arrivals Terminal.

Porters

As with most informal services in South Africa, the porters are self-employed and rely on gratuities for their income.

Airport Upgrade

Long term planning to cope with an estimated 14 million passengers by 2015, includes; construction of a second runway, and remote parking alongside satellite terminals linked to the main complex by an underground passage.

Cape Town International Airport is a sophisticated point of arrival and departure, situated 20km east of Cape Town.

Even though it caters for over 6 million travellers a year, it has managed to retain the friendly, informal feel of a provincial airport. Arriving passengers seem to relax the moment they step into the Cape sunshine. Look straight ahead and the recognisable shape of Table Mountain confirms that you really have arrived in one of the most beautiful cities in the world!

Cape Town International Flight Enquiries tel: 021 934 0407. Website: www.airports.co.za

AIRPORT ACCOMMODATION

Only business travellers and those with a very early flight tend to stay at close proximity to the airport, the closest accommodation being the new, value for money 90-room Road Lodge Hotel (www.citylodge.co.za, tel: +27 21 943 7303). By car you can be in Central Cape Town, the V&A Waterfront or overlooking a gorgeous beach in just 20-30 minutes (outside rush hours).

TRANSPORT

Cape Town International Airport is not known for its public transport. In fact you will be hard put to find any! There is no train link or regular bus service, but there is a door to door microbus run by Magic Bus, which must be booked at least a day in advance. Cost is R140 per adult if more than one, or R195 for a single passenger. Tel: 021 505 6300, fax: 021 534 9111, email: capemagic@magic.co.za, There are plenty of private taxis, car hire firms, hotel courtesy buses and tour guides meeting clients. Add to this throng, a welcoming committee of Capetonians collecting friends and families, and the Arrivals Hall often becomes quite festive and chaotic. Watch your step outside the terminal building, as 'stop and drop' cars are so busy discarding people or looking for their passengers, they don't always notice you on the designated crossings.

VAT REFUND

International passengers exiting the country from Cape Town or Johannesburg Airports, can reclaim VAT at Cape Town International Airport. It is very easy and only takes a few minutes. Before checking in, follow the signs to the VAT Reclaim and show them your VAT receipts for goods purchased within the past 3 months. Have the items packed at the top of the bag for the clerks to see. They process the receipts and give you a VAT refund cheque, which can be cashed into any currency at a bank on the other side of customs control.

ENJOY MORE
convenience and comfort
at the airport

**Premier Club
Departures Lounges**

**Premier Club
Arrivals Lounge**

Whatever airline you fly and whatever class of ticket you hold, the Premier Club Lounges make the airport a place of productivity and pleasure.

JOHANNESBURG INTERNATIONAL AIRPORT
International Departures   +27 11 921 6459
Domestic Departures   +27 11 394 0727
Arrivals Lounge   +27 11 390 3860

DURBAN INTERNATIONAL AIRPORT
Domestic Departures   +27 31 469 2811

PORT ELIZABETH AIRPORT
Domestic Departures   +27 41 581 6381

CAPE TOWN INTERNATIONAL AIRPORT
International Departures   +27 21 936 2127
Domestic Departures   +27 21 936 3014

The Premier Club
Airport Lounges

Everyone's Lounge

LUXURY TRAINS
Blue Train

The state-owned Blue Train is the luxurious option for travelling between Cape Town and Johannesburg.

Rovos Rail

There is also Rovos Rail, who claim to be "The Most Luxurious Train in the World," because of the size of their cabins. You will experience silver service, champagne in crystal glasses, haute cuisine and superior comfort on both these trains. Blue Train tel: 021 449 2672, torros@transnet. co.za. Rovos Rail tel: 021 421 4020, reservations@rovcos.co.za, www.rovos.co.za.

Old Donkey Cart

Drive Africa

FINDING YOUR WAY AROUND

Table Mountain is bang smack in the middle of Cape Town, which makes a direct route to anywhere pretty impossible. It does however, provide a good reference point to help you find your way around. Seeing the city by foot, scooter or car is easy, but good public transport in the city centre or between main areas of interest is sadly lacking.

TRAINS

Cape Town Station in Adderley Street services local and national rail networks. Spoornet operates all mainline services (tel: 086 000 8888), and Cape Metro Rail runs the suburban services (tel: 080 065 6463). Trains run once a day from Cape Town to Johannesburg departing 10am, and take about 24 hours (not taking delays into account). Cost one-way is approximately R495. Website: www.spoornet.co.za

COAST TRAIN

The local train from Cape Town to the end of the line at Simon's Town, runs right along the coast from Muizenberg, giving fabulous sea views, which from July-September may include whales. There is a special restaurant carriage offering breakfast, lunch and snacks, tel Biggsy's: 021 449 3870. Please exercise caution with your belongings. To check on train safety ask the Tourist Information Centre tel: 021 426 4260.

BUSES

Golden Arrow buses do not service Cape Town CBD, but they do run along the Atlantic Seaboard to such towns as Seapoint, Camps Bay and Hout Bay, and to other suburbs and townships. Buses depart from the central bus terminus in Strand Street opposite the Railway Station. Surprisingly, they often run on time and apart from rush hour (4-6pm), are pretty empty. For information tel: 080 121 2111.

COACH SERVICES

Inter city coaches run between Cape Town and most other cities. They depart from the coach terminus beside Cape Town's railway station. Tel Greyhound: 021 505 6363, Translux tel: 021 449 3333, Intercape tel: 0861 287287

TAXIS

Metered taxis are usually ordered on demand by the restaurant or hotel. They don't just drive around waiting to be hailed like New York or London taxis, although you are likely to find some at night outside clubs and bars. Ask the expected fare before getting in e.g. from the V&A Waterfront to Long Street is about R45-50 one way in a metered taxi. Seapoint Taxis tel: 021434 4444, Marine Taxis tel: 021 434 0434, Unicab tel: 021 448 1720.

MINIBUS TAXIS

These are usually battered minibuses often booming with music and shouting passenger touts. They drive like lunatics through main thoroughfares and pull out and stop without warning. Beware of them on the road. This is the main form of transport from the townships, but for safety reasons are best avoided by the visitor.

CAR HIRE

There are many car hire companies in Cape Town. You can collect and dropoff at the airport or take delivery at any address. An International Driving Permit is required' if your licence is not printed in English. Don't forget to drive on the left. Hertz tel: 0861 600136, Avis tel: 021 934 0330, Tempest Car Hire: 021 424 5000, Budget tel: 086 101 6622, Britz 4x4 Rental tel: 021 981 8947. Automobile Association Tel: 021 419 6914, website: www.aasa.co.za

PETROL/GASOLINE

All types of petrol and diesel are available. Credit cards cannot be used to pay for petrol, you will need cash for this. Don't even bother getting out of your vehicle, as an attendant will fill your tank, clean the windscreen and check your oil, water and tyres. Garage attendants survive on tips, so keep some R2 coins handy.

BICYCLES, MOTORBIKES, SCOOTERS & QUAD BIKES

Several companies offer bicycle tours in the beautiful surroundings of Cape Point Nature Reserve or the Winelands. This is far preferable to cycling in the car-crowded city. Daytrippers tel: 021 511 4766, Adventure Village tel: 424 1580.

Scooters are pretty popular too and can be hired all over the place. Adelphi Enduro tel: 021 439 6144, South African Motor Cycle Tours tel: 794 7887.

Cruise the coast on a BMW or Harley Davidson; BMW Motorcycles & Scooter Hire cell: 083 377 8833, www.motoberlin.co.za. Harley Davidson Rentals tel: 021 434 2603. Quad bike trips can be fun, contact Cape Quad, tel: 021 556 6724.

AIR

Cape Town International Airport is an easy car journey 20km east of central Cape Town. Flight Enquiries Tel: 021 934 0407, www.airports.co.za

There is no train link or regular bus service, but there is an airport to city shuttle bus run by Magic Bus. Tel: 021 505 6300, email: capemagic@magicbus.co.za. Cost is minimum R140 one way. Hotels, backpackers and tour organisers normally collect you if notified in advance. For more information see Cape Town International Airport section.

Rikki's Rickshaw Taxis

Rikki's taxis are distinctively different and great for hopping around safely. You can flag down their odd-looking vehicles if you happen to see one, or pre-book at reasonable rates. For central areas tel: 021 423 4888, for Simon's Town and South Peninsula tel: 021 786 2136.

Rikki's Rickshaw Taxi

Speed Limit

Suburban roads - 60km per hr.

Rural areas - 100km per hr.

Motorways - R120km per hr, unless otherwise stated.

Speed cameras are dotted along several Cape Town routes and police with radar traps often operate at the entry and exit routes of small towns.

Safety

Whatever your mode of transport, you need to feel safe. Don't walk around with an open handbag or wearing lots of jewellery, and keep your camera tucked away when not using it. As a matter of course, lock car doors when you get in and wear a seat belt (which is law in South Africa). With such standard precautions as these, you should have a safe and wonderful experience in Cape Town.

CABS CAR HIRE

CABS Car Hire and United Kombi Van & Bakkie Rental, are customer-driven, national vehicle rental companies. Operational in South Africa since 1990, they are represented in Cape Town (plus the suburbs of Blaauwbergstrand and Camps Bay), and Johannesburg, Port Elizabeth and Durban.

All vehicles in the CABS and United fleet are owned and not subject to frequent rental rate fluctuations, so working in close conjunction, CABS and United are able to offer a wide range of vehicles and services. Proud to serve, they are committed to meet your individual needs.

Free Cell Phone

As an added bonus, a free cell phone is available with each vehicle reservation. There is no phone hire fee - you just pay for calls and phone insurance. You also qualify for free travel insurance with each cell phone reservation. When you book your phone and car simultaneously, your cellular phone number will be provided before your departure, so that you can notify your friends and family in advance.

Your trip may include several South African cities and towns, with hops on internal flights. With CABS and United there is no need to pay more as a result of to interrupted travel. CABS and United are able to combine contracts in different cities, so that the rate applicable is that of the total number of rental days.

Free Rental Days

Now you can earn free rental days for every 15 days that you rent a vehicle (at undiscounted or standard rates). And you will be rewarded with one rental-free day, in the same class, on your next rental with CABS.

Speak to a consultant today to arrange an affordable tailor-made self-drive tour, allowing you complete independence. Let CABS and United make your holiday truly unforgettable.

For more information contact CABS Car Hire, tel: 021 683 1932, fax: 021 683 1957, or on email: info@cabs.co.za

CABS
CAR HIRE

Customers Appreciate Better Service

- ESTABLISHED 1990
- FREE DELIVERIES AND COLLECTION (INCLUSIVE)
- NATIONAL – PORT ELIZABETH & CAPE TOWN, JOHANNESBURG, DURBAN INTERNATIONAL AIRPORTS
- FULL COVER INSURANCE AND UNLIMITED KMS ON RENTALS LONGER THAN 7 DAYS
- FIRST TIME VISITORS ESCORTED TO FINAL DESTINATION (ON REQUEST)
- CHAUFFEUR DRIVE ON REQUEST
- ALL MAJOR CREDIT CARDS ACCEPTED
- SELF-DRIVE TOURS
- ARRANGE ACCOMMODATION (IF REQUIRED)

Telephone (021) 683 1932
24 hrs: 082 707 8071
Fax: (021) 683 1957
Email: info@cabs.co.za

For more information
on vehicle rental,
visit our website at
www.cabs.co.za

For information on self-drive tours, visit our website at
www.southafricaholidaytours.co.za

NATIONAL ALAMO CAR RENTAL

National Car Rental has been an industry pacesetter throughout its 56-year history. National was formed on August 27, 1947, as a group of 24 independent car rental operators with 60 locations and 800 vehicles. They incorporated as a for-profit corporation in 1959 and quickly established an identity as "the best in localized, personal service."

As National continued to grow and evolve, so too did its identity. While being one of the earliest companies to initiate corporate account business in the late '70s, the 1980s and beyond for National can be characterized by its commitment to the corporate traveler. In 1987, National introduced the industry's first, comprehensive frequent-renter program, "Emerald Club", along with the "Paperless Express Rental Agreement," which made car rental faster by using information stored in the computer to process the whole transaction in seconds. National continued to develop ways to make the car rental process more efficient to time-sensitive business travelers.

Through tremendous growth, organizational changes and new travel industry innovations, National has remained a leader in both business and leisure rentals. Today, the National Car Rental brand is one of the world's largest rental car companies and serves the most popular domestic and international travel destinations through a network of more than 2,000 locations in the United States, Canada, Europe, Latin America, the Caribbean, Asia-Pacific, Africa and Australia.

In 1999 Combined Motor Holdings brought National Alamo Car Rental to South Africa to expand on these global expertise and services. In addition we have a service agreement with Alamo, America's largest car rental group, to serve their SA bound clients.

SMILES PROGRAM

Cost saving can be achieved by joining the Smiles Program, which rewards the renter one day free rental in an air-conditioned vehicle, after they have rented 9 times. The redemption vouchers can be issued to the client on a monthly or quarterly basis.

ROADSIDE DIRECT ASSISTANCE PROGRAM

Our FREE Roadside Direct Assistance program, has been a tremendous success due to the fact that our renters know that they are covered, 24 hours a day, for emergencies such as, Flat tyre assistance, Battery jump-start, Vehicle lockout service, Emergency fuel delivery, Extrication/winching service, Towing service and Message relay service.

SHOW 'N GO

Show 'n Go is a speed rental service which is offered to our corporate renters as well as individual renters. The simplicity of this product is that the renter or corporate company signs a master rental agreement when an account is opened. This means that they will never be required to sign a rental agreement at the point of rental. There is also no need to produce a rental voucher.

Airport Desk

CAR RENTAL

South Africa
Special Rates

24h FREE Roadside Assistance

Enjoy South Africa with 24 Hour FREE Roadside Assistance!

Going with the Internationally trusted name in car rental has certain benefits, like "24h FREE roadside assistance".

Choose National Alamo Car Rental and enjoy South Africa, enjoy peace of mind!

We provide car hire at competitive rates in the Western Cape. Our fleet of cars consists of small, medium and large size saloons as well as minivans and microbuses. Deliveries and collections are possible in and around Cape Town as well as at Cape Town International Airport.

Tel: +27 (0) 21 447 3001
337b Main Road, Observatory, CT
www.gopassport.com/

Cape Corporate Car Rentals provides a 24-hour reliable, quality, personalised service. With our head office in Cape Town and an association with other quality suppliers throughout South Africa, we can offer a national service at competitive prices. We operate a new fleet of vehicles, which are covered by a 24-hour roadside assistance for total peace of mind.

Tel: +27 (0) 21 532 0430
Unit 2, Techno Square, 42 Morningside Rd, N'dabeni
www.gopassport.com/

Based in Cape Town, South Africa for over 20 years, Vineyard Car Hire offers new, clean vehicles at competitive car rental rates. We offer a free delivery and collection service, including personally meeting clients at the airport at no charge. Good old-fashioned personal service ensures a trouble-free hire.

Tel: +27 (0) 21 761 0671
298 Main Road, Kenilworth
www.gopassport.com/

We're the Long-Term Rental Specialists with a difference, the 'Original Rental Purchase.' Did a vehicle purchase ever include a buy-back guarantee in the sale? Now it can, and save up to 60% on rental prices. Special offers for students and backpackers on long and short-term rentals.

Tel: +27 (0) 21 447 1144
P O Box 13924, Mowbray, 7705
www.gopassport.com/

Custom tours and transfers for families and small groups. Experience your own unique itinerary in and around Cape Town, the Peninsula, Winelands, Western, Southern and Northern Cape. We can also do the regular tourist routes. Complete flexibility: you call the shots, we drive.

Tel: +27 (0) 21 558 6817
Mobile: David +27 (0) 82 378 5072
www.gopassport.com/

OVERVIEW
&
ORIENTATION

BRIEF OVERVIEW

Cape Town lies at the head of a small peninsula, which dips into the sea at the south-western tip of Africa, (not quite the southern-most point, which is a couple of hours drive east at Cape Agulhas). If you head south from Cape Point, the next stop is Antarctica.

GETTING AROUND

The Table Mountain range runs down the length of the Cape Peninsula and is the reason you cannot always go direct to your chosen destination. You have to follow one of the roads that run either side of the mountains, and then cross at one of the few passes or valleys.

Well maintained arterial roads head out of Cape Town; east towards the Garden Route, north along the West Coast, north-east into the mountainous Cape Winelands and south to Cape Point. To head west you will need a boat. Additional information can be found in the 'Getting Around' section.

CAPE CULTURE

There is nothing black and white about Cape Town's racial mix, which is populated by skin shades of every colour. Cape Town is unlike anywhere else in South Africa, with the majority of its population calling themselves Cape Coloureds (referring without any offence, to their mixed race heritage). Originating from a mix of slaves from Africa and South East Asia, Dutch settlers and Khoikhoi herdsmen, the Cape Coloureds first language is Afrikaans - an Africanised old Dutch.

Black Africans of the Xhosa tribe makes up more than a million of Western Cape's 4.5 million population, with English and Afrikaners in the white minority.

Cape Malay people are also a small minority, but their strong culture and distinctive cuisine has influenced the Cape for hundreds of years. Immigrants and refugees from other African countries like Angola and Congo, add a touch of the exotic to the many languages that can be heard in Cape Town.

TOWNSHIPS

Apartheid policy decided that blacks and coloureds, many of whom had come to the cities in search of work, should be neither seen or heard. They were banished to unappealing stretches of land well outside the cities. Townships and squatter camps arose and grew to great proportions on these windswept Cape Flats. Townships have expanded considerably in the new South Africa, and many now contain suburbs sporting fancy brick houses.

Road Signs

Just when you think the signposts are good, they stop altogether. They also switch languages between English (South Africa's official language) and Afrikaans. 'Airport' may appear firstly in English, but the next sign will say 'Lughawe'. So look out for a pictorial illustration of an aeroplane instead. Maps are easily obtainable and a wise acquisition. An excellent alternative is to use Table Mountain as your point of focus, as it is very rarely out of sight, even from great distances.

Crime

Traditional village values where tribal chiefs maintain law and order, don't apply in the cities . As a result crime has spiralled, (some would say out of control). However, a visitor to Cape Town is unlikely to encounter any crime at all. There may be opportunistic bag snatchers, but normal vigilance will limit risk. Most violent crimes and shootings occur in gangland drug-dealing territory, which you should avoid at all cost.

Lifestyle

Some people say that Cape Town contains a very spiritual force, with Table Mountain exuding a rare and calming energy. This may be true and Cape Tonions are renowned for being laid back, with a slightly slower pace of life than other cities. As a result you need to relax into 'Africa time' and start to enjoy the wait between courses and unhurried departures. Being surrounded by water helps to develop an easygoing temperament, which you should have attained by the time you leave Cape Town.

These happily rub shoulders with tin and wood shacks, which are likely to flood or fall down in the first winter storm. Satisfy your curiosity and take a Township Tour, which will almost certainly reveal a lifestyle very different from your own. Not only will you get a better perspective on South Africa, but it will help uplift the lives of your township hosts.

CAPE TOWN'S POPULATION CENSUS 2001		
	CAPE TOWN	**WESTERN CAPE**
BLACK AFRICAN	916,520	1,207,429
COLOURED	1,392,656	2,438,976
INDIAN / ASIAN	41,490	45,030
WHITE	542,580	832,901
TOTAL	2,893,247	4,524,335

THE WEATHER

Cape Tonions love talking about the weather, as you usually get a bit of everything all in one day. As a result it is wise to carry a bathing costume on a cool day and a sweater on a warm day.

The Table Mountain range is so dominant that it creates microclimates along its flanks, and acts as a windbreak against the stormy winter northwester and the sand-blasting summer southeaster. The northwester brings rain and storms, while the southeaster can batter you into submission. Misnamed as the 'Cape Doctor', its habit of swirling against the mountainsides gathering dust and pollen, give some people instant hay fever. Luckily, you can escape the worst of the wind by retreating to the opposite side of the mountain, where you can bask in calm sunshine on a wind-free beach (see section on Cape's Best Beaches).

OCEANS

The city of Cape Town stares out over the chilly Atlantic Ocean, where a dip in the water will leave you zinging like a mentholated mint. The water may be icy but the sand is hot and the beaches close to Cape Town are sizzling with beautiful bodies. The further south you go on the Atlantic side, the wilder it gets and the less people you encounter. Once you have rounded Cape Point, you enter False Bay, where the water is decidedly warmer.

SHIPWRECKS

False Bay isn't quite the Indian Ocean (satellite images show a major meeting of currents further east at Cape Agulhas), even though you can often see a distinct colour separation in the water. False Bay is a large body of water with Cape Hangklip at its far end. Ships rounding either of these Capes, thought it was safe to head up the coast, but often found themselves unable to turn against the strong wind, when they realised they were heading straight for a rocky coastline. Many shipwrecks are easily visible around the Cape, with tragic stories to go with them (see section on Famous Shipwrecks).

Windsurfing

Huts at St. James Beach

CITY & WATERFRONT

THE CITY

Cape Town is an easy city to negotiate as it has two major factors limiting its expansion; Table Mountain and the Atlantic Ocean. These two natural restraints create a very unique atmosphere that might be compared with San Francisco or Sydney, but isn't! Cape Town is one of a kind.

Cape Town is where Nelson Mandela's 'Rainbow Nation' really exists and thrives. The city streets are trodden by rich and poor - there is a place for everyone, although not everyone likes their place!

BEGGARS

At every large robot (traffic light), you are likely to be propositioned by one or two sellers or beggars (often small children). It is hard to know who to give your charity to, as every homeless child and poverty stricken mother is deserving of a better life. If you decide to donate to an organisation rather than direct to the street, don't feel guilty, just give a polite "No" and the beggars will quickly move on. If you can afford to give to those less fortunate, but don't, shame on you.

WALK THE CITY

The best way to experience the city of Cape Town is to walk it. Leave major valuables behind and tuck your camera into a closed bag, then enjoy the stroll. Look at the amazing mixture of architecture and similarly amazing mix of people (see section entitled Cape Town By Foot).

V&A WATERFRONT

The Alfred part of the Victoria & Alfred Waterfront is named after Queen Victoria's son, who tipped the first load of stones for construction of the new breakwater in 1880. It has come a long way since then and is now the premier entertainment, dining and hotel area in Cape Town. The vast car parks are often very full and there is a buzz of activity inside the malls and at the water's edge bars and restaurants. There is also an open-air amphitheatre, street musicians and marquees with all sorts going on.

You can jump on any number of boats for jaunts into Table Bay or the speedy catamaran to Robben Island. Helicopters give you an aerial view of the ocean, while the Two Oceans Aquarium take you under it. It is easy to spend a couple of days at this venue alone.

The best way to experience the city of Cape Town is to walk it.

Bo-Kaap

Cape Town Harbour

HISTORY
&
PEOPLE

Sweet Cape Wine

It was during the heyday at the end of the 18th century that the sweet Cape wines found favour in Europe. Napoleon it is said, preferred to drink nothing but Constantia wines!

Slave Lodge

Groot Constantia Gable

Groot Constantia

PAST TO PRESENT

You can see and feel Cape Town's history all around you. There are many ways in which the past inhabits our lives, but we usually forget to notice. As a visitor, you are more likely to observe aspects of the past that flourish perfectly well in the present.

ARCHITECTURAL ELEGANCE

Cape Town developed a certain style and elegance, which came to the fore in the latter part of the 18th century to mid 19th century. It revelled in the talents of German sculptor Anton Anreith and Parisian architect Louis Thibault. They collaborated several times and Anreith's German Baroque style, somehow managed to blend with Thibault's neo-classic designs as favoured by French King Louis XVI.

THE CHERUB THAT LOST HIS MANHOOD

Thibault and Anreith created masterpieces that can be admired today, such as at Groot Constantia - South Africa's most famous wine estate. The exuberant sculpture on the pediment above the wine cellar, flows over the strict boundaries of Thibault's design, but its frivolous nude bacchantes (male cherubs who worship the Greek God of wine), seem to know no boundaries. When the pediment was restored in the early 1990's, one bacchante lost his manhood and required a sex change! Go and see if you can spot him/her!

SAD STALLION AND DRUNKEN LION

Anreith was commissioned to sculpt the British Coast of Arms, with a stately Lion and Unicorn on the pediment of British Government Offices (now called The Slave Lodge in Adderley Street). The sculpture was unveiled to reveal a sad old unicorn glancing over his shoulder at a drunken lion. The British couldn't have minded too much as it remains there to this day. See it for yourself as you head up Parliament Street.

SLAVERY

The site of the Slave Lodge ironically became the Supreme Court, then the Cultural History Museum, but now returns to its roots to be known once again as The Slave Lodge. Slavery was abolished in the British Empire on 1 December 1834, but economic benefits of a more accessible workforce, presided over philanthropic reasons. A 'Heritage of Slavery in South Africa' website has been launched: www.museums.org.za/iziko/slavery.

Noon Day Gun

In 1795, the British began firing their latest 18-pounder cannon every day at noon from the castle battlements, to give a time signal to ships in Table Bay. Since 1806 this tradition has continued daily except Sundays. The noise in town was so great that in 1902 the gun was moved the Lion Battery on the slopes of Signal Hill overlooking Cape Town. This is where it is fired today, so if you hear an almighty explosion in the middle of the day, there is no need to look at your watch.

Just Nuisance

In 1940 the Great Dane dog - mascot of Simon's Town sailors - became a menace to anyone not in uniform. When accompanying sailors on a night out, he insisted on occupying several seats on the train, much to other passenger's annoyance. After numerous complaints, the British parliament agreed to enlist the dog so he could legally own a train ticket. For the enlistment papers the sailor was asked the dog's name ."*Nuisance Sir,*" he stated. The form also required a first name, but the sailor insisted it was, "*Just Nuisance, Sir.*" Able Seaman Just Nuisance became a legend in his own lifetime and even married his sweetheart 'Adinda' in 1941. He was an irrepressible character and died after leaping from a moving vehicle - probably chasing something. His life-size memorial statue stands in Jubilee Square, Simon's Town and his grave is at the top of the hill inside Navy grounds.

Chapman's Peak Drive

A coast road between Hout Bay and Noordhoek, cut into sheer rock, seemed like a "mission impossible' in 1916. But Sir Nicholas De Waal - Administrator of the Cape - was a stubborn man and ordered construction to begin. With the help of convict labour, the road took 6 years to build and opened in May 1922. Chapman's Peak Drive became renowned as one of the most scenic drives in the world. But, in late December 1999, after several rock falls had endangered road users, a motorist died as a rock crashed onto her car. Only a couple of months later, forest fires raged over the mountain, loosening and cracking rocks which plunged onto the road. Chapman's Peak Drive was closed indefinitely. Experts discussed ways of making the road safe again, but it was a daunting prospect. But, once again 'mission impossible' was achieved, with huge wire-mesh nets to catch falling rocks and a roof over parts of the road. Chapman's Peak Drive opened again in December 2003, but now you must pay a toll for the privilege of using this spectacular drive.

Just Nuisance

Chapman's Peak Drive

Bushman

Bushman Paintings

Democratic Elections

The first free elections in South Africa were in 1994 and Nelson Mandela was elected President.

South Africa held its second election in 1999 and the third in 2004. On both occasions the ANC won the required two thirds majority to form a government with Thabo Mbeki as President.

Uncut Diamond

A quick exam-cram of history will go a long way to help understand what makes Cape Town tick. Read on for a condensed irreverent dip into South Africa's history, or skim the history time line for a quick fix.

RHYMING CONDENSED HISTORY OF SOUTH AFRICA

Bushmen certainly had little fun, when the white man arrived here with his gun.

It was the Portuguese who came here first, but the land did little to quench their thirst,

They sailed on to other places, while the Dutch took a liking to the Cape's graces.

Scared that they might lose their land, the Dutch asked the British if they wouldn't mind,

To look after the Cape from Napoleons grasp, and give it back later whenever they asked.

To everyone's amazement the British gave back, the land that they had babysat.

But it wasn't long before they decided, to return and lay claim to the land they most prized.

In 1803 the British moved back and set up a bureaucracy without any slack.

They abolished slavery and taught English in school, but the Afrikaners would not suffer such fools.

They packed up their stuff and trekked over the mountains, to lusher valleys with pools and fountains,

But they fought with the Zulus in great bloody wars, and with God on their side they nursed all their sores,

Revenge against Dingane the Zulu King, turned Blood River red with many of his kin.

Diamonds were discovered in Kimberly, and Cecil Rhodes took charge quite nimbly.

Gold was found in the Boer Republic, and Rhodes was impatient to get his hands on it.

He sent a party to topple the Boers, but only succeeded in starting some wars.

The Boers commenced with guerrilla tactics, but the Brits soon discovered some far worse antics,

They burnt their farms and starved them into a corner, and ended the war with no great honour.

An Act of Union followed with no vote for the blacks, which fuelled more discontent behind their backs.

20th century South Africa was without human rights, and blacks of this land had no choice but to fight.

Mine workers strikes were brutally crushed and any defiance was immediately hushed.

Apartheid ruled with an iron hand, but softly softly the ANC readied their hand.

With courage they opposed injustice to blacks, and when the tide turned they got their land back.

Nelson Mandela is a man most humble, but his unflinching approach made apartheid crumble.

South Africa is now a land of the free, where all colours live in proud democracy.

HISTORY TIMELINE

500 years ago - Khoisan, (Khoikhoi pastoralists and San hunter-gathers), live in the Cape.

1450-1500 - Portuguese sailors visit the shores of southern and east Africa. Bartholomew Dias lands in Mossel Bay to a volley of Khoikhoi stones.

1652 - The Dutch East India Company sent Jan van Riebeeck to establish a base in the Cape, supplying food and water to trading ships. Company employees were soon freed to start farms, more manual labour was needed.

1658 - Slaves arrived from Angola and West Africa, then Madagascar, Mozambique and Dutch controlled Java in Indonesia. A mixed-race Coloured population began to evolve.

1688 - French Huguenots came to Franshoek (French corner) of the Cape Winelands.

1795 - The British occupied the Cape during the Napoleonic wars at the request of William of Orange, and amazingly enough, gave the colony back in 1803.

1806 - The British regretted leaving the Cape and returned to re-claim it and govern it. They implemented bureaucratic laws much resented by the Dutch.

1834 - The British abolished slavery, a decision opposed by the Afrikaners.

1836 - The Great Trek began. As the Boers (Afrikaner farmers) travelled east, one hundred years of frontier wars ensued against the Zulus.

1852 - Sand River Convention between the British and Afrikaners guaranteed the trekker communities independence. The South African Republic was formed. Pretoria grew into the Afrikaner capital, led by Paul Kruger.

1867 - Diamonds discovered at the Orange River, then in Kimberly. By 1888 Cecil Rhodes had formed De Beers Company and acquired the entire Kimberly diamond mines.

1871-1899 - Gold was discovered along Witwatersrand. Miners had their wages cut by 40% over 5 years.

1877 - Britain proclaimed that the first South African Republic (SAR) ceased to exist and had officially been annexed.

1895 - A party led by Dr Jameson (instigated by Cecil Rhodes) rode towards Johannesburg in a covert operation to topple Paul Kruger. The raid was bungled and they ended up in jail.

1899 - The Boer War began. Afrikaners had initial advantage using 'commando' style tactics, but the tables turned and the British took Pretoria. Their 'scorched earth' policy, setting fire to Afrikaner farms, proved devastating. Prisoners, women and children were held in concentration camps under appalling conditions.

1902 - Exhaustion brought Boers to the conference table, where they gave up their independence and recognised King Edward IV. An act of Union followed bringing the four South African colonies under one flag. It failed to unite the country and by excluding blacks it sowed seeds of discontent.

1924-46 - By mid 20th century, Africans couldn't even retain what few rights they had. The Natives Land Act divided South Africa into black and white areas. Africans were stripped of the vote.

1948-76 - Afrikaner nationalism reached a height under D.F. Malan. Black resistance failed to halt or even retard apartheid policies. Coloured people removed from voters roll

1960 - 69 - people were shot at Sharpeville, while protesting against pass laws. ANC and PAC political parties banned. Liberation movements turned from non-violent protest to armed insurgency and sabotage. Police retaliated with greater oppression.

1963 - Nelson Mandela was jailed for life.

1976 - Children shot by police during a protest in Soweto, over forced use of Afrikaans language in schools. Seventeen black consciousness organisations banned. Steve Biko dies in police detention.

1984 - Bishop Tutu wins the Nobel Peace Prize

1985-89 - President P.W.Botha repealed Apartheid laws. Seventeen anti-apartheid organisations un- banned.

1988 - F.W. de Klerk becomes Prime Minister and arranges to meet Nelson Mandela. Eight prominent political leaders released from prison. Public amenities opened to all races.

1989 - Nelson Mandela released from 27 years in prison and hailed as a hero. All banned organisations freed and press restrictions lifted.

1992 - Almost 70% of whites vote for further reform.

1993 - Nelson Mandela and P.W. de Klerk jointly win the Nobel Peace Prize.

1994 - First free elections in South Africa are peaceful and Nelson Mandela is elected President.

1999 & 2004 - South Africa holds its second and third free elections, in which the ANC wins a two thirds majority with Thabo Mbeki as President.

2004 - Nelson Mandela announces his retirement at the age of 85.

Cape Minstrels

CULTURAL MELTING POT

A masala of African, Malay, Indian, European and indigenous 'coloured' influences merge to produce the faces, lifestyles and accents of the 4.5 million people who inhabit this ever-expanding metropolis.

Also, a growing number of White – especially young – South Africans prefer to identify themselves as African, proudly claiming their roots and a close identity with the continent on which they were born and raised.

FACES OF A NATION

You are best placed to study the faces of Cape Town by sitting at a sidewalk café. Traders and business people, students and street children - a combination of faces that have the makings of a Benetton advertisement.

Cape Town's forebears hail from the hot islands of Malaysia, coffee plantations and palm groves of East Africa, African savannah and crowded Indian villages, not to mention Dutch, German, British, and Lithuanian Jewish heritage. Some arrived as slaves or labourers, others as colonists and settlers. There is also the recent flood of new immigrants and refugees to consider, often displaced from countries like Congo and Angola.

The black population of Cape Town is overwhelmingly Xhosa, but even they migrated here from the Eastern Cape in mid to late 19th century. The only indigenous people of the Cape were the Khoikhoi herders and San Bushmen hunter-gatherers, commonly linked in name as Khoisan. Decimated by smallpox epidemics and marginalised by colonists, their lifestyles became untenable and few bushmen survive to this day.

PAROCHIAL CAPE TOWN

Capetonians believe firmly that the world begins and ends in their city. They go so far as to appropriate Table Mountain as their own, referring to it as, *"My Mountain."* Cape Town cliques could be accused of being class conscious in a parochial sense, through their habit of making fun of non-locals as well as fellow Capetonians.

LIFE ON THE STREET

The impact of HIV/Aids is not making life on the streets any easier. It is an undisputed fact that many AIDS orphans will go on to live as adult 'bergies'. Help is at hand in the form of street shelters and training and job creation programmes, but it seems that despite such help, many still choose their familiar stomping grounds and a life on the street.

'Bergies'

Street people, who eagerly assist you in parking your car by flailing their arms like a human windmill as they guide you into a tight spot, are often referred to as 'bergies'. This informal (translate: illegal) 'employment' is based on tips, and their good humour, toothless grins and sometimes incredible stories of survival, should serve as a reminder of your own good fortune.

"Bergie"

You will also see many unique personalities as well as the abject poor begging at traffic lights. Some sell things you don't really want, another may offer to take your rubbish in return for a tip and others send their small children begging with a jangling can. Those brandishing newspapers or the monthly Big Issue magazine - an incredibly successful job creation programme - are trying hard to lift themselves off the breadline. Please treat the poor people of Cape Town with respect and buy one of their magazines.

Cape Town's relaxed notion of 'African Time' is one of the city's most charming traits.

SUB-CULTURES WITHING SUB-CULTURES

A useful way to get a feel for the people of Cape Town is to check out some of the organisations they belong to and activities they take part in. This ranges from the conventional (Friends of Lion's Head Hikers) to the slightly mad (Cape Town Skeptics) – there is something for everyone.

A major sub-culture, it could be argued, is to be found within the sporting world. Rugby, cricket and football take precedence over matters of state, and marathons and cycle races close down the entire city. At the first hint of the summer south easter (wind), Capetonians of all shapes and sizes start preparing for "The Argus".

To the uninitiated, the annual Cape Argus Cycle Tour every March, sees about 35,000 cyclists negotiating 105 kilometres of twists, turns and hills just for the fun of it. If you haven't got the constitution for this gruelling race, then relax and sit back in true Cape Town style. Whip up a skottel braai breakfast at the roadside (a fry up on a concave gas hotplate), and shout encouragement to the thousands of puffing and panting passers by.

CAPE TOWN TIME

Capetonians are renowned for their ability to put their own lateness down to 'Cape Town Time.' While this may annoy some people, visitors have to understand that this Cape Town take on 'African time' is one of the city's charming Unique Selling Points (although it takes some getting used to)!

If you live in the shadow of Table Mountain, would you not also be tempted to skip that 8a.m. meeting and head out for a morning stroll? Sit back, breathe in, take up yoga – do whatever it takes – you will soon find that you cannot fight the system. Visitors to Cape Town should learn to do things the local way - slowly.

Cape Town Personalities

Nobel Peace Prize winners - former President FW de Klerk and Archbishop Desmond Tutu.

Another Nobel prize winner, this time for Literature, is the secretive J.M Coetzee.

First African in Space and internet billionaire Mark Shuttleworth.

Funnymen adding their own brand of humour to the Cape are: comedian Mark Lottering, 'cultural terrorist' Zebulon Dread, and drag artist Pieter-Dirk Uys.

Nelson Mandela

FAMOUS FACES

Cape Town has more than its fair share of visiting celebrities and quite a few of its own. After all, there is no one more famous in the entire world than Nelson Mandela, and South Africans are rightly proud to claim him as their own.

NAME DROPPING

A few others who regularly grace Cape Town are: Bill Clinton; Oprah Winfrey; Dalai Lama; Naomi Campbell; U2 and André Agassi. Actor Will Smith has been spotted house hunting and Simon Le Bon supposedly owns a home in Llandudno. Jean-Paul Gaultier likes De Waterkant Steambaths and Michael Schumacher was heard to shout, *"I vont to verk out!"* at an annoying autograph hunter while exercising at a well-known Green Point gym.

STAR SPOTTING

To see faces you might recognise visit the Planet Bar at The Mount Nelson (the likes of Colin Farrell, Charlize Theron, Tiger Woods) and The Nose Bar or The Tank within De Waterkant's trendy Cape Quarter. Royals would feel at home in the Cape Colony Restaurant at The Mount Nelson or La Colombe in the Constantia winelands. The bold and beautiful prefer to be visible in Beluga Restaurant or Pigalle - both in Green Point, Verandah at the Metropole, Eclipse in Camps Bay or 95 Keerom Street. During hours of darkness, there is nowhere more choosy than Sting's upmarket night club Rhodes House in Queen Victoria Street. Round off a night on the town at Kennedy's Cigar Lounge in Long Street or sip one of any of the 400 or so brands of whisky at Cape Grace's Bascule Bar.

CAFÉ SOCIETY

Media24's coffee store Nazwebe, Heerengracht Road in the city, is where magazine doyens interview mafioso or models. Swedish designer types hang out at Vida e Café, Kloof Street in Tamboerskloof, and Cape Town's delectable gays love De Waterkant's Dutch coffee shop. It's all jodhpurs and jewellery at Melissa's café in Constantia's old money belt, but understated elegance for 'Tea at The Nellie' (Mount Nelson Hotel).

SEASONAL EVENTS

Confusion reigns (or reins) in February, with beauty queens and fillies competing for attention at the glamorous J & B Met Horse Race at Kenilworth Race Course. Dress up for the Cape Town Fashion Festival in November or December, and round off the year in December by painting the town pink at the much-hailed Mother City Queer Project outrageous party.

FW DE KLERK

Nobel Peace Prize winner - former President FW de Klerk

DESMOND TUTU

Nobel Peace Prize winner - Archbishop Desmond Tutu.

BOBBY SKINSTAD

Springbok rugby icon Bobby Skinstad

MARK SHUTTLEWORTH

First African in Space and internet billionaire
Mark Shuttleworth

PIETER DIRK UYS

Funnyman and drag artist Pieter-Dirk Uys adds his own
brand of humour to the Cape

INTERESTING SIGHTS & ACTIVITIES

Bo-Kaap (previously the Malay Quarter)

The Bo-Kaap Museum on Wale Street, is within the culturally rich Malay Quarter of Cape town, a short walk from the city centre. It portrays the lifestyle of a 19th century Malay family, whose origins date back to slaves brought here from Java. Take a guided walk through the cobbled streets lined with colourful houses and learn its true history. Or allow Tana-Baru Tours (tel: 021 424 0719), or Bo-Kaap Community Guided Tours (tel: 021 481 3939) to take you on an enlightening stroll.

Bo-Kaap

GET YOUR BEARINGS

Make Cape Town Tourism (corner Castle/Burg Streets, tel: 021 426 4260) your starting point. You can grab a cup of coffee here while looking through their one-page low-down on the city's finer points of interest. You won't have time to stop at all the suggested places of interest below, so select your choice.

GUIDED TOURS

Privately guided walking tours are the best way to see Cape Town, with such renowned walking tour guides as Ursula Stephens or Garth Angus, both bookable through Cape Town Tourism. The Cape Art Deco Society puts out a free map of self-guided walks within the CBD, Sea Point and Vredehoek. Pick up the Art Deco map at Cape Town Tourism, or call the society Chairperson Brent Meersman (tel: 082 568 9940).

MOUNTAIN RAMBLING AND THINGS THAT GO BOOM

Ascending the Grande Dame of mountains by foot - Table Mountain - commands proper precautions or the services of a professional guide from the likes of Active Africa Adventures & Touring, tel: 021 788 8750. There's also Lion's Head and Devil's Peak to conquer, just for the fun of it or for photographic memories of incredible views. And worth the stroll, err schlep, is a visit to the Noon Gun at the top of Military Road in Bo-Kaap. In time-honoured tradition the gun lets the whole city know it is midday and scares the uninformed half to death. Recover at the Noon Gun Restaurant with tea, lunch or dinner (tel: 021 424 0529).

COMPANY'S GARDENS

Horse, bicycle and foot patrols ensure safety and security in the Company's Gardens, which was the Cape's first vegetable patch supplying Dutch East India Company ships in 1652. It still boasts an ancient saffron pear tree, believed to date from this time. You might also notice an old oak tree that has almost enveloped an old water pump in its trunk dated 1842. Wander around, sit on park benches and feed squirrels with peanuts from street vendors. Or imitate Cecil John Rhodes pointing north to the land he wished to colonise, with a plaque quoting, *"Your hinterland is there."*

SLAVE LODGE

The Gardens were worked by over 300 slaves, conveniently supplied by the Slave Lodge at the entrance to the Gardens. Dating back to 1679, these foundations have seen several masters since its original gory use. At the rear is a small round plaque set in the central island of Spin Street, proclaiming the site where slaves were sold, lest we should ever forget.

PARLIAMENT

On Government Avenue, at the base of the Gardens and adjacent to St George's Cathedral, lie the Houses of Parliament where you can see South Africa's democracy in action on a morning guided tour, or in the Gallery during an afternoon Parliamentary session

MOUNT NELSON

THE MOUNT NELSON

Opposite the top of Company's Gardens is the 'Pink Palace', or 'Nellie' as The Mount Nelson Hotel is sometimes called. The bastion of Cape colonial life and unofficial headquarters of the British Army during the Anglo Boer War, there is nowhere better than the 'Nellie' to take tea.

iziko
museums of cape town

SLAVE LODGE

Dating back to 1679, The Slave Lodge is one of the oldest buildings in Cape Town and its foundations have seen several masters since its original gory use. The Gardens were worked by over 300 slaves, conveniently supplied by the Slave Lodge at the entrance to the Gardens.

Tel: +27 (0) 21 460 8240
Corner of Adderley and Wale Streets
www.gopassport.com/

iziko
museums of cape town

BO-KAAP MUSEUM

Established in 1978 and furnished as a house depicting the lifestyle of a nineteenth-century Muslim family, exhibitions include photographic impressions of life in the Bo-Kaap and highlights its social history and the influence of Apartheid. Older exhibitions show the material culture of the Muslim community at the Cape.

Tel: +27 (0) 21 4813939
71 Wale Street, Bo-Kaap, Cape Town
www.gopassport.com/

iziko
museums of cape town

SOUTH AFRICAN MUSEUM

The South African Museum was founded in 1825. In 1897 the Museum moved to its present building in the historic Company's Garden. Since then millions of visitors have wandered its halls and corridors to be stimulated and inspired by its collections and exhibitions. They have left the Museum with a better understanding of the earth and its biological and cultural diversity, past and present.

Tel: +27 (0) 21 481 3800
25 Queen Victoria Street, Gardens
www.gopassport.com/

Tea at the Nellie

CULTURE VULTURES

Still in the Gardens is the excellent South African National Art Gallery, whose African art acquisitions provide an interesting contrast to the old masters. And the historical South African Museum, with an atmospheric Whale Well, San artworks and 'Eve's' footprints dating back 117,000 years (see Ancient Ancestors, West Coast section). For a starry experience, go next door to the Planetarium, which hosts regular astronomical and scientific presentations (see Museum's page for opening times.)

SA JEWISH MUSEUM

Next to the Art Gallery and adjacent to South Africa's first synagogue is the fascinating SA Jewish Museum (entrance in Hatfield Street). Here you'll find a vibrant history of the country's thriving Jewish community. Neighbouring is the highly acclaimed Cape Town Holocaust Centre, even more moving than its Jerusalem equivalent.

ANTICS AT THE CASTLE

Any good walking tour will include the Castle of Good Hope (1666), immediately to the west of the Grand Parade. Although it now stands high and dry, the ocean originally filled its moat and its pentagonal shape offered effective defence. Cutting across the central quadrangle is the famed Kat Balcony with its long dining room. Over the centuries there have been many revellers on its parapet, including an irreverent crowd of fancy and cross-dressers at the Mother City Queer Project 2002! Guided tours of the Castle are on offer on the hourly strike of the clock, after which you can wine and dine in the courtyard.

GRAND PARADE

The expansive Grand Parade next to the Castle, is the former military parade and public execution ground. Now home to a lively market each Wednesday and Saturday. You can't fail to notice the imposing Italian Renaissance style City Hall, from whose balcony Nelson Mandela addressed the people of South Africa on his first day of freedom, 11 February 1990. City Hall also plays host to regular concerts by the Cape Philharmonic Orchestra.

DISTRICT SIX

Head down Buitenkant Street to Number 25a and the District Six Museum. This documents the city's, thankfully now defunct policy, of forced removals of people of colour and its consequences. This small museum is big on impact and brings Cape Town's past and present into sharp focus - a must for the visitor. Contrasting this in Buitenkant Street, is the 18th Century Rust-en-Vreugd former house of the State Prosecutor and now containing more of the William Fehr collection, plus paintings by John Thomas Baines depicting early colonial Cape Town, and much else besides.

SOUTH AFRICAN NATIONAL GALLERY

South Africa's premier art museum houses outstanding collections of South African, African, British, French, Dutch and Flemish art. Selections from the Permanent Collection change regularly to enable the museum to have a full programme of temporary exhibitions of paintings, works on paper, photography, sculpture, beadwork, textiles and architecture.

Tel: +27 (0) 21 4674660
Government Avenue, Gardens
www.gopassport.com/

This museum which is a vehicle for education, information and dialogue narrates the story of the SA Jewish community from its early beginnings against the backdrop of South African history. Interactive and high-tech, it includes an exclusive documentary on Nelson Mandela, international exhibitions and cultural programmes and houses a reconstructed Lithuanian shtetl. The Centre provides online information on European origins and a search facility for family trees.

Tel: +27 (0) 21 465 1546
Address: 88 Hatfield Street, Gardens
Web: www.gopassport.com/

CASTLE OF GOOD HOPE

Although it now stands high and dry, the ocean originally filled The Casle's moat and its pentagonal shape offered effective defence. The Castle of Good Hope now offers many attractions to suit every taste and hosts daily tours.

GRAND PARADE

Flanked by The Castle of Good Hope and The City Hall, host to concerts by the Cape Philharmonic Orchestra, the expansive Grand is the former military parade and public execution ground. It is now home to a lively market each Wednesday and Saturday.

The District Six Museum tells the history of apartheid through an intimate look at ordinary people's stories and memories. It is celebration of local triumph which resonates with people globally who have experienced marginalisation. As an award-winning, community Museum, the District Six Museum is considered to be an essential stop in Cape Town for the culturally and eco-sensitive tourist.

Tel: +27 (0) 21 461 8745
25A Buitenkant Street, Cape Town
www.gopassport.com/

Greenmarket Square

Formerly a fruit and vegetable market supplying passing trading ships, Greenmarket Square is now a thriving flea market, flanked by pavement restaurants and coffee shops. Leave the high heels behind or the original cobblestones will surely trip you up. The adjacent Old Town House's was built in Greenmarket Square in 1755, and now houses the Michaelis Collection of old Dutch and Flemish masters. Parallel to Greenmarket Square is the pedestrian St George's Mall, with street stalls and buskers and singers entertaining you as you snack or stroll.

Greenmarket Square

The Planetarium

The Pan African Market

LONG STREET

Running the length of the CBD, Long Street throbs with a life of its own, gained over hundreds of years, as seen by the assortment of fine architecture from an old Mosque to Cape Dutch, Georgian and fancy Victorian filigree balustrades. Long Street has a split personality from night to day, both of which are equally eccentric. During daylight hours peruse the second-hand furniture, book and genre clothing shops, as well as small photographic and interior stores. While at night revel in the lively atmosphere provided by bars and nightclubs pounding their beat onto the street. You could always end your day with a massage in the Long Street Baths and a dip in the warm waters of the Turkish steam bath. Don't forget to drop into the Pan African Market for a Djembe drum lesson, or enjoy a traditional meal, have your hair braided, and buy a flowing caftan or Madiba shirt.

ADDERLEY STREET

One Sir Charles Adderley championed the cause of the Cape Colonists against turning the place into a convict settlement, and was promptly presented with £100 and had a street named after him. Adderley Street is one of Cape Town's arteries, which leads down to the reclaimed Foreshore where it becomes Heerengracht (gentleman's canal). A most colourful and photographic part of Adderley Street is the flower market, where you can buy huge brazen bunches at very low prices.

The Golden Acre Shopping Mall linking Adderley Street with the Cape Town Station is not of great interest, other than to take in the 1663-constructed reservoir – the oldest remaining such structure in South Africa.

STRAND STREET

The Lutheran Church (tel: 021 421 5854) stands victoriously tall at 98 Strand Street and displays a swan on its exterior indicative of the Lutheran faith. Followers of this faith were granted the right to worship in 1779, where previously a One Faith law applied.

Nearby is the impressive Gold of Africa Museum - the world's first Museum to African gold, its heritage and traditional goldsmithing skills. There's a wine bar and coffee store in here too.

Museums mentioned here have a fuller description and opening hours in the Museums section of this book.

PLANETARIUM

Next door to the SA Museum is the unmistakable dome of the Planetarium. The southern hemisphere night sky is revealed on Tuesdays at 2pm and 8pm, Thursdays at 2pm and Saturdays at 2.30pm, with additional shows during school holidays. Top of Queen Victoria Street. Tel: 021 481 3901. Entry R20 adults, R6 children.

GREEN MARKET SQUARE

Adjacent to The Old Town House which was built in 1755 and which now houses the Michaelis Collection of old Dutch and Flemish masters lies Green Market Square. Formerly a fruit and vegetable market supplying passing trading ships, the Square is now a thriving flea market, flanked by pavement restaurants and coffee shops.

FLOWER SELLERS

Along the busy pavements of Adderley Street are shops and businesses of every description, as well as the inimitable flower sellers who add both colour and life to the business district and have become part of the day-to-day life of the bustling city centre.

ST GEORGES MALL

Parallel to Greenmarket Square is the pedestrian St George's Mall, with street stalls and buskers and singers entertaining you as you snack or stroll. It leads to Long Street which throbs with a life of its own

The Pan African Market located in a national monument on Long Street, comprises 33 stores and stalls representing 14 African countries including art and crafts, hair dressing, tailoring, holistic healing and catering. The traders man their stalls and is so structured as to allow them to showcase the work they choose and in so doing, bring a beautiful and unrestricted multi-ethnicity to this space.

Tel: +27 (0) 21 426 4478
76 Long Street, Cape Town
www.gopassport.com/

PLANETARIUM

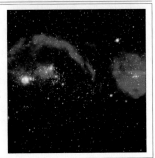

Housed in the SA Museum building is a celestial theatre in the round, which transports the audience through the wonders of the universe. Inside the domed auditorium, we can recreate the night sky, so whatever the weather outside, the Planetarium sky is always clear, an extraordinary audio-visual experience for old and young.

Tel: 27 (021) 481 3900
Address: 25 Queen Victoria Street, Cape Town
Web: www.gopassport.com/

Robben Island Museum

Proclaimed a UN World Heritage Site in 1999, Robben Island is the icon which symbolises South Africa's struggle against apartheid and its successful transformation into democracy. Crowds of visitors take the super-fast catamaran for a guided tour of this former island prison, whose most famous resident was Nelson Mandela.

Tours lasts 3½ hours and depart from the Nelson Mandela Gateway, Clocktower Precinct, V&A Waterfront. Booking is essential. Tel: 021 555 3100/3600 or the Waterfront Tourism Office tel: 021 405 4500. Tickets R150 adults, R75 children 4-17 years old.

WATERFRONT MUSEUMS

Cape Medical Museum

Of interest is the display about Dr James Barrie, a woman who disguised herself as a man so she could practice as a doctor. In 1818 she performed the Cape colony's first successful Caesarian (read her story in the Ghosts & Legends section). Portswood Rd, Greenpoint, near the V&A Waterfront. Tel 418 5663. Entry donation.

SA Maritime Museum

This quirky museum is dedicated to the preservation of South Africa's Maritime Heritage. It has all sorts of things maritime, like a model ship workshop, multi-media lighthouse display and a children's discovery cove. Next to the Aquarium, V&A Waterfront. Tel 021 405 2880. Open 10am-4.45pm daily. Entry R10 adult, R2 child.

CITY MUSEUMS

DISTRICT SIX MUSEUM

Township tours often begin here to help forge an understanding of the pass laws, which were responsible for the forced removal of people of colour from the city. District Six was an inner city area almost completely bulldozed, and remains barely inhabited today, although former residents are slowly being repatriated. 25a Buitenkant Street. Tel: 021 461 8745. Open Mon 9am-3pm, Tues-Sat 9am-4pm. Entry R10 adults, R5 children.

BO KAAP MUSEUM

Inside a 1763 house is the Bo Kaap Museum, portraying the lifestyle of a 19th century Malay family, whose origins date back to slaves brought here from Java. Add to your enjoyment of this culturally rich area, with a guided walking tour through the Malay Quarter's cobbled streets. 71 Wale Street. Tel: 021 424 3846. Open Mon-Sat 9.30am to 4.30pm. Admission R3.

GOLD OF AFRICA MUSEUM

Africa is the home to the world's largest gold deposits and this museum is dedicated to the history and artistry of African gold. They even hold workshops and courses in gold leafing, cuttlefish casting and jewellery making. 96 Strand Street. Tel: 021 405 1540. Open Mon-Sat, 9.30am to 5pm. R20 adult, R16 pensioners/students, R10 children.

CAPE TOWN'S MUSEUM MILE

SA MUSEUM

This oldest museum in South Africa continues to draw visitors to its giant whale well, Eve's 117,000 year old footprints, san rock art and many fascinating exhibits. Top of Queen Victoria Street, entrance in Company Gardens. Tel: 021 421 3800. Open 10am-5pm daily. R10 adults, R2 children.

NATIONAL GALLERY, in the Company Gardens
- see Artists & Galleries section

SA CULTURAL HISTORY MUSEUM/SLAVE LODGE.

After extensive excavations in the courtyard, the museum is putting together an exhibition on slavery and its history in the Cape. Corner of Wale/Adderley Street, Tel: 021 460 8200. Open Mon-Fri 9am-4.30pm, Sat 9am-1pm. Entry R10 adults, R2 children.

CAPE TOWN HOLOCAUST CENTRE

Small but emotionally effective with a moving video from holocaust survivors. Hatfield Street. Tel: 021 462 5553. Open Sunday-Thursday 10am to 5pm, and Friday morning until 1pm. Admission free - donations appreciated.

SOUTH AFRICAN JEWISH MUSEUM

This museum narrates the story of the South African Jewish community from its early beginnings, against a backdrop of South African history. High-tech and interactive, you can search for a family tree, see an exclusive Nelson Mandela documentary and watch a video wall entitled 'Culture Among Cultures'. 88 Hatfield Street, Gardens. Tel: 021 465 1546. Open Sunday - Thursday , 10am to 5pm, Friday close at 2pm. Closed on Saturdays and Jewish holidays.

SOUTHERN SUBURBS

IRMA STERN MUSEUM

Irma Stern (1894-1966) is considered to be one of South Africa's most important pioneer artists, who achieved international recognition in her lifetime. The museum, which was her home, has a permanent collection of her portraits, exotic figures, fecund landscapes and still lifes, in various mediums. Contemporary South African artists exhibit upstairs. Cecil Road, Rosebank. Tel: 021 685 5686. Open Tuesday-Saturday 10am to 5pm. Entrance R8 adults, R4 pensioners & students.

TRANSPLANT MUSEUM

On 3 December 1967 the world's first human heart transplant was performed at Groote Schuur Hospital by Dr Chris Barnard. This museum dedicated to that event, is situated on the very site of the theatre in which the operation took place. It contains many items of historical interest. Groote Schuur Hospital. Tel: 021 404 5232. Open Monday - Friday 9am to 2pm. Entry R5.

JOSEPHINE MILL

This old mill dates to the early 1800's and is Cape Town's only surviving operational watermill. You can buy freshly milled flour, pasta and biscuits or eat these in their restaurant. Boundary Road, Newlands. Tel/Fax: 021 686 4939. Open Monday-Friday 9am to 4pm. Guided tours by arrangement. Entry R8 adults, R5 children.

GROOT CONSTANTIA MUSEUM

The Manor House of this ancient wine estate - first planted in 1685 - is a magnificent example of Cape Dutch architecture. The museum's pediment by Anton Anreith (circa 1792), is a masterpiece, which required a recent alteration - read the Past to Present page in our History Section to find out how a cherub lost his manhood! Walk around the grounds, do some wine tasting and dine in the tasty Simon's Restaurant. Groot Constantia Wine Estate. Tel: 021 795 5140. Open daily 10am to 5pm. Entrance R10.00 adults, R1 children.

SOUTH PENINSULA MUSEUMS

Muizenberg Toy Museum

This museum and shop for the avid toy collector, houses a unique collection of current and obsolete model cars and other collectibles like dolls, early steam trains, rocking horses and clockwork toys, dating from 1890-1970. 8 Beach Road Muizenberg. Contact Ray Butters Tel/Fax: 021 788 1569,

Simons Town Museum

Housed in the 1777 'Residency', the building has a long history as a hospital, post office, school, customs house, police station, gaol and magistrate's court. It is a fascinating museum covering the cultural history of Simon's Town and its connection with the Dutch East India Company and Royal Navy. Court Road, signposted off the main road in Simons Town. Tel: 021 786 3046. Open Monday-Friday 9am to 4pm, Saturdays 10am to 1pm, Sundays & Public Holidays 11am to 3pm. Entry fee R5 adults, R2 pensioners/ students, R1 children.

Gold of Africa Museum

Rhodes Memorial

Picnic spots

UNUSUAL PLACES TO VISIT

Some lesser trodden places can give the well-travelled visitor a new angle on a destination like Cape Town. Let your curiosity take you to some places off the beaten track...

OBSERVATORY

The site of the former Royal Observatory is now SA National Observatory HQ. Public are welcome on the second Saturday of every month at 8pm, for a guided tour and a look at the stars (weather permitting). Mention Observatory to locals, and they will think you mean the trendy, laid back, studenty suburbs of narrow streets, cool restaurants and arty shops. Come for a meal out or to the intriguing street market on the first Sunday of every month, where a multiracial crowd indulge their esoteric inclinations.

MOSTERT'S MILL

From the M3 highway, the bulging white body and magnificent sails of Mostert's Mill stand proud against the skyline. Built around 1796, the mill is still working over 200 years later, thanks to a full restoration in 1995. Guided tours and milling demonstrations are held most Saturdays between 10am and 2.30pm. Call the Friends of Mostert's Mill, tel: 088 129 7168.

RHODES MEMORIAL

Cecil John Rhodes was a formidable man who attained much in his relatively short life. You will have to count the steps in front of this memorial to find out what age he died! Founder of De Beers diamond mining company, Prime Minister of the Cape, acquirer of land in the name of British Imperialism and a country named after him to boot. His memorial (and a coffee shop) are on the slopes of Table Mountain above the university, signposted off the M3. Open daily, no charge.

PICNIC SPOTS

Picnic from a basket of temptations at Buitenverwachting Wine Estate, Constantia. Booking essential, tel: 021 794 5190. Create your own mix at Spier's Deli, and eat at tables around the lake (on R310 outside Stellenbosch), tel: 021 809 1159. Put your own picnic together from; Melissa's in Constantia Village or Claremont, Giovanni's in Main Road Greenpoint, Barnyard Farmstall in Tokai or Noordhoek Village Farmstall.

PICK YOUR OWN

Hillcrest Berry Orchards, between Stellenbosch and Franschhoek, grow raspberries, Cape gooseberries, cherry guavas, strawberries, blueberries and blackberries. Most of these luscious berries are at their peak in November and December, but the best strawberry picking is in August. Tel: 021 885 1629, Email: info@hillcrestberries.co.za, Website: www.hillcrestberries.co.za.

The delicate scent of roses will entice you to Chart Farm in Cape Town's southern suburb of Wynberg Park, where they grow about one hundred different varieties. From January to May wander around and select your perfect rose at R2.50 per stem. From September-October to February you can also pick sweet Hanepoort grapes straight off the vine. They also sell apples and lemons from their Ceres farm, a couple of hours north of Cape Town. Tel: 021 761 0434.

AFRICAN DRUMMING

You don't have to be African to get some rhythm! Just go to the Drum Café in Glynn Street, (back of Roeland Square). Don't let its dark and dingy appearance fool you - it's quite safe and will probably be one of your most memorable evenings ever. Hire a djembe drum and take your lead from the expert Rastafarian drum teachers. Group lessons start at 9pm on Monday, Wednesday and Friday nights. Tel: 021 461 1305, www.drumcafe.com

Drumming at Mama Africa

SOUTH PENINSULA LIVE MUSIC

Wednesdays and Saturdays are hot nights out for locals, but the Red Herring in Beach Road, Noordhoek is packed on Sunday night from 5.30-8.30pm. Dave Gommersal's local cover band plays plenty of foot-tapping, sing-along numbers and the vibe is great - particularly in summer when the sea-view balcony is full, (and by the way, the pizzas are delicious). Tel: 021 789 1783. Dave also plays at The Southern Right Hotel in Glencairn on Wednesday nights, and there is a DJ on Friday, a local band on Saturday, and jazz on Sunday nights. Tel: 021 782 0314. Would you believe it, Dave also plays at Café Pescado in Simon's Town on Tuesdays, while on Saturdays they have a mixed show of music and comedy. The Railway House Restaurant in Muizenberg has some sophisticated jazz music on Sunday evenings, tel: 021 788 3251.

African Restaurants

Dine to the accompaniment of the boisterous, drummers, singers and dancers at traditional African cuisine restaurants: Africa Café - 108 Shortmarket Street, tel: 021 422 0221, email: africacafe.co.za, and Mama Africa - 178 Long Street, Tel: 021 424 8634.

SIMONSTOWN WATERFRONT

Uniformed sailors and holidaymakers mingle in this quintessentially English seaside village and navy port, on the False Bay coast near Cape Point. Curio shops and cafés pack the single main street, which is full of whitewashed Cape Dutch gables rubbing shoulders with intricate Victorian balustrades. Simon's Town is vibrant during the day (especially in summer), but empties out in the evening, for no other reason than everybody has gone home!

Simon's Town awoke from a contented slumber after the opening of its new Waterfront complex. Shops and restaurants are now jangling with summertime activity and it success has created a vibrant atmosphere in this little seaside town. The Waterfront is small and friendly and its 4 star Quayside Hotel retains an intimate quality (tel: 021 786-3838, info@quayside.co.za).

RESTAURANTS

Lunch at Boulders Beach Lodge

It is really worth staying in Simon's Town, not least for the chance to dine at some of its great restaurants; Bertha's caters for everyone (Simon's Town Waterfront, 021 786 2138), Seaforth Restaurant has a selection of seafood (out of town towards Cape Point, tel: 021 786 4810), Café Pescado for fresh seafood and great pizza, (opposite Jubilee Square, tel: 021 786 2272), The Meeting Place is the best bistro (opposite Jubilee Square, tel: 021 786 1986). Bon Appetit is Simon's Town's top restaurant, serving authentic French haute cuisine of an exceptional standard, (along the main drag, tel: 021 786 2412).

SEA KAYAKING

Boulders Beach Shops

There are lots of watery things to do in Simon's Town like sea kayaking around the yacht basin, or beyond the harbour past Cape fur seals to the penguins at Boulders Beach. A guided paddle to the penguins, on very stable sit-on kayaks, equipped with life jacket costs R200. Contact Real Cape Adventures Tel/Fax: 021 790 5611, Cell: 082 556 2520 or 082 920 3696, website: www.seakayak.co.za.

WHALE WATCHING BY BOAT

Simonstown Waterfront

From July-October, Southern Right Whales come to mate and calve in False Bay. Ocean View & Masiphumelele Fishing Co. have the only local whale watching boat licence and advertise daily departures from late July until mid Nov. They depart from the town pier by the Waterfront at approximately 11am or 2pm, but phone to check and book a place. Tel: 021 783-5016. Price approx. R150 for 1½-2hrs.

Legend has it that Van Hunks was an early 18th century pirate who got into a smoking contest on the top of Table Mountain, with the devil. The table cloth of cloud that cascades over the mountain is said to be the smoke from this contest.

GHOSTS AND TALL STORIES

The Cape's ghosts and legends arise mainly from apparitions that you may well see for yourself - with a little imagination of course!

TABLE MOUNTAIN'S TABLE CLOTH

It is perfectly likely while you are in Cape Town, that you will encounter the fruits of the smoking competition between Van Hunks and the Devil. Namely the Table Cloth of cloud, which cascades over the edge of the Table Mountain plateau during a southeaster.

Table Mountain's Table Cloth

Van Hunks was an early 18th century pirate who retired from his capricious life to a more sedate existence in the Cape. He spent his days at the top of Table Mountain sitting on Devil's Peak, where he would light up his pipe and stare out to sea. After bragging about his smoking capabilities to a stranger, the two decided to have a competition. They smoked and smoked for days, but finally Van Hunks defeated the stranger, who was revealed to be the Devil who vanished in a puff of smoke. Van Hunks of course, can still smoke up a storm, as you can see for yourself on many a windy summer day.

THE FLYING DUTCHMAN

Cape Point Light House

The ghost of this schooner has been seen many times in the waters around Cape Point, moving under full sail even in no wind. The Flying Dutchman sank as it was trying to round the Cape in 1641 and Captain Hendrik van der Decken, vowed that he would sail on forever. This it seems he has done, and his phantom ship has been recorded several times, by some very important people.

King George V of England saw it in 1881, as did thirteen other crewmen in the squadron. Keepers of Cape Point lighthouse often reported seeing her during storms and in 1911 an American whaler reported almost colliding with The Flying Dutchman.

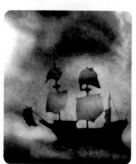
The flying Dutchman

Such tales have inspired novelists and composers over. centuries, including Wagner's Der Fliegende Hollander opera. The lack of regular passenger liners and trading ships bearing many hands, means that The Flying Dutchman doesn't encounter so many boats anymore, but that doesn't mean she isn't out there!

AINTJIE SOMERS

"Be good or Aintjie Somers will get you," is what some South African mothers still tell their children. Poor little Annette, was a slave who worked herself to death and now avenges her hard life by throwing stones and scaring people. Or was she a man in woman's clothing who attacks and robs travellers? Or were her misdemeanours actually the work of early 19th century outlaws, one of whom was a cross dresser? No-one really knows.

Phantom animals feature in several South African tales such as, the kloof haunted by horse and rider after they were both shot dead during the Boer war.

DR JAMES BARRY

Perhaps it was something about the early eighteen hundreds, but Dr James Barry was another cross dresser. Not man to woman this time, but the other way around. This cultivated and attractive, if somewhat effeminate, young man, had a penchant for getting into trouble, but was such good society company he managed to wriggle out of punishment.

Dr Barry was renowned as an excellent doctor and was promoted to the rank of Medical Inspector only weeks after his arrival in the Cape. Even though he cultivated a reputation as a ladies man, there were rumours of homosexuality. He was subsequently posted abroad and it was only several weeks after his death in 1865, that news arrived in South Africa that Dr James Barry was a woman!

QAMATA OR ADAMASTOR?

According to some African legends, Qamata created the world, but not without a fight against Nganyamba, a mighty dragon who sleeps under the sea. The one-eyed earth goddess Djobela, helped by creating four giants to guard the land, but they failed and before dying asked Djobela to turn them into mountains so they could continue their vigilance. The watcher of the south became Table Mountain - Umlindi Wemingizimu.

However, some would say that the mythical monster Qamata, is actually Adamastor, the alarming spirit of the Cape of Storms (first written about by the Portuguese in the 1500's). It seems Adamastor was punished by the Gods for warring with the titans and was turned into a mountain to guard the southern seas. He appears as a giant storm cloud to warn of dangers and disaster for anyone daring to round the Cape. Bartholomew Diaz's crew threatened mutiny on the basis of this legend and forced the ship to turn back.

A phantom car is sometimes seen near Mossel Bay along the Garden Route. So if you see a driver swerving onto the wrong side of the road, you should consider blaming the ghost car before the booze.

CASTLE GHOSTS

When Cape Town's castle was built in 1666, the sea lapped its bastions and the moat was filled by the tide (now the land has been reclaimed). This ancient building has towers and cells, which have had centuries to develop ghosts of all sorts.

When you walk around the castle, you may sense its eeriness, especially in the windowless dungeon that also served as a torture chamber, or the winding corridors leading to narrow stone stairs. A ghost has been seen on the battlements, sometimes leaning over the parapet, and inexplicable footsteps are sometimes heard. It could be the spirit of a guard who hung himself with the rope bell, which now rings on its own from time to time.

On a lighter note, the ghost of the romantic and frivolous Lady Anne Barnard, first lady of the colony in the late seventeen hundreds, is said to appear at parties. She was renowned for being seen bathing nude in the Dolphin Pool (accessible in a rear courtyard), which has been reconstructed according to her drawings and descriptions.

HAUNTED HOUSE

Another haunted house rivalling the antiquity of the castle, and said to be connected to it by a secret passage, is Rust-en Vreugd (Rest and Gladness). A ghostly woman appears at an upstairs window next to a baby cot, and just stares out. Or she floats around the ground floor in a long dress and taps people on the shoulder.

KHOIKHOI LEGEND

There is something about a stone cairn that invites you to add a piece to the top. The Khoikhoi - the indigenous inhabitants of the Cape - used to do this too. They would create a cairn to identify a sacred site to Heitsi-Eibib - a roguish character who was likely to fill your mind with bad suggestions. To avoid this, the Khoikhoi would cover the back of their head while walking away from the cairn.

THEATRICAL HAUNTINGS

The University of Cape Town's Little Theatre is housed in some old city buildings near the Company Gardens - an area settled by the first Europeans in the Cape. A long-standing caretaker and a lecturer at the Little Theatre, both experienced unexpected performances and peculiar happenings, such as a piano playing in an empty theatre and being shoved from behind when painting scenery.

It was perhaps the actress who died in the Green Room still playing her role, and/or Cecil, the deceased perfectionist scenery painter.

Even though the wild horses of Kleinmond are considered by some to be merely a spectre - they are in fact very real!

THE CHOKING BRIDE

Many ghostly sightings are explained by stories of unfortunate and gruesome tales, and none more so than the bride who choked on a giant oyster during her wedding feast.

The bridegroom had sent his farm labourers out to collect oysters along the De Hoop coastline, and they returned with one so large that he wanted to present it to his bride. She unfortunately asphyxiated on it, and in a state of total despair, the bridegroom fetched his gun and shot his own head off.

The giant oyster shell was hung outside the doorway and the wooden ceiling still bears the jagged hole where the bullet exited nearly two centuries ago. The dark-haired bride appears on full moon nights and during low spring tides - the best time for gathering oysters!

HORSEMAN OF TOKAI

The owners of Tokai Manor in the early nineteenth century, were known to throw a good party and one New Year's Eve, young Petrus Michiel Eksteen was dared to ride his horse around the dining room. This he did with great gusto (hoof prints were seen on the wooden floor for years afterwards), but the horse took fright and bolted out of the door. It either slipped or leaped off the top step of the veranda and both horse and rider came crashing down breaking both their necks. They are reputed to re-appear each New Year's Eve.

An almost identical story is attributed to the Old Nectar Cape Dutch house near Stellenbosch, where a cavalier on a white horse would ride up to the house before turning and cantering out to crash to his death. Other mysterious spirits are said to visit this house and the new owners in 1942 were welcomed by a ghost knocking insistently at the door.

CAPE LIGHTHOUSES

Submerged rocks, miasmic mists, and phantom ghost ships are just a few of the hazards of the Cape Coastline, so it's not surprising that numerous lighthouses are required to warn of these dangers.

ROBBEN ISLAND

As early as 1657, Robben Island had fire beacons to warn ships of its dangers, but there are nevertheless many shipwrecks along its shores. A lighthouse with a range of 24 sea miles replaced the beacons in 1863. By this time Robben Island was home to the 'living dead' - the sick, mad, criminal and politically inconvenient were dumped here to live without much prospect of seeing their friends or relatives again.

GREENPOINT LIGHTHOUSE

The red and white candy-striped Greenpoint Lighthouse was the first of two built along this hazardous shipping stretch, often enveloped by winter fog. When the mist descends, its booming foghorn can be heard for miles out to sea. The distinctive Green Point lighthouse is sometimes erroneously referred to as Mouille Point Lighthouse, which was built in 1842 and demolished in 1908.

SLANGKOP

Slangkop Lighthouse shines out across the 'Outer Kom' reef of Kommetjie, created by dangerous hidden rocks. The 33 metre white minaret is the tallest cast iron tower on the South African coast and spreads its light 33 miles out to sea. This deserted section of coast is renowned for its variety of seabirds, especially after a winter storm.

CAPE POINT

The most powerful light of the South African coast beams out from Cape Point, to forewarn sailors of its notorious dangers. On a calm day the ocean looks mild mannered, but changeable winds, criss-crossing currents and submerged bedrock have brought many ships to disaster.

CAPE AGULHAS

This lighthouse warns of the Agulhas Bank at the southern most point of Africa. The area is beset with dense fog, unpredictable currents and dangerous seas and worth a visit for its portentous atmosphere. This lighthouse is very distinctive with a red and white banded tower in the Egyptian style of the Pharos of Alexander, and hosts a fascinating museum to its 150-year old history. Nearby is the Bredasdorp Shipwreck Museum exhibiting relics dating back to 1647.

DANGER POINT

The name says it all! The lighthouse warning of this menacing and rocky point came 43 years too late for the HMS Birkenhead (1852) - one of the most infamous of all maritime disasters (see Shipwrecks page).

Lighthouse Signals

Each lighthouse emits a different signal, and it is the groupings and duration of the flashes that allow ships and yachts to identify exactly where they are and what they should be avoiding.

Lighthouse at Slangkop

Fog horn

The Green Point lighthouse fog horn has not stopped many ships being wrecked right under its nose, including the 'Sea Farer' who ran aground in 1966 directly in front of the lighthouse.

Cape Point's First Lighthouse

The original Cape Point lighthouse was too high up and often enveloped in mist, so a new one was built lower down in 1914, which emits an incredible 10 million candlepower.

Cape of Needles

Many ships have come to grief on the 'Cape of Needles' - as 15th century Portuguese navigator Bartholomew Dias called Cape Agulhas.

SHIPWRECKS OF THE CAPE

Ships continue to be in need of good hope as they travel along the Cape of Storms, because even to this day vessels are wrecked with surprising frequency. Sophisticated equipment, detailed maps and vigilant harbour masters, still cannot stop the effects of stormy seas, mechanical failure and human error.

The Cape has about 2,700 wrecks around its coast, only about 10-15% of which have been accurately pinpointed. Many are very visible in the sand or surf and all have a dramatic story to tell.

The Cape Shipwreck Route will soon have information signboards telling you the traumatic stories of each wreck. In the meantime, use this as your guide to allow each shipwreck to come alive with drama and history.

VISIBLE CAPE SHIPWRECKS

ATHENS - Mouille Point - 1865: Mountainous seas of the Great Gale extinguished her boiler fires and the Athens was quickly driven onto the rocks. Although close to shore, the immense waves made it impossible for onlookers assist and all 29 of her crew perished. The engine remains can still be seen in the surf.

KAKAPO - Noordhoek Beach - 1900: It is not quite clear why the captain of the Kakapo thought he had rounded the Cape, but he came full steam ahead right onto Noordhoek Beach. The sailors didn't even get their feet wet as they stepped off! Its skeletal ribs and boiler can be seen today in the middle of the sand.

CLAN STUART - Simon's Town - 1914: No lives were lost when this small steamer dragged anchor in a southeaster. The boilers and cylinder tops are easily seen from the road.

ANTIPOLIS & ROMELIA - 1977: These ships were being towed to a breakers yard in the Far East, when the cables broke just south of Cape Town. They both found visible resting places; the Antipolis can be seen at low tide at Oudekraal and local landmark Romelia recently slid into deeper water off Llandudno.

Cape Town's Great Gale of 1865

Wednesday 17th May 1865 was an ominous day for sailors. Seas turned from heavy to ferocious and ships could no longer steer or hold anchor. By about 2pm, more than ten vessels had crashed into each other or run ashore in Table Bay - amazingly without loss of life. Unfortunately as the day progressed the shipwrecks increased and many lives were lost. Numerous ships were subsequently re-floated, but seven left their shattered hulls forever in the bay.

HMS BIRKENHEAD - 26 February 1852

This sad tale of the Birkenhead remains one of South Africa's worst maritime disaster. Carrying passengers and British troops, she struck a rock off Danger Point that all but ripped her open. As she sank, the Captain insisted that women and children leave first, thereafter it was every man for themselves and 455 men died on this tragic day.

Clifton Beach

Wind Surfers

Worshipping the sun

CAPE TOWN'S BEST BEACHES

Choosing a beach should depend not just on your personal preference, but on which way the wind is blowing. The perfect beach of yesterday, might be your worst nightmare today. As a general rule, if the southeaster is blowing, sunbathers should head for the Atlantic side.

Another determining factor is whether you want to swim, be sporty, sunbathe or just be seen. The Atlantic water is so cold (8-14°C) that however hot the bodies, most are loath to take a dip without a 7mm wetsuit. The beaches of False Bay may not be so chic, but the water is warmer (11-22°C), and is usually safer for swimming.

ATLANTIC BEACHES (north to south)

Cape Town looks west over the Atlantic Ocean, into which the sun disappears each night. Beaches closest to the city attract beautiful people onto their soft pale sands. Beaches on the northern edge of Table Bay offer a classic Table Mountain backdrop perfect for photographs.

A coastal drive south provides magnificent rocky coastal views, especially from Chapman's Peak Drive, which ends with an sensational view of 3.4 km of pure white sand at Noordhoek Beach. Even further south are the wild empty beaches of the Cape of Good Hope Nature Reserve.

BLOUBERG - BIG BAY AND LITTLE BAY

Take the perfect Table Mountain photograph from these popular long sandy swimming and windsurfing beaches in Table Bay, 20 km north of Cape Town. Beyond the breakers Robben Island - Nelson Mandela's island prison - can be seen 13 km offshore. Activities: swimming, windsurfing, hobie cats, paddle skiing.

CLIFTON

The glamour of beautiful bodies and moored yachts attract sun worshippers to Clifton. Granite boulders divide Clifton's four white sandy beaches and shelter them from the south easter. Activities: sunbathing and being seen, watching paragliders land at Club Med beach bar.

CAMPS BAY BEACH

Lined with palm trees and pavement cafés, Camps Bay has a decidedly Mediterranean feel. Activities: sunbathing and strutting a beautiful body, beach volleyball, meeting friends. Parking can be difficult.

LLANDUDNO

A narrow road winds its way through a concealed hillside suburb to this charming beach, hemmed in by huge granite boulders. Activities: body boarding, sheltered sunbathing, sandcastles and sunset picnics. Watch out for a strong undertow and avoid high tide when there is little beach left.

CLIFTON BEACH

...glamour of beautiful bodies and moored yachts attract sun worshippers to Clifton. Granite boulders divide Clifton's four white sandy beaches...

LLANDUDNO BEACH

...through a concealed hillside suburb to this charming beach, hemmed in by huge granite boulders.

NOORDHOEK BEACH

This gorgeous long horseshoe curve of fine white sand is unspoilt and deserted...

CAMPS BAY BEACH

Lined with palm trees and pavement cafés , Camps Bay has a decidedly Mediterranean feel.

DIAZ BEACH CAPE TOWN

...just before Cape Point and is the south-western most tip of Africa. Feel the freedom.....

THE BEST BEACHES

SANDY BAY

Narrow paths from the high dunes of Hout Bay or the southern end of Llandudno lead to this unofficial nudist beach, favoured by Cape Town's gay community. Activities: getting an all-over tan.

HOUT BAY

Hout Bay Beach and Mariner's Wharf provide everything for a family day by the sea. There is a one kilometre safe swimming beach and large fishing harbour with boat trips to Seal Island and fresh fish n' chips for lunch. Activities: swimming, paddle skiing, sea kayaking, surfing and seafood.

NOORDHOEK BEACH

This gorgeous long horseshoe curve of fine white sand is unspoilt and deserted. About half way along are the remains of 'The Kakapo' shipwreck preserved in the sand since 1900. Activities: horseriding, kite flying, long walks and advanced surfers and boogie boarders. Muggings have occurred on the far reaches of this beach, so stay where you can see other people.

CAPE OF GOOD HOPE

This is the small sandy bay just before Cape Point and is the south-western most tip of Africa. Feel the freedom of space as you look at an endless ocean. Activities: bird watching, walking through unique flora and fauna. Watch out for cheeky baboons.

FALSE BAY BEACHES - almost Indian Ocean (north to south)

The water is warmer in False Bay, but most beaches take the full force of the summertime south-easterly wind. The bay has long sandy beaches interspersed with seaside towns and is connected to the centre of Cape Town by a scenic railway (see Trains section in Getting Around).

MUIZENBERG SUNSET BEACH & SURFER'S CORNER

With 40 kilometres of uninterrupted beach from Muizenberg to Strand, Sunset Beach offers constant gentle waves perfect for learning to surf. Activities: swimming and novice surfing

FISH HOEK BEACH

Fish Hoek is a popular safe swimming beach with firm sand, a coastal path dotted with viewing benches, and a café, restaurant and play area. Activities: safe swimming, hobie-cats for hire, sunbathing and family fun.

BOULDER'S BEACH, SIMON'S TOWN

Just south of Simon's Town, is one of the Cape's most delightful beaches. Not only is Boulder's Beach scenically beautiful with warm coves sheltered from the south easter, but it contains a rare land-based colony of African Penguins. (see Eco Tourism - Birds section), and there is a small entry fee. Activities: swimming with penguins, wheelchair-friendly boardwalk to the nesting beach, learning to snorkel. Scuba divers can explore Castle Rock a few kilometres south.

Clear Blue Water

Kids at play

HOUT BAY BEACH

…everything for a family day by the sea. There is a one kilometre safe swimming beach and large fishing harbour with boat trips to Seal Island…

FISH HOEK BEACH

…a popular safe swimming beach with firm sand, a coastal path dotted with viewing benches, and a café, restaurant and play area…

MUIZENBERG BEACH

…40 kilometres of uninterrupted beach from Muizenberg to Strand, Sunset Beach offers constant gentle waves…

BLOUBERG BIG BAY BEACH

…perfect Table Mountain photograph from these popular long sandy swimming and windsurfing beaches in Table Bay,…

GORDON'S BAY BEACH

The water is warmer in False Bay,… The bay has long sandy beaches interspersed with seaside towns…

EVENTS CALENDAR

JANUARY
J&B MET

One of the most prestigious events on CT's social calendar, this is not only about thoroughbreds, but glamorous fashion, entertainment, sophistication and J&B Scotch Whiskey. The R1.5-million prize money is in keeping with its status and the official after-party is a highly rated post-race event that continues the festivities well into the early hours.

Venue: Kenilworth Race Course

www.tabgold.co.za

MARCH
CAPE ARGUS PICK N PAY CYCLE TOUR

The Cape Argus Pick 'n Pay Cycle Tour is the world's largest individually timed cycle race - and the first event outside Europe to be included in the International Cycling Union's Golden Bike Series - sees over 35 000 cyclists tackling a 109km route around Cape Town that is as spectacular as it is gruelling. This is SA's biggest one-day sporting event is fast becoming a big international drawcard - and increasingly a boon for tourism and business in the region.

www.cycletour.co.za

MARCH
THE CAPE TOWN FESTIVAL

Since 1999 the City has been host to the festival to promote cultural tolerance, through showcasing the many different cultures we have, by using arts and cultural events as a vehicle.

www.capetownfestival.co.za

MARCH
THE NORTH SEA JAZZ FESTIVAL

The North Sea Jazz Festival 2004, which is now known simply and affectionately as "Africa's Grandest Gathering", is about to celebrate its 5th anniversary in 2004, and it will be doing so in style in its new home at the Cape Town International Convention Centre on the Mother City's Foreshore.

Venue : Cape Town International Convention Centre
www.nsjfcapetown.com

APRIL
OLD MUTUAL TWO OCEANS MARATHON

More than 12000 competitors line up under a floodlight start and race in either the 56km or 21.1km marathon. Thousands of supporters line the streets and television cameras record all the excitement. The marathon has become one of the premiere running events in South Africa and draws both local and international competitors. Held on Easter Weekend each year.

www.twooceansmarathon.org.za

APRIL
DECOREX

South Africa's premier lifestyle and interior design show from furniture, fabrics and floors, to lighting, leisure spaces, kitchens and bathrooms.

Venue : Cape Town International Convention Centre

www.decorex.co.za

MAY
CAPE TIMES WATERFRONT WINE FESTIVAL

This relaxed and well-organised annual wine and cheese tasting festival represents the entire spectrum of Cape wine producers, from top-notch estates to superb boutique wineries and groundbreaking garagistes. Visitors are able to tour all the wine routes in one evening at a convenient and secure venue. At the Cheese Hall housed next door you can sample and buy boutique cheeses and deli products such as olives, olive oils, oysters, sushi and organic foods.

Venue: V&A Waterfront
www.waterfront.co.za

MAY
CAPE GOURMET FESTIVAL

A festival which celebrates food and wine in abunance! "Taste the Good Life".

www.gourmet.co.za

JUNE
RED BULL BWA (BIG WAVE AFRICA)

Dungeons, one of the best big wave surfing spots in the world hosts this 20 day surfing spectacle. Renowned International and local big wave surfers will converge on Hout Bay under the watchful eye of the sentinel waiting for waves in excess of 15' (5 metres), only once the waves have reached the required height and consistency will the contest run.

Venue: The Sentinel Hout Bay Convention Centre
www.redbullbwa.com

JULY
PICK N PAY KNYSNA FESTIVAL
(previously Knysna Oyster Festival)

All the favourites of the Festival will be back and more. Don't miss the chance to attend Knysna's famous Oyster Cooking and Eating Competitions, to play in the golf and bowls tournaments, participate in the various running marathons, angling competitions and adventure races, or just chill out with a glass of the famous local beer and a plate of fresh oysters while you listen to the wonderful sounds of the SA Navy Band.

Venue : Knysna
www.tourismknysna.co.za

EVENTS CALENDAR

AUGUST
CAPE TOWN FASHION WEEK 2004

About 50 top designers from South Africa and the rest of Africa will showcase the best they have to offer in high Fashion in this glamorous and glitzy high profile fashion event.

Venue: Cape Town International Convention Centre

AUGUST
STELLENBOSCH WINE FESTIVAL

Fine wines in beautiful surroundings.

Venue: Paul Roos Sentrum

www.stellenbosch.org.za

SEPTEMBER
SIMON'S TOWN PENGUIN FESTIVAL

Let's talk penguinese ! Experience the best of what Simon's Town has to offer during this exciting annual 5 day event which raises funds for SANCCOB who protect our friends, the African Penguin. A selection of Sporting Events, Evening Entertainment, Art & Culture, Environmental, Children's Activities and Markets will fill our programme.

Venue: Simon's Town

www.simonstown.com

SEPTEMBER
WineX

How many Capetonians can truly say that they get to visit the neighbouring winelands as often as they would like? But city residents and visitors can, however, look forward to a three-day showcase of some of South Africa's top wines during WineX

Venue: Cape Town International Convention Centre

www.winex.co.za

SEPTEMBER
THE HERMANUS WHALE FESTIVAL

The ultimate enviro-arts festival! This Festival held at peak whale watching season attracts thousands of visitors who come to marvel at these giant and graceful creatures. Enjoy guided whale watching walks, boat-based whale watching and 4 x 4 trips into the Fynbos reserve.

Venue: Hermanus

www.whalefestival.co.za

OCTOBER
CAPE TIMES /FNB BIG WALK

This event, one of the oldest in Cape Town, attracts over 20 000 people from all walks of life. Distances range from a 5km stroll to the more gruelling 80km. Alternatively you can choose between a 10km,15km, 20km, 25km, 30km or 50km

Venue: Cape Town and the surrounding Areas finishing at Hartleyvale stadium

www.bigwalk.co.za

NOVEMBER
INTERNATIONAL DRAGON BOAT FESTIVAL

This spectacular and exciting team sport originated in China over 2300 years ago, and came to South Africa in 1992 when two beautiful ceremonial wooden dragon boats were presented to Cape Town by Taiwan. This Festival now in its 10th year in Cape Town contains a special and exciting atmosphere created by the glorious mixture of Chinese, South African and International cultures.

Venue : V&A Waterfront

www.dragonboat.org.za

NOVEMBER
SOUTHERN AFRICAN INTERNATIONAL FILM AND TELEVISION MARKET (SITHENGI)

Producers, directors and financiers from Africa and abroad trade products and form partnerships at Africa's premier market for film, broadcasting and allied industries.

Venue : Artscape Theatre Centre

www.artscape.co.za

DECEMBER
MCQP - MOTHER CITY QUEER PARTY

MCQP presents Cape Town's 10th annual Mother City Queer Project - The party of the year where people fly in from all over the world for a night of unrivalled parting and fun.

Venue : Cape Town International Convention Centre

www.mcqp.co.za

DECEMBER
GOOD HOPE FM / VODACOM CLIFTON BEACH CHALLENGE

Clifton's trendy 4th Beach plays host once more to this challenge featuring exciting strength, speed and fitness contests between celebrity Springbok rugby stars and the Clifton Beach lifesavers. Mr & Ms Clifton contests provide the eye candy.

Venue : Clifton 4th Beach

TOURIST ATTRACTIONS

THE VICTORIA & ALFRED WATERFRONT
WHERE THE WORLD MEETS AT THE WATER'S EDGE

The V&A Waterfront is the most visited tourist destination in the Southern Hemisphere, with some 22 million visits each year. Situated in the heart of Cape Town's working harbour against the dramatic backdrop of Table Mountain, the Victoria & Alfred Waterfront is widely acknowledged as Cape Town's premier shopping and tourist destination and a well known entertainment hotspot. Here, an innovative fusion of history and modern convenience has resulted in a multi-purpose, dockside environment unlike any other in the world.

SHOPPING

With over 400 stores, the Victoria & Alfred Waterfront provides the opportunity for serious shopping, with an incredibly diverse scope and something for everyone. Its spectacular blend of Victorian architecture, maritime tradition, and African culture ensures a shopping environment that is lively and cosmopolitan, with a distinctive African twist.

The stylish Victoria Wharf Shopping Centre forms the bulk of the retail space at the Waterfront and boasts over 240 unique retail outlets that offer a vibrant mix of luxury items, designer brands, and craft emporia. For those looking for a more traditional selection of art, antiques and jewellery, the Alfred Mall, situated within the historic Pierhead, offers a selection of stores for the discerning shopper.

HISTORIC CLOCK TOWER PRECINCT

Across the Pierhead's swing bridge, you can find the latest addition to the Waterfront's retail offering – The Clock Tower Centre. This brings South African crafts, arts, designs and foods together under one roof, as well as the Waterfront Information Centre. There are also several sites of historical interest here, including the Clock Tower built in 1882 and the old Chavonnes Battery - the fascinating ruins of the Dutch East India Company military installation dating back to 1724. There are also spectacular views of Table Mountain and the working harbour, and there are usually a few enormous Cape fur seals lolling around in the water or on a platform where they sunbathe. Old rubs shoulders with the new in the Clock Tower Precinct with the Nelson Mandela Gateway to Robben Island, from where the high speed catamaran departs regularly throughout the day.

Parking is no problem as there are over 6,000 open-air and covered parking bays, patrolled and monitored 24 hours a day.

AFRICAN ARTS & CRAFTS

The Waterfront also takes local crafts seriously and has two craft markets that provide the curious shopper with a traditional view of South African products.

The Red Shed Craft Workshop, adjoining the Victoria Wharf Shopping Centre, is filled with an eclectic mix of handmade merchandise and art while providing an opportunity to see crafters at work. Adjacent to the Two Oceans Aquarium, The Waterfront Craft Market is one of the largest and most vibrant indoor craft markets in Cape Town, open seven days a week. It represents the Waterfront's culture of entrepreneurship and small business development and features a diverse assortment of innovative designs and traditional handcrafts, antiquities and holistic lifestyle accessories.

From fashion and accessories, to jewellery, homeware, curios and gifts, novelties, books and stationery, audiovisual and electronic equipment, food, wine and flowers, there is sure to be something to suit every shopping taste at the V&A Waterfront. For ultimate shopping convenience, all stores are open until 9pm seven days a week.

RESTAURANTS

When it comes to restaurants, one would be hard-pressed to find such a wide selection in one venue, anywhere in South Africa. Some 68 restaurants, taverns and eateries are complimented by seven of Cape Town's finest hotels, each with its own unique style. From ice-creams and take-aways, to elegant dining in five star restaurants and a vast range of international cuisine, the Waterfront has something for every taste. A restaurant guide 'Savour', detailing each and every culinary establishment, is produced regularly by the V&A Waterfront Company, and can be viewed at www.waterfront.co.za.

ENTERTAINMENT

There is no need for visitors to the Victoria & Alfred Waterfront to search for entertainment — it surrounds you as soon as you enter the Waterfront complex. From street buskers demonstrating the art of mime, or musicians performing anything from Southern Jazz to traditional South African folk songs, entertainment keeps the Waterfront alive. A full programme of entertainment is planned every year for the Amphitheatre, where visitors can enjoy free concerts, music and dance performances.

V&A Amphitheatre

On weekends and during holidays, the Waterfront also has an extensive programme of events and activities to capture the imagination of visitors of all ages. The Waterfront's year-round calendar is packed full of exciting and fun-filled happenings like the international yacht races – the BT Global Challenge and the Volvo Ocean Race – which attract sailing enthusiasts from around the world. Other annual events include the V&A Waterfront Wine Festival, the Spring Flower Festival, Winter Food Fair, Dragon Boat Racing and the country's largest Jazzathon. Kids really enjoy scrabbling around for semi-precious gems at the Scratch Patch, while the SA Maritime Museum exposes all sorts of marine and shipping revelations.

WATERFRONT HOTELS

The Cape Grace Hotel

Whether you are simply looking for a place to sleep or wanting to indulge in 5 star luxury, you'll find it all at the V&A Waterfront. Bustling or tranquil, modern or classic, budget or luxurious - staying at one of the eight accommodation facilities will put a world of opportunities right on your doorstep. See the Accommodation Guide at www.waterfront.co.za.

Seal

MARINE LIFE

Being built around a working harbour, the fishing industry and the ocean still takes centre stage, providing visitors with the chance to see the catch of the day being off-loaded, while seals, dolphins and seabirds add to the unique maritime experience. The world-class Two Oceans Aquarium reveals many more marine creatures, including several sharks that cruise around their enormous circular aquarium.

One of the best ways to enjoy the spectacular scenery in and around Cape Town's Table Bay is to take any one of the many boat or helicopter trips that depart from the Waterfront daily. For the adventurous, the Ocean Sailing Academy will teach would-be sailors the art of sailing. Waterfront leisure attractions can be downloaded from www.waterfront.co.za

For more information on shops, restaurants, events or anything you need to know about the V&A Waterfront, contact Waterfront Information at Tel: 021 408 7600, email: info@waterfront.co.za, www.waterfront.co.za

Victoria Wharf

View of Table Mountain

The Victoria & Alfred Waterfront
is located within the breathtaking
setting of a dynamic working harbour and
includes over 400 comtemporary
stores, a wide selection of top
restaurants, an aquarium, boat and
helicopter charters, art
and craft markets, a variety of leisure
attractions as well as a choice of world
class conference and hotel facilities.

The V&A Waterfront
offers a range of
cultural landmarks including
museums, historic buildings and
exclusive access to one
of South Africa's
essential heritage
sites, Robben Island. All
of this, coupled with on-
going events and
entertainment within a
vibrant cosmopolitan
atmosphere ensures that
the V&A Waterfront is the
heart of your visit.

The Warm Heart of Africa

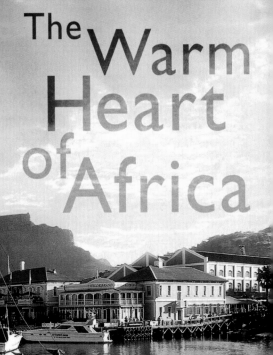

VICTORIA & ALFRED WATERFRONT (PTY) LTD. CAPE TOWN SOUTH AFRICA
Victoria & Alfred Waterfront (Pty) Ltd. P.O. Box 50001, Waterfront 8002, Cape Town, South Africa
Tel:+ 27 (0)21 408 7600 Fax:+ 27 (0)21 408 7605
Email: info@waterfront.co.za Website: www.waterfront.co.za

THE ROBBEN ISLAND STORY

Robben Island is known the world over as a place of banishment, exile, isolation and imprisonment. For nearly 400 years, colonial and apartheid rulers banished those they regarded as political troublemakers, social outcasts and the unwanted of society, to this 575-hectare rocky outcrop in Table Bay.

The Island's unwilling inhabitants included; slaves; political and religious leaders who opposed Dutch colonialism in East Asia; troublesome local Khoikhoi and African leaders who resisted British expansion in South Africa; Leprosy sufferers and other sick and the mentally disturbed; French Vichy prisoners of war; and most recently, political opponents of the apartheid regime in South Africa and Namibia.

ROBBEN ISLAND'S MOST FAMOUS PRISONER

During the apartheid years Robben Island became internationally known for its institutional brutality. Some freedom fighters spent more than a quarter of a century in prison for their beliefs. Yet people such as Nelson Mandela emerged to lead South Africa to democracy, with a message of tolerance, reconciliation and hope.

Those imprisoned on the Island succeeded on a psychological and political level in turning a prison "hell-hole" into a symbol of freedom and personal liberation. Robben Island came to symbolise, not only for South Africa and the African continent, but for the entire world, the triumph of the human spirit over enormous hardship and adversity.

In doing so it has offered a troubled world, hope for the future.

Nelson Mandela's Cell

WORLD HERITAGE SITE

Robben Island Museum (RIM), aims to develop the island as a national and international heritage and conservation project in the new millennium. In managing its resources and activities, RIM strives to maintain the unique symbolism of the island, nurture creativity and innovation, and contribute to socio-economic development with the transformation of South African society and the enrichment of humanity.

MISSION

In implementing its vision, the RIM constantly focuses on the following core essences:

Maintaining the political and universal symbolism of Robben Island.

Conserving and managing the natural and cultural heritage and resources of Robben Island.

Promoting RIM as a platform for critical debate and life long learning.

Managing RI in a manner that promotes economic sustainability and development.

THE NELSON MANDELA GATEWAY TO ROBBEN ISLAND

The Robben Island visitor experience begins at the Nelson Mandela Gateway to Robben Island, at the Clock Tower Precinct inside Cape Town's V&A Waterfront.

The Gateway is the "mainland front door" to Robben Island, symbolising the importance of the island in South Africa's young democracy. The Gateway houses a 150-seater auditorium, boardrooms and a Robben Island Museum shop, among other facilities. Digital, interactive exhibition spaces on all three floors of the Gateway building provides the visitor with a historical context of Robben Island's Maximum Security Prison, as well as reflecting the broader span of the island's history.

The Gateway is open to the public from 7.30am to 6pm. Opening times may be extended during peak holiday periods.

Ferries generally leave each day at 9am, 10am, 11am, 12 noon and 2pm. The ferry schedule is subject to change and may be affected by inclement weather and r ough seas.

FARES

R150 for adults, R75 for children (4-17). Disadvantaged or community groups of 15 or more, meeting special requirements, may be granted concession fares on application. Even though their fares are free, children under 4 must be booked.

The 3½ hour Robben Island tour includes:

• Return boat trip across Table Bay

• A visit to the Maximum Security Prison

• Interaction with an ex-political prisoner

• A 45- minute bus tour, with a guide providing commentary

• The opportunity to explore Murray's Bay Harbour

• Attractions including the African penguin boardwalk and bird hide, plus the museum shop

Robben Island receives upwards of three hundred thousand visitors each year, with the highest percentage being South Africans. This shows the importance given to Robben Island as a symbol of 'the struggle', with lessons to be learned for the successful continuation of democracy in South Africa.

Table Mountain looks so close and offers the perfect photograph. But the prisoners knew that between them and the mainland was freezing Atlantic Ocean, strong currents and great white sharks!

More than 95% of the visitors described their visit to Robben Island in positive terms with such comments as: "well worth a visit", "historical, informative and amazing ", "Uplifting, emotional, empowering and informative", "eye opening", "very impressive and alive".

Robben Island and Table Mountain

Robben Island Maximum Security Prison

A visit to the prison is a highlight for most visitors and the Robben Island Museum tour has several components:

A Section. A bleak area of 40 isolation cells containing artefacts on loan from ex-political prisoners. This stark place recreates the bleakness of prison life. Prison songs and cell stories reverberate in this interactive space.

B Section. This part of the sprawling prison complex includes Nelson Mandela's tiny cell. The former South African president spent 18 of his 27 years of incarceration on Robben Island. This section held many leaders isolated from the other prisoners.

Ex-Prisoner - Now Guide

Who better to guide you around the cells, than the very people who were once imprisoned here. In April 1964, Lionel Davis was sentenced to six years on Robben Island, after being found guilty of conspiring to commit sabotage. Lionel is now a guide and lives on Robben Island with his family and is the chairperson of the Robben Island Village Association.

Today, Lionel speaks evenly of his former jailers, and the appalling conditions he had to endure in the early 1960s and 1970s at the Robben Island Maximum Security Prison. Guides such as Lionel bring to life a South African heritage, which speaks to all people of heroic endurance in the face of adversity and the triumph of the human spirit.

The Island Bus Tour

The tour takes in the historic village and selected parts of the 2km-wide, 4km-long Island:

• The prison house of Robert Sobukwe (founding leader of the Pan Africanist Congress)

• The Lime Quarry

• The Male Leper Church

• The 19th century lighthouse

• Second World War fortifications, including big gun emplacements

• Shipwrecks and Table Bay views

• The Cape Gothic-style Garrison Church

• The Commissioner's Residence: now a guest house/conference venue

Robben Island Wildlife

Robben Island provides a sheltered haven for about 132 bird species, some of which are endangered. The most popular feathered residents are the African penguins, who have re-established a breeding colony, after having been previously wiped out from the island. There are several species of mammals too, including the antelopes bontebok, springbok and eland. In the surrounding waters are Cape Fur seals, Southern Right whales and Dusky and Heaviside Dolphins and Great White Sharks.

Robben Island Contact Information:

Tel: 021 413 4200, email: info@robben-island.org.za,

website: www.robben-island.org.za

Robben Island
MUSEUM

The Robben Island experience includes:

- An opportunity to explore the many layers of the history of the island through the multi-media exhibitions at the Nelson Mandela Gateway.
- A return boat trip across Table Bay.
- A visit to Maximum Security Prison.
- Interaction with an ex-political prisoner.
- A 45-minute bus tour, with a guide providing commentary.
- Robben Island memorabilia and books are available at the Robben Island Museum shops on the Island and at the Nelson Mandela Gateway.

Fares: R150 for adults and R75 for children (4-17 years)

Tel: +27 21 413 4200
Fax: +27 21 419 1057
Email: info@robben-island.org.za
Website: www.robben-island.org.za

TABLE MOUNTAIN AERIAL CABLEWAY

Table Mountain Aerial Cableway started operating on the 4th October 1929. The Cableway has become as much of a landmark in Cape Town at Table Mountain itself, and has carried almost 15 million passengers to the top. Some of its better-known visitors include Oprah Winfrey, Arnold Schwarzenegger, Margaret Thatcher and Jackie Chan, to name just a few.

Work on a complete upgrade began in January 1997, and the new Cableway was officially opened on the 4th October 1997 - the anniversary of the original launch almost 70 years previously.

Table Mountain provides a magnificent backdrop to Cape Town, and is famous for the tablecloth of clouds that pours down its slopes when the south-easter blows. This is a mountain of many moods and offers walkers and hikers a range of routes at various hiking levels. If you want the view without the effort, catch the state-of-the-art revolving cable car to the top, and have lunch or dinner in the table-top restaurant.

ROTATING CABLE CAR

Unlike their predecessors, the new cable cars (or Rotairs), transport you to the top in under 10 minutes. Each car has a carrying capacity of 65 people and a revolving floor giving a 360-degree view of the city and mountain as you glide to the top. The cars also offer excellent aerodynamics in high winds, enabling a more reliable service.

On the top of Table Mountain, designated walkways lead you all over the tabletop to experience extraordinary views past Robben Island, to the very edge of the world as it curves into the Atlantic Ocean. Then look south along rocky mountain ridges leading to Cape Point. The curio shop allows you to take home momentos bearing the insignia of Table Mountain - South Africa's premier tourist attraction. Visitors can also enjoy a hot or cold buffet meal in the self-service restaurant or a drink in the Cocktail Bar.

BIODIVERSITY HOT SPOT

Table Mountain is a biodiversity hot spot with many endemic species. Some of the most conspicuous fynbos plant species on the mountain are proteas, including South Africa's national emblem the King Protea.

One unusual animal you can expect to encounter on the mountain is the Dassie or Rock Hyrax. About 50cm in length, it resembles a guinea pig, but is actually the closest living relative to the elephant! The Table Mountain dassies are very sociable and have lost their natural fear of humans, but don't touch or feed them as they bite.

OPEN DAILY

The Cableway is open 365 days a year, with late cable cars for evenings a the top of the mountain during the summer months. The cablecar will be closed during gale force winds and for annual maintenance. Table Mountain Aerial Cableway tel: 021 424 0015, Website: www.tablemountain.net.

HIGH LIFE

VISIT CAPE TOWN'S PREMIUM
TOURIST ATTRACTION, TABLE
MOUNTAIN AERIAL CABLEWAY,
OFFERING SPECTACULAR VIEWS
OF THE CITY AND THE PENINSULA.

FOR MORE INFORMATION VISIT OUR WEBSITE
WWW.TABLEMOUNTAIN.NET

Photograph by Neil Austen

TABLE MOUNTAIN AERIAL CABLEWAY Co. Ltd.

TABLE MOUNTAIN NATIONAL PARK

Take a hike, a ride, a walk, a stroll. Fly your kite, catch a wave, dive, snooze or picnic. If you are a nature addict and need a fix then the stunning sunsets, exquisite flora and fauna, vast white beaches and waves crashing endlessly against sheer cliffs, should satisfy your cravings.

All these elements combine to form the essence of Table Mountain National Park (TMNP). Established in 1998, TMNP starts in the City of Cape Town and extends along the Table Mountain chain from Signal Hill in the north, to Cape Point in the south. The park incorporates 24,000 hectares and an additional 1,000 square kilometres of marine and coastal reserve.

Part of the Cape Floristic Region World Heritage site, TMNP is the heart of the unique Fybos plant kingdom - the only plant kingdom on earth contained in one country. It is also the smallest yet richest kingdom in the world, with an area smaller than the City of London boasting no less than 2,285 plant species, many of which are endemic to the park. Because TMN is a park within a city, the conservation land is fragmented by urban development and private land. Few people realise that it is in fact one single Park, offering a diversity of attractions.

Within the SANParks stable, the TMNP is unique in that it is largely an open access park, offering locals and visitors free entry at the majority of its access points. In certain sections of the park, entrance fees are charged, which get channelled straight back into conservation initiatives and environmental education.

TMNP Head Office is open from 8am– 5pm, Monday to Friday.

Tel: 021 701 8692, email: tablemountain@sanparks.org.

Cape Point

Table Mountain National Park

A Park for All, Forever   'n Park vir almal, vir Altyd
iPaka yoluntu lonke ngonaphakade

More than just a walk in the park

With spectacular views of majestic mountains plunging into mighty oceans, Table Mountain National Park is Cape Town's natural treasure and extends for 60 kilometres from Signal Hill to Cape Point.

Home to *fynbos*, the world's smallest yet richest floral kingdom, the TMNP is world renown for her unique flora and fauna – both terrestrial and marine.

The TMNP has something for everybody from adrenaline junkies, anglers and hikers to nature-lovers, dreamers, and photographers.

Welcome to our Park but please, tread lightly and help us conserve our priceless environment for generations to come.

Legend

Hiking Path	Penguins
Picnic Site	Angling
Braai Fires Only	Mountain Biking
Tidal Pool	Cable Car
Main Gate	Diving
Restaurant	Main Roads
Wheelchair Access	Hiking Trail
View Site	Table Mountain National Park
Toilets	Marine Protected Area
Slipway	Marine Restricted Zone
Whale Watching	

South African NATIONAL PARKS

Tel: +27 (0)21 701 8692
Fax: +27 (0)21 701 8773
e-mail: tablemountain@sanparks.org
website: www.tmnp.co.za

THE CAPE OF GOOD HOPE

With Cape Point at its tip, this is perhaps the most popular section of Table Mountain National Park, and is one of the top tourist destinations in South Africa. Visitors can see a variety of wildlife such as antelopes like bontebok, eland and red hartebeest, cheeky chacma baboons, an array of reptiles and a great selection of birds - it literally teems with life.

This area of Cape Town's South Peninsula, is also steeped in history, for it is here that the great Portuguese voyagers Bartholomew Dias and Vasco da Gama historically rounded the Cape in the 16th century, and opened up the sea trade routes between east and west. This revolutionised global economics (although some historians argue that this is a Eurocentic record of history and that Persian and Arabic seafarers should claim this honour).

Cape Point

SHIPWRECKS

The coastline is littered with the wrecks of ships that fell prey to the violent storms and deceiving reefs that have earned this passage the accolade, "Cape of Storms". The original Cape Point Lighthouse still stands and visitors can take the funicular up the hill to see for themselves, the treacherous conditions that caused it to be erected in the first place. While at Cape Point, dine at the Two Oceans Restaurant, which boasts spectacular sea views. If you prefer a picnic, head down to Buffels Bay – but you may have company, so look out for baboons. Be sure to visit the Buffelsfontein Visitor Centre for coffee and a snack, while looking at the exhibits showing all the plants and animals in each season. The centre also provides first class conference facilities.

OVERNIGHT IN THE PARK

For a really awesome experience, book yourself a night or two in the Olifantsbos cottage. Remotely situated in the far south of the Park, this isolated getaway affords you star spangled nights with only the sound of the waves, and the nocturnal animals in moonlight. A rare treat indeed.

For the more active, a two-day hike in this section of the park gives a true wilderness experience with exceptional views. Or for the serious hiker, book on the six-night Hoerikwaggo Trail - a hike starting in Cape Town and finishing at Cape Point. You stay overnight in renovated park accommodation along the way. This trail will open in stages, starting in early 2005.

CONTACT DETAILS

Two Oceans Restaurant and Buffelsfontein Visitor Centre are both open 9.30am– 5.30pm Monday to Sunday. Two Oceans Restaurant tel: 021 780 9200. Buffelsfontein Visitor Centre tel: 021 780 9204.

BOULDERS PENGUIN COLONY

Visit the famous Boulders Beach colony of African Penguins. This is a truly special experience, with the option of a guided tour. After you have fallen in love with the penguins, swim in the comparatively warm sheltered coves, ideal for children. But don't touch or feed the penguins - they can give a nasty bite. Boulders Visitor Centre, tel: 021 786 2392.

SIGNAL HILL, LIONS HEAD AND DEVILS PEAK

These three peaks flank Table Mountain and together hold Cape Town in a rocky embrace. Signal Hill is home to the noonday gun, which marks midday in Cape Town with a bang. A drive to the top of Signal Hill offers uninterrupted views of Table Bay and endless Atlantic Ocean. Lions Head peak has become something of a pilgrimage for Capetonions, who make the rocky climb to witness the full moon rising. Devils Peak protrudes from the flat line of Table Mountain and has challenging slopes.

PICNIC SITES

Silvermine picnic and braai sites and wheel chair-friendly boardwalk (half an hour south of the city), overlook a picturesque reservoir in which you can take a refreshing swim. Half way back to the city is the popular jogging and picnic area in Newlands Forest, while on the Atlantic coastline is the beachside Oudekraal braai and picnic site. These areas are available for functions too, call: 021 715 0011.

THE MARINE PROTECTED AREA

The most recent addition to TMNP is the newly proclaimed Marine Protected Area. Extending from Moullie Point to Muizenberg. It aims to regulate recreational and commercial activities to ensure sustainable use of our seas. The oceans of TMNP are exceptional for biodiversity, and whales are a favourite visitor.

THE HOERIKWAGGO TRAIL

The Hoerikwaggo six-night trail will run from Cape Town to Cape Point, with terrain ranging from ragged slopes to endless beaches. Beginning with the Slave Route in the city and winding south through the mountains, hikers will overnight in restored historic buildings or campsites. This trail will open in stages, starting in early 2005.

Silvermine Waterfall

Hikers

Two Oceans Restaurant

KIRSTENBOSCH BOTANICAL GARDENS

Kirstenbosch National Botanical Garden has been voted one of the top seven botanical gardens in the world and one of the top ten most desirable tourist destinations in South Africa. This garden is renowned for the beauty and diversity of the South African flora it displays and for the magnificence of its setting against the eastern slopes of Table Mountain.

This is a garden where mainly plants indigenous to South Africa are grown. Those which are not indigenous are plants introduced to the garden many, many years ago. The estate covers 528 hectares and supports diverse fynbos flora and natural forest. The cultivated 36-hectare garden displays collections of South African plants, particularly those from the winter rainfall region of the country.

The Visitors' Centre provides several opportunities for those wishing to take a little of Kirstenbosch home with them including a letterbox, coffee bar and facilities for conferences and exhibitions.

ART IN THE PARK

A stroll around the park will reveal unexpected guests in the form of exquisite stone sculptures in the Shona style of art peeking out of flower beds. Most are for sale. There are also regular Art Exhibitions showing off considerable local talent.

TRAILS AND MOUNTAIN WALKS

For visitors wishing to explore the Kirstenbosch Nature Reserve on their own, there are some several trails including two well marked access routes which ascend to the top of Table Mountain. Other services are volunteer guides conducting regular free tours, shuttle car tours, The MyGuide™ self-guiding system (available in English and German) as well as wheelchair-friendly walks in the garden with wheelchairs available. Tours can be booked via the Visitors Centre Information Desk on Tel: 021 – 799 8783.

EATING AT KIRSTENBOSCH

The Kirstenbosch Restaurant is divided into the Silver Tree à la Carte Restaurant and the Fynbos Food Court and caters for a wide range of both foreign and local tastes. Reservations & Enquiries: Tel 021 762 9585; Fax 021 762 9625. The Kirstenbosch Tea Room's menu of all day breakfasts, light meals and decadent teas. Reservations and enquiries: Tel 021 797 4883

Other facilities include a Centre for Home Gardening - a one stop outlet, featuring an indigenous plant nursery, a garden design and landscaping advice desk, demonstration gardens and a hall for flower shows and horticultural lectures.

CONCERTS

On Sundays during the summer months from December to March, sunset musical concerts are held on the lawns from 5pm-6.30pm. Bring a blanket, a picnic basket and a bottle of wine. For more details call the Information Desk on Tel: 021 799 8783

In Winter the musical concerts are held at the Silvertree Restaurant on Sunday evenings. For further details contact the restaurant, tel: 021 762 9585.

CRAFT MARKETS

Craft Markets are held at the Stone Cottages (opposite Kirstenbosch) on the last Sunday of every month (except during the winter months of June, July & August). For more information contact the Botanical Society, tel: 021 671 5468.

Kirstenbosch, Cape Town

South Africa's

Garden Getaways

Visit the National Botanical Institute's three
magnificent outdoor meanders
in the Western Cape

Harold Porter, Betty's Bay

NATIONAL
BOTANICAL
INSTITUTE

Welcome

Karoo Desert, Worcester

**For more information call +27 21 799 8783 or
Fax +27 21 761 4687 or email info@nbi.ac.za
or visit our web site at http://www.nbi.ac.za**

GRANDWEST CASINO AND ENTERTAINMENT WORLD

Only 15 minutes drive from the centre of Cape Town, is one of South Africa's premier leisure venues - GrandWest Casino and Entertainment World. Nearly 4-million people visit GrandWest every year and there is something here to entertain every member of the family.

EVOCATIVE CAPE ARCHITECTURE

GrandWest lives up the 'grand' part of its name from the moment you catch sight of it. The eclectic neo-classical facades are evocative of the beauties of Early Cape Town in its late 19th century heydey. GrandWest's design recognises the beauty of some of Cape Town's disappeared buildings and historical photographs provided the basis for replication of this stylish period, when Cape Town was at the height of its economic power. Landscaped gardens lead towards the complex and the Old Cape theme continues inside, creating a stylised Cape ambience.

FOOD GLORIOUS FOOD

There are so many styles of restaurants, that choosing one can become a problem. There is the elegant Union Castle Grillroom - which naturally enough serves some of the best steaks around or Squire's Grill and Chop House. Bukhara is arguably the Cape's top Indian Restaurant, while the Cape Town Fish Market serves fish fresh from the sea. Asian tastes are satisfied by Kyoto Japanese and Lai Kung Chinese. The Cape Village is a Cape Dutch-themed fast food court, with a mini ice rink in the centre for the kiddies to slide around on, while more competent skaters take to the large Ice Station rink, right next door.

Alongside the casino floor is The Quarterdeck Restaurant, which is an all you can eat buffet of gargantuan proportions, at an incredibly good value price. Pace yourself in the salad and cheese valley and don't fill yourself up on the tempting range of fresh breads and rolls. Stroll the Fish Counter and sample oysters, crayfish, prawns and crab. Hopefully you still have room for the meat aisle which starts with African dishes, and leads to the Roast Carvery, with a full range of vegetables. There's still more.....with a choice of Italian, Greek or other regional dishes. Last but by no means least, is the Dessert Den, with about 40 different delectable sweets to finish off your feast.

GrandWest's success lies in the breadth and quality of its entertainment, with its Casino a big draw card. There are plenty of other activities too; go-karting, ice-skating, adventure golf, arcade games, night clubs and a wide variety of restaurants.

The Movies

"Cinema Starz", one of the most comfortable cinema complexes in the Western Cape, screening the very latest Hollywood blockbusters, as well as films for the more discerning movie-goer. The latest Bollywood titles are proving popular as are monthly movie premiers.

The Ice Station

GrandWest's Ice Station, with its Olympic-standard ice rink, is the leading ice skating facility in South Africa. It has changed the face of the old fashioned ice rink into a modern Ice Venue, where social skating remains popular, but international ice shows, ice hockey and figure-skating competitions crete much excitement. Skates are for hire and the rink offers an energetic experience that takes the visitor off their feet in more ways than one.

Children

The Magic Company offers varied entertainment that will keep children occupied for hours. Amusements include go-karting, adventure golf, a mini roller coaster, merry-go-round and a large range of the latest and best in interactive games. The Magic Company also provides individually-themed venues for children's birthday parties.

The District

Exhilarating nightlife and tempting eating is what the District is all about. The District recalls the unique vibe of the Old District Six, before this mixed-race suburb of Cape Town was demolished. The District - GrandWest style -is inspired by buildings found on the original streets. This is the hub of GrandWest's nightlife and comprises various restaurants offering a unique and delicious selection of different dining delights. Some of the more adult attractions located within 'The District' include Hanover Street, with a unique and exotic atmosphere for party animals. Jackson Hall gets you dancing to a live DJ playing a varied mix of today's sounds, and Roxy's Revue Bar is renowned for offering the best live music shows such as; Forever Young, 70's Revolution, Joker in the Pack, DIVA's and Diamonds & Dust.

GRANDWEST CASINO

The core of GrandWest is its spectacular casino with 1,750 slot machines and 60 gaming tables. The casino is decorated with a rich colour palette enhancing the nautical theme, and is surrounded by bars and restaurants, all open twenty four hours a day, seven days a week. The Casino caters for smokers and non-smokers in separate sections on the casino floor. Exciting promotions add to the thrill and increase your chances of winning big.

Of special interest to first time gamblers is GrandWest's Gambling Information Centre, which provides instruction on how to play all the table games, as well as the slot machines. Spending a short time here first, will ensure you make your debut on the casino floor with greater confidence. For the higher stake gambler there is an exclusive Salon Privé, situated between the Grand Hotel and the Union Castle Grill Room.

GRANDWEST HOTELS

Sun International's 4-star Grand Hotel is a recreation of the historic establishment which used to grace the main street of Cape Town in the late nineteenth century. Its stately historic façade recreates an era long since forgotten in the modern metropolis of 21st century Cape Town. The Grand Hotel is conveniently situated within Grand West's main complex, next to 'The District'. This hotel has 39 rooms and an executive suite, plus the luxury of a swimming pool. Standard amenities include a mini bar, computerised safe, colour satellite TV, radio, hairdryer, telephone, air conditioning and 24-hour room service.

The more affordable City Lodge Hotel is immediately adjacent to the complex and is modelled on a Cape-Dutch homestead, complete with traditional gable. The City Lodge has 120 rooms.

LOCATION

GrandWest Casino and Entertainment World is located in the bustling Goodwood area, just north of the beautiful City of Cape Town. Pedestrians and groups arriving by train from Goodwood Station enter the complex via the Welcome Centre, for those arriving by car there is ample parking.

For a look at what GrandWest has to offer, take a look at their website: www.suninternational.co.za.

GRANDWEST

· CASINO AND ENTERTAINMENT WORLD ·

THE BEST GAME WATCHING IN AFRICA

For untamed entertainment come to South Africa's grandest casino and entertainment world. Experience Mystery Jackpots. Slot Machines and Tables. Digital Cinemas. Themed Restaurants. Nightclub and Revue Bar. It's wild.

LIVE THE GRAND LIFE

FOR MORE INFO: (021) 505 7777

 Sun International

An amazing opportunity to dive in a gigantic shark-filled aquarium, presents itself at the incredible Two Oceans Aquarium in Cape Town's V&A Waterfront.

FISH-EYE VIEW

Swim freely alongside ragged-tooth sharks and come face to face with a multitude of fishes cruising around the gigantic aquarium. You need to be a qualified scuba diver to dive in Two Oceans Aquarium two main exhibits; the I&J Predator Exhibit and the swaying Kelp Forest.

The I&J Predator Exhibit contains two million litres of water and is home to several notorious ragged tooth sharks, who patrol the tank. There are also a variety of beautiful rays gliding silently thought the water, shoals of silvery fish and a turtle.

Qualified divers can put on wetsuits and scuba gear, then swim without the hindrance of a cage in this extraordinary marine environment. Close encounters with these formidable sea creatures are absolutely thrilling.

The Kelp Forest Exhibit is open to qualified advanced divers to swim in this swaying underwater forest and feed a multitude of fish. Containing 800,000 litres of water, the Kelp Forest is one of the best on display in the world, and is typical of the cold waters along the West Coast of South Africa.

OLD FASHIONED COPPER HAT DIVE

The Two Oceans Aquarium also offers qualified divers the opportunity to experience an original copper hat dive. Wearing an Imperial Navy Diving suit, comprising a copper helmet and bulky canvas suit, divers are lowered via a diving stage into the I&J Predator Exhibit. Weighted down with lead-weighted boots and a weight-belt, you can stroll amongst the creatures as they circle above and around you. What a marvellous sensation!

CASTLE OF GOOD HOPE

The Castle of Good Hope is the oldest colonial building in South Africa. Built between 1666 and 1679 by the Dutch East India Company, better known as the VOC (Vereenigde Oost-Indische Compagnie), this pentagonal fortification replaced a small clay and timber fort built in 1652 by Commander Jan Van Riebeeck, founder of the maritime replenishment station at the Cape of Good Hope.

On 26 April 1679 the five bastions were named after the main titles of Willem, the Prince of Orange. The western bastion was named Leerdam, followed in clockwise order by Buuren, Catzenellenbogen, Nassau and Oranje. In 1936 the Castle was declared a National Monument. As a result of an extensive, ongoing restoration programme launched in the 1980's, the Castle of Good Hope remains the best preserved fortification of its kind built by the VOC in regions where it had interests.

The Castle of Good Hope was the regional headquarters of the South African Army in the Western Cape, and houses the famous William Fehr Collection of historic artworks, the Castle Military Museum and ceremonial facilities for traditional Cape Regiments.

ENTRANCE & BELL

The main entrance of the Castle bears the emblems of the VOC which ruled the Cape for nearly one and a half centuries. This entrance is a unique example of 17th century Dutch classicism. The bell, cast in 1697 by Claude Fremy in Amsterdam, still hangs in the tower from its original wooden beams.

CASTLE MILITARY MUSEUM

The museum depicts the military history of the Cape, the Castle and Cape Regiments.

WILLIAM FEHR COLLECTION

This collection consists of artworks reflecting many aspects of cultural life at the Cape from the early VOC days until the middle of the 19th century. Exhibitions of a contemporary nature are occasionally presented.

TRADITIONAL MILITARY CEREMONIES

Daily performances of ceremonies echo traditions of earlier years.

MOAT

Sections of the moat, once a part of the Castle's system of defence, were rebuilt during recent restoration.

THE CASTLE FORGE

The Castle Forge is located in the earliest blacksmith workshop in South Africa. The Forge was initially built for the upkeep and maintenance of the Castle's hardware and steel goods.

DE GOEWERNEUR RESTAURANT

Home of South African cuisine. Enjoy freshly baked scones and sample a selection of typically South African dishes, with a beautiful view of Table Mountain as your background.

HET BAKHUYS & DOLPHIN POOL

During the restoration of the inner courtyard, the foundations of the early 18th century bakery and pool were discovered. The building, currently known as Het Bakhuys ('t Bakhuijs), has been reconstructed on these foundations. Het Bakhuys also caters for functions and conferences.

PUBLIC TOURS

Guided tours of the Castle are conducted daily by professional tour guides. The Castle is uniquely equipped to provide tours for the physically challenged.

GENERAL INFORMATION

Opening times: 09h00 to 16h00 Mondays to Sundays
Public tours: 11h00, 12h00, and 14h00 daily

Self guide maps available in English, Afrikaans, Spanish German, Dutch, French and Italian.

CASTLE OF GOOD HOPE

OPENING TIMES:
09H00 TO 16H00 MONDAYS TO SUNDAYS
PUBLIC HOLIDAYS: 11H00, 12H00 AND 14H00 DAILY

DRAKENSTEIN LION PARK

This privately-funded park is a sanctuary for captive born, hand-raised animals that cannot be rehabilitated to the wild. Our animals are housed in large sprawling camps and can be viewed from an overhead walkway. The park is also home to the endangered cheetah, as well as ostrich and a host of farmyard animals. Admission is R27 for adults and R10 for children.

Tel: +27 (0) 21 863 3290
Old Paarl Road (R101), Klapmuts
www.gopassport.com

100 Landscaped walk-through aviaries with 3000 birds, monkeys and small animals.

Tel: +27 (0) 21 790 2730
Valley Road, Hout Bay
www.gopassport.com

Butterfly World

Cape Town's very own butterfly sanctuary is just a flutter away. Housed in a lush tropical garden, butterflies fly free in amongst the palms and ponds. Open Monday to Sunday, 9am to 5pm, Butterfly World offers a craft shop, Coffee shop informative displays and insectariums. 30 minutes from Cape Town: Take N1 towards Pearl, Exit 47 towards Klapmuts on R44.

Tel: +27 (0) 21 875 5628
N1 towards Paarl, Exit 47 on R44
www.gopassport.com

MONKEY TOWN
PRIMATE CENTRE SOMERSET WEST

Sanctuary for 25 amazing exotic monkey species. Guided tours through leafy garden park. Feeding times. Interaction. Restaurant. Farm yard. Play park.

Open daily 09:00 -17:00.

Tel: +27 (0) 21 875 5628
Outside Somerset West on N2
www.gopassport.com

This world-class science centre is packed with over 300 interactive displays and is geared towards everyone, from the very young to the young at heart! Call from a giant cell phone, visit a walk-in room size camera or weigh yourself on a different planet. Open 7 days a week, this is edutainment at its best.

Tel: +27 (0) 21 529 8100
407 Canal Walk, Century City
www.gopassport.com

Own your very own Madiba shirt

An invitation to visit and view the Presidential Shirt range

Tel: +27 (0) 21 421 1695
Shop 007 Clock Tower, V&A Waterfront,
Cape Town
www.gopassport.com

The District Six Museum tells the history of apartheid through an intimate look at ordinary people's stories and memories. It is celebration of local triumph which resonates with people globally who have experienced marginalisation. As an award-winning, community Museum, the District Six Museum is considered to be an essential stop in Cape Town for the culturally and eco-sensitive tourist.

Tel: +27 (0) 21 461 8745
25A Buitenkant Street, Cape Town
www.gopassport.com

iziko
museums of cape town

PLANETARIUM

Housed in the SA Museum building is a celestial theatre in the round, which transports the audience through the wonders of the universe. Inside the domed auditorium, we can recreate the night sky, so whatever the weather outside, the Planetarium sky is always clear, an extraordinary audio-visual experience for old and young.

Tel: 27 (021) 481 3900
25 Queen Victoria Street, Cape Town
www.gopassport.com

iziko
museums of cape town

SOUTH AFRICAN MUSEUM

The South African Museum was founded in 1825. In 1897 the Museum moved to its present building in the historic Company's Garden. Since then millions of visitors have wandered its halls and corridors to be stimulated and inspired by its collections and exhibitions. They have left the Museum with a better understanding of the earth and its biological and cultural diversity, past and present.

Tel: +27 (0) 21 481 3800
25 Queen Victoria Street, Gardens
www.gopassport.com

KIDS ATTRACTIONS

Ratanga Junction

According to a spokes person (in March 2004), Africa's largest theme park, Ratanga Junction is selling off all its rights. So phone before you go. Tel: 0861 200 300

Ice Skating

Cut a fine figure at the Grand West Casino Complex's ice-rink (to the left of the N7 motorway, 10 minutes drive north of town, tel: 021 505 7777).

Beautiful Butterflies

Some beautiful winged creatures are found in the hot steamy fairytale setting of Butterfly World, near Stellenbosch in the Cape Winelands (Klapmuts Road, Stellenbosch, tel: 021 875 5628).

Farmyards

Family fun can be had at Firlands Farm World (Firlands, tel: 021 856 3130), Stodels Nurseries (Eversdal Road, Bellville, tel: 021 919 1107), Phillippi's Adventure Farm, (Weltevreden Road, tel: 021 371 5246), or by talking to the animals while parents have brunch at the Barnyard Farmstall (Steenberg near Tokai, tel: 021 712 6934).

Something Cerebral

Stimulate grey matter at the Planetarium, or allow budding scientists to create some chemistry in the MTN ScienCentre (Exit 39 of N1, follow Canal Walk signs, tel: 021 529 8100) or the Telkom Exploratorium (Union Castle Building, Victoria & Alfred Waterfront, tel: 021 419 5957).

ANIMAL MAGIC

Take a jaunt on the Table Mountain rotating cablecar (tel: 021 424 0015), but at the top don't chase the funny little dassies (rock hyrax) as they might nip you.

Boulders Beach Penguin Colony (just outside Simon's Town, tel: 021 789 2329) is another place with kid appeal. The penguins may also bite if annoyed and are best left to their own devices, which include looking really cute and flashing past you while you swim in the sheltered coves.

There are some interesting and unusual animals at Imhoff Farm, Kommetjie, with camel and horse rides, a snake park, plus peacocks and emus wandering around the paddocks, (Kommetjie Road, tel: 021 783 4545). Giddy up at several other stables - see details on Horse & Camel Rides page. Solole Game Reserve, Kommetjie has a waterhole frequented by buffalo, springbok, ostrich and other creatures that you can watch while dining at Mnandi's Restaurant (tel: 021 785 1992).

Get up close to sharks and other sea creatures and dip your fingers in the touch pool at The Two Oceans Aquarium (V&A Waterfront, tel: 021 418 3823).

Other wildlife can be seen at Tygerberg Zoo (Exit 39, N1 Motorway, tel: 021 884 4494), and 20 exotic species of monkey roam around Monkey Town, (signposted on the N2 motorway at far end of Somerset West, tel: 021 858 1060).

SPEED FREAKS

Take a mountain bike flip in the beautiful Tokai Forest or through the Cape of Good Hope Nature Reserve. (Downhill Adventures, tel: 021 422 0388). Kids upwards of 1.2 metres will revel in the noisy Formula 1 go-kart tracks at Kenilworth (tel: 021 683 2670) and Canal Walk (tel: 021 551 8570).

Cut a fine figure at the GrandWest Casino ice-rink (10 minutes drive north of town on the N1, then follow the signs to GrandWest, tel: 021 505 7777).

WATCH THE BIRDIE

The smart Cape Point ostrich show farm runs short tours where you might witness an ostrich being born. Its upmarket shop has highly priced curios. (Opposite Cape Point entrance, tel: 021 780 9294).

Hout Bay's World of Birds (Valley Road, tel: 021 790 2370), contains fascinating feathered friends - many of whom are being nursed back to health after injuries. While in this neighbourhood, chug out to Seal Island (Circe Launches tel: 021 790 1040), for an incredible glimpse of this large Cape fur seal breeding colony (but hold your nose when downwind)!

hoff Farm offers a warm welcome with something for the whole
mily to enjoy. In the converted farm buildings you will find a
rm shop with our own bakery and tea garden, local craft and
ft shops, art studios, cheese dairy, herb nursery, restaurant and
offee house, pottery studio, surfboards, clothing and magical
eans. Visit the snake and reptile park or take horse and camel
des. Children can have fun in the play areas including donkey
des in the courtyard.

**Open Tuesday – Sunday 10h00 till 17h00
including Public Holidays.**

**The Gift Restaurant open Tuesday
and Sundays 9h00 till 17h00 and
from 9h00 till late on Wednesday, Thursday,
Friday and Saturday.
Closed on Mondays.**

Tel: +27 (0) 21 783 4545
Mobile: +27 (0) 83 735 5227
www.naturefarm.co.za   Kommetjie Road, M56

TOURING

Putting the Umuntu into Ubuntu

"The spirit of Ubuntu – that profound African sense that we are human only through the humanity of other human beings – is not a parochial phenomenon, but has added globally to our common search for a better world." – Nelson Mandela.

Township Kids at Play

Children having fun at home

Township Child with Tourists

TOWNSHIP LIFE

The Ubuntu of township culture dictates that the community is placed above the needs of the individual (Umuntu). Prepare to re-evaluate your perspective on life and do as some of the locals do, with an inter-dependent society, where everyone knows and helps their neighbours.

Democratic South Africa was born on these township streets and Cape Town's townships roll out the welcome mat for you to see it for yourself.

THE TOWNSHIPS

Apartheid-era 'Homelands Policy' allocated areas according to ethnicity. This has left its mark on the ethnic distribution of Cape Town to this day, and townships are there in all their squalor for everyone to see. The spectacle greets you before your plane lands, as many of Cape Town's informal settlements are adjacent to the airport. These overpopulated areas are distinguishable by their lack of infrastructure and services, but adhere proudly and defiantly to a mixture of traditional and western ways.

Don't be afraid to head into a township (probably best on a guided tour), to see, feel, smell and touch a side of life very different from you own. Your visit will be most rewarding and your fears will be quickly allayed by the dramatic transformation taking place by the provision of homes, water, electricity, schools and sport facilities. This has led to a positive outlook by the residents, evidenced by their optimism and warmth.

DISTRICT SIX

It is also worth paying a visit to District Six, which is a vast and until recently all but empty tract of land on the edge of the city centre. District Six was previously a thriving mixed community, but residents were forcibly removed from their homes during the 1960s to the early 1980s. Today, settlement of land claims, mean that many displaced people can return to their rightful place and District Six can live again. The excellent District Six Museum is at 25a Buitenkant St, Cape Town. Tel: 021 461 8745.

DOOM AND THE GLOOM

Some tin shanties have been accorded 'shack chic' status, but in reality the townships are rough and tough. Before you judge township residents, remember you have not walked in their shoes. There is great news of hope and change but this is countered with some harsh realities. HIV/Aids is rife and there are a growing number of AIDS orphans. The lucky ones have grandmothers who are left holding the baby. Rape, wife beating and child abuse is common. Disabled people are neither seen nor heard but kept in a backroom.

Unemployment is rife. Some kids take to the streets for a life of crime or join drug gangs who rule the streets.

NOT ALL DOOM AND GLOOM

Please remind yourself that, "Never in the history of the world has a country the size of South Africa housed 20 per cent of its most disadvantaged people in ten years." There are a large number of both public and private initiatives that are engaged in social upliftment and awareness programmes such as aids and family counselling, youth and drug rehabilitation, skills development, food gardening and re-cycling of waste as a means of income. Many still need proper homes but slowly and surely progress is being made. There is a middle class on the rise within the townships, and an ever increasing number of residents building houses or upgrading their shacks. The well educated and well funded rarely give up the township spirit of Ubuntu to join their counterparts in Cape Town's leafy suburbs.

LIVELY TOWNSHIP STREETS

Feisty township residents trade from their homes, their backyards, and out of shipping containers or shopping trolleys. Despite the dense living conditions and high unemployment, they realise that they need to help themselves, so ambitious entrepreneurs are to be found everywhere.

SIMPLE PLEASURES

With few material possessions, most township children manage to convert waste matter into toys and seem to derive great pleasure from doing so. Witness a child taking delight in rolling an old tyre along the road with a stick, or playing with a car fashioned from cardboard and wire. Mothers who are lucky enough to have work, leave their children with grandparents, siblings or at overcrowded crèches, who charge for one month less than you would pay for one meal out.

LIFE-ALTERING EXPERIENCES

On a visit to a township (or informal settlement), capture the resident's warmth, creative energy, adaptability, faith, community spirit and indomitable humour. This is best reflected in their fashion, music, homes, taverns, businesses and distinctive cuisine. A township visit is quite simply a pilgrimage that every tourist and every South African should make. According to Cape Town Tourism, township tours are selling as well as wine tours, so be sure not to miss out on this humbling and enlightening experience on the "other side of town".

Township Streets

Township streets are hectic with speeding mini-bus taxis dodging carts pulled by patient donkeys. Spaza shops sell anything from groceries to gearboxes and traders peddle hubcaps and skin creams, potatoes and cigarettes, on the side of the road. Sangomas (traditional healers) 'throw the bones' to tap into the wisdom the ancestors for those that need assistance, while the same people crowd into Churches on Sundays.

Township Children

TOWNSHIP TOURS

Township Store

While in the Kayelitsha-Gugulethu region, make the township-based Sivuyile Tourism Centre, (next to Sivuyile College), your starting point - tel: 021 637 8449. Or board the red double-decker bus for a Township Music Tour whose highlights include, a drumming circle, traditional African instruments, story-telling, and a stop for a 'washdown' (usually referring to a beer), at a shebeen (tavern - often unlicensed). Tel: 021 790 8825.

KHAYELITSHA

Visit Khayelitsha, South Africa's second largest township, which has traditionally been the point of arrival for job-hunters from the former Transkei and Ciskei black homelands. Your stay in Khayelitsha is not complete without a visit to Philani Nutrition Centre (Walter Sisulu Road, Site C, tel: 021 387 5124). Here you can snap up township-inspired tapestries, pillows and shirts. Also visit the Khayelitsha Craft Market (St Michael's Church, Ncumo Road, tel: 021 361 5246). For Khayelitsha township tour bookings tel: 021 970 3172.

LANGA

Gugas' Thebe Arts and Cultural Centre in Langa, (cnr Washington Avenue/Church Street, tel: 021 695 3493), is testimony to a collaboration between architects and the community, that is both functional and fun. The ceramic-adorned walls watch over drama, music, beading and photography initiatives. The on-site Eziko Restaurant (tel: 021 694 0434) is also worth a visit. Book a Langa tour on tel: 021 694 000. The Tsoga Environmental Resource Centre (Washington Street, tel: 694 0004), welcomes visitors to their environmental organisation.

MASIPHUMELELE

On the way to Cape Point, visit Masiphumelele Township and their Two Oceans Craft & Culture Centre selling beautiful locally made crafts. Situated on the Kommetjie Road, South Peninsula. Tel: 021 783 4545, email: toccc@mweb.co.za.

Right opposite this is the Solole Private Game Reserve and Mnandi's Restaurant, who offer a combined Township and Game Tour including a tractor ride through the private nature reserve. Tel: 021 785 3248, email: info@solole.co.za, website: www.solole.co.za

IMIZAMO YETHU

Imizamo Yethu - meaning 'Through Struggle We Achieve' - is the informal settlement on the mountain slopes of Hout Bay. They know all about struggle as too often their shacks are swept through by forest fires. For an interesting walk around this community tel: 021 790 1264.

SEE THE CAPE FROM THE AIR

It's always a good idea to get orientated to your surroundings at the start of a holiday, and Cape Town has the perfect way to negotiate its impassable mountains and ragged coastline - in a helicopter, light aircraft or supersonic jet!

V&A WATERFRONT HELIPORT

The V & A Waterfront has a boulevard just for helicopter companies, which can get quite noisy as the choppers come and go. They all offer scenic trips and you can also hire a helicopter to take you anywhere you please. The good thing is you only pay for the time you are in the air.

The Flying Company: Based in the Franschhoek winelands, they offer scenic flights and pioneering helicopter activity trips such as heli-biking, heli-hiking and heli-fishing. Tel: 021 876 3367, info@flyingcompany.co.za.

Sport Helicopters: Sport have a range of helicopters including a Huey called 'Sea Wolf' seating nine passengers. Tel: 021 419 5907, info@sport-helicopters.co.za, or visit their website www.sport-helicopters.co.za

Civair: Civair have been around a while in this competitive business and have a Jet Ranger and Long Ranger. Tel: 021 419 5182, civair@mweb.co.za, www.civair.co.za

NAC Makana: Their V&A Waterfront helicopter operation is part of a much larger organisation offering charter aircraft from South Africa's major airports. Tel: 021 425 3868, info@nacmakana.com, www.nacmakana.com

Helicopter & Marine Services: Their claim to fame is a Vietnam-style Huey in camouflage colours, for a simulated combat mission extreme ride. Tel: 421 1195.

Win Aviation: They have a helicopter and seaplane for scenic peninsula flights. Depart from the heliport and V&A Waterfront quayside respectively. Tel: 418 0207, tours@winholdings.com, www.winholdings.com

FIXED WING CHARTER & FLIGHT TRAINING

Cloud 9 Charters have 25 aeroplanes from twin engines to executive jets, with numerous different operating licences for just about anything aerial. Tel: 021 934 9994, info@cloudn9air.co.za, www.cloud9air.co.za

Federal Air is a charter airline with aircraft seating from 4 to 10 passengers, plus they can supply a 727 or 737. Tel: 021 934 1383, Capetown@fedair.com, www.fedair.com.

Cape Aero Club is a flight training school at Cape Town International Airport. The basic Private Pilots Licence can be achieved in 8 weeks study and practical (minimum), costing around R45,000. If you already have your PPL, you can hire one of their light aircraft. Tel: 021 934 0234, aeroclub@iafrica.com, www.capeaeroclub.co.za

Helicopter Tour Prices

2004 Helicopter ride prices average out at around R9,500 per hour for a six-seater Long Ranger or R7,200 for a four-seater Jet Ranger. Divide this by the number of passengers and you have an affordable luxury tour.

Also available are Vietnam-style Huey's and a seaplane. Most helicopter operators charge the same price, so it doesn't harm to ask if one operator will give you a discount in return for your business.

Nac Makana Helicopter

Supersonic

Thunder City Entertainment have their own hanger at Cape Town International Airport with options for the jet set and speed freaks. Take a supersonic flight in their Lightening, at a cost of €9,500. Or up to an hour in their Hunter at €3,500 and Buccaneer at €7,500. They also have a Helicopter School where tuition and 50 hours in the air costs R120,000. Tel: 021 934 8007, ulf@thundercity.com, www.thundercity.com.

Thunder City Jet

Snoek Braai (barbecue)

Local wisdom dictates that a long thin silvery snoek is best braaied over a deep-sunken sand pit on the beach full of smoked oak shavings, or poached in foil on the grid in a sauce of apricot jam, lemon juice and tons of garlic butter. Delicious!

Trawler

Fishy Tails

For The Record … A 92.55 kilogram Yellowfin Tuna was caught off Gordon's Bay in 2002!

"Good Luck and Stywe lyne - (tight lines!)" The writer caught no less than six Yellowfin Tuna off Cape Point (plus the one that got away!) on her inaugural one-day big game fishing excursion.

Old Cape Fishermen's Tales

• If the day's catch is good, don't count the haul before you pull in your lines, or your luck may change!

• If you whistle at the sea, the wind will soon visit.

• A boiled egg in a lunch box will result in a 'mombakkies' ('blank' - no fish will be caught).

• If a baboon is viewed sitting or playing on the sand dunes near Cape Hangklip, decent catches of geelbek will follow.

• 'Red sky in the morn, fishermen forlorn. Red sky at night, fishermen's delight'

SEA FISHING

With the meeting of the cold south to north Benguela current, with the warm Agulhas current from the east, Cape Town arguably offers the best deep sea angling in southern Africa.

With most of the world's oceans fished out or polluted, the fishing nations of the world are increasingly looking to South Africa as one of the last frontiers. Cape Town is especially renowned for trophy-size tuna, swordfish, carp, yellowfish, skipjack, yellowtail, yellowfin and longfin tuna (albacore).

Eighteen international teams attended the 2002 European Federation of Sea Angling Game Fishing Championships hosted in Cape Town. Recent sport fishing developments include the South African Deep Sea Angling Association (SADSAA, tel: 011 794 6950, tatpled@iafrica.com), who were recently approached by the International Federation of Sea Anglers to bid for the World Games in 2006.

WHERE THE BIG 'UNS HANG OUT

Catch your piece of the action from Strandfontein to Saldahna Bay (along the West Coast), or try the Saldahna Bay to Table Bay and Cape Point stretch. There is also the slightly warmer water of False Bay from Cape Point to Cape Hangklip. SADSAA can advise as to local boating clubs, or contact Cape Town Tourism (corner Castle/Burg Streets, tel: 021 426 4260) for deep sea angling tour operators. Other useful resources include SADSAA's Year Book as well as 'Strike!' - the book on Salt Water Fishing in Southern Africa.

FISHFULL THINKING

Locals are best placed to advise as to how to braai your catch. Strike it lucky and you may reel in any of the following: kabeljou, white and red stumpnose, roman, elf (shad), mackerel, maasbanker, white steenbras, silverfish, panga, Hottentot, steentjies, jakopever, galjoen, Broadbill swordfish, black, blue or striped marlin, bigeye, yellowtail and longfin tuna, geelbek (Cape salmon), carp, barbell, kob, snoek, skipback, or hake. Shark catches include mako, blue shark, bronze whaler, thresher, spotted guller, and ragged tooth.

BOATING

Buy a slice of the bold and the beautiful lifestyle on some stunning yachts and cruisers in Table Bay or False Bay. Whether on a state-of-the-art speed boat or traditional sailing vessel – it is hard to ignore the temptation to experience the ultimate Cape Town sunset and Table Mountain view from the water.

V & A Waterfront

The V&A Waterfront is a great place to select from a number of sailing adventures. Stroll along the embankments and choose from gentle cruises under sail, to exhilarating high-speed adventures.

A cruise south towards Hout Bay, reveals spectacular views of the central city, Table Mountain, Devil's Peak, Lion's Head, and the Twelve Apostles. You also have a bird's eye view of the luxurious beachfront apartments of Bantry Bay, Clifton, and Camps Bay.

Waterfront Charters specialise in Table Bay trips and exclusive sunset dinner cruises, also a once in a lifetime 'Around the Cape' experience. They also operate short harbour tours and a Robben Island cruise. Tel: 021 418 5806, www.waterfrontboats.co.za.

The Robben Island Tour commences with a speedy catamaran, departing from the V&A Waterfront Clocktower every hour on the hour. Booking essential, tel: 021 419 1300, website: www.cue.co.za.

Not for the faint hearted is the 12-seater inflatable operated by Atlantic Adventures. It takes you across Table Bay at high speed for a thrilling and (sometimes bumpy) ride. Tel: 021 425 3785, website: www.atlanticadventures.co.za.

A little slower and steadier is 'Steamboat Vicky', offering a sedate half-hour Waterfront cruise (tel: 083 651 0186.) also potter around the harbour amongst the seals and through the working docks is The Queen Victoria (tel: 021 425 0200, victoriacharters@webmail.co.za) and The Flagship Dawn (tel: 021 418 5806, website: www.waterfrontboats.co.za)

The stylish catamaran Tigresse (tel: 021 419 7746) explores the coastline between Table Bay and Clifton on excursions up to two hours. Hot summer days present you with an opportunity to pose aboard the 66-foot Maharani, which parks off in front of Clifton Beach (tel: 082 412 2222, email: classicsailing@worldonline.co.za).

Yacht Racing

Aspirant or experienced 'yachties' can offer themselves as crew (or ballast), for the Wednesday evening and Saturday afternoon summer races and regattas at Royal Cape Yacht Club (tel: 021 421 1354) or False Bay Yacht Club (Simon's Town, tel: 021 786 1703).

Catamarans

Hout Bay

Hout Bay boat operators. Hout Bay's Tigger Too Charter (tel: 021 790 5256, www.tiggertoo.co.za), specialise in the ubiquitous Chapman's Peak sunset cruise, while large groups should hire the Nauticat ferry-style catamaran (tel: 021 790 7278, www.nauticatcharters.co.za). Many visitors visit Seal Island - easily accessible on a Drumbeat Charter's glass-bottomed boat (tel: 021 791 4441) or Circe Launches (tel: 021 790 1040).

Simonstown

In the slightly warmer waters of False Bay at Simons Town, the Spirit of Just Nuisance offers short excursions around the harbour and into the Naval base (tel: 082 737 5263). Other yachts and whale watching boats (during season) depart from the town jetty.

andulela *experience*

Opportunities for unique and powerful experiences start with authentic people, original venues and inspiring environments.
- Accompany nature conservationists on wildlife excursions
- Share a table with Capetonians and learn to cook a traditional meal
- Surf the oceans with our local heros…

Wir sprechen Deutsch. Nous parlons francais.

Tel: +27 (0) 21 790 2592 / +27 (0) 82 695 4695
Suite 286, Private Bag X4, Hout Bay 7872
www.andulela.com

Enjoy, learn, regenerate.

Your trip is not complete until we meet….
* Winelands Tours * Golf Tours & Events
* Cultural Interaction Tours- a taste of township living!
* Corporate Events / Teambuilding
* Custom Tours & Travel Centre

Tel: +27 (0) 21 421 1660
67 Dock Road, Waterfront
www.gopassport.com

Founded in 1995, Out of Africa Safaris is a reputable, well established company organising quality camping and lodge tours to some of these untouched and wild places. Our several exciting tours will leave you with a lasting impression of this wonderful area.

Tel: +27 (0) 21 424 4540
P O box 1293, Milnerton
www.gopassport.com

ECO-TOURS SA
THE OVERLAND & UNDERSEA TOUR COMPANY

ECO-TOURS SA offers unique and authentic South African travel experiences to natural wilderness areas actively promoting conservation of our wildlife, heritage, flora and fauna and especially our rich cultural way of life whilst visiting the finest destinations and viewing spectacular attractions all over South Africa. We proudly support responsible Eco Cultural Tourism in SA.

Tel: +27 (0) 21 788 5741
www.ecotourssa.co.za
www.gopassport.com

QUINTESSENTIAL TOURS
Your travel companion

Enjoy the freedom and relaxation of having every detail of your visit taken care of while leaving you the flexibility to alter your itinerary. After a decade of enjoying Southern Africa with our clients, we can arrange your ideal package according to the season, events, festivals and your personal preferences.

Tel: +27 (0) 21 761 3208
Mobile : +27 (0) 83 324 0987
www.gopassport.com

Day Trips
Tailor-made Tours
Packaged Tours
Day & Overnight Safaris
Specialised Tours
Garden Route Tours
Township Tours
City Tours

INFORMATION CENTRE

All
Bookings &
Reservations

ADVENTURE

Bungy Jumping
Mountain Biking
Surfing
Quad Biking
Abseiling
Paragliding
Kite Surfing
Horse Riding

ACCOMMODATION

All Hotels & Guest Houses
Private Game Lodges
Luxury Homes & Apartments
Backpackers
Self Catering

VEHICLE RENTALS

All Groups
4x4 Vehicles
Luxury Cars
Exotic

www.ctic.co.z

CHARTERS

Aircraft
Yachts / Boat Trips
Helicopters
Shuttle Services

Tel: 27(21) 422 4611
Fax: 27(21) 422 4610
47 Burg Street
Waldorf Arcade
Cape Town
8001

Monday - Friday (9am - 6pm)
Saturdays (9am - 2pm)

info@ctic.co.za

Fancy a stroll through the vineyards, a trek through the Cedarberg or Table Mountain, a tour of our colourful townships? Walk with the whales or discover Cape Town icons alongside professional Field and Mountain Walking Guides. Eclectic accommodation arranged under thatch or stars with local cuisine to taste!

Tel: +27 (0) 21 788 8750
P O Box 30993, Tokai, 7966
www.gopassport.com

NAC Makana Aviation

Operating from the V&A Waterfront we specialise in Helicopter Flights in and around the heart of the Cape, providing the ultimate personal experience for the discerning traveler, business executive and aviation enthusiast through exploring the breath taking wonders of the fairest Cape by helicopter... where high up in the sky we will exhilarate your mind and fill your heart with beauty!

Tel: +27 (0) 21 425 3868
V&A East Pier Road, V&A Waterfront, CT
www.gopassport.com

Take an interactive, insightful journey into the heart of our dynamic people. Witness the everyday life of South Africas many varied cultures. Share in the struggles, hopes and achievements. And understand why the birth of the New South Africa was such an important day in our lives. Including District Six, Langa and Khayelitsha, the tour can be extended to include a visit to Robben Island.

Tel: +27 (0) 21 706 1006
4 Eastbank Road, Zeekoevlei
www.gopassport.com

Discover how the squalor and the deprivation of the townships of our previously disadvantaged community is being transformed with modern schools, clinics, electricity, clean water, liveable homes and sport facilities. Their struggle against apartheid and their efforts during these difficult years to liberate and uplift themselves through the establishment of street committees, community centers and informal trading initiatiuves like "spaza shops"and "shebeens".Get an idea of what is being done about HIV and AIDS through aids clinics,youth centers and counselling programs. We visit three areas that affected so-called "non-whites", namely the Black, Indian and Coloured people. A portion of the tour fee is contributed to township projects.

Tourist Guide of The Year 2003/4
Tel: +27 (0) 21 448 3117 Mobile: +27 (0) 83 358 0193
Email: tourcape@mweb.co.za
www.gopassport.com

AFRICAN EAGLE

Established in 1993, African Eagle is one of the biggest inbound wholesale operators in Southern Africa. Our network of seven branches, in South Africa, Namibia, Zimbabwe, Kenya, Tanzania and France enbables us to service clients worldwide.

Our own fleet of vehicles, tailormade computer programs and reservation system, mobile luxury tented camp and highly competitive rates enable us to ake care of all your requirements from flights and airport transfers to accommodations, venues, tours- both scheduled or private.

For more information contact your nearest African Eagle Branch or visit our website at www.africaneagle.com

Cape Town
Tel: +27 (0) 21 464 4260
Fax: +27 (0) 21 447 6300
Email: daytours@aecpt.co.za

Johannesburg
Tel: +27 (0) 11 807 2939
Fax: +27 (0) 11 803 1347
Email: henrim@ae.co.za

Namibia
Tel: +264 (0) 61 259 681   Fax: +264 (0) 61 259 680
Email: nicolas@ae.com.na

Zimbabwe
Tel: +263 (0) 13 43501   Fax: +263 (0) 13 43334
Email: aevfa@samara.co.zw

Kenya
Tel/Fax: +254 (0) 2 573 986 or 577 8414
Email: cecilel@africaneagle.co.ke

SELF DRIVE TOURS

SOUTH PENINSULA DRIVE

Here is a short description of some of the places you might like to include in a self-drive tour of the South Peninsula.

Cape Town to Hout Bay: Hug the Atlantic coast most of the way from Cape Town to Hout Bay and stop in the harbour for a boat ride to see thousands of frolicking seals.

Hout Bay to Noordhoek: Chapman's Peak Drive (toll road), is one of the most spectacular cliff roads in the world. Sensational Noordhoek beach greets you at the last bend. Stop at Noordhoek Farm Village to see local art and original curios.

Noordhoek to Kommetjie: Solole Private Game Reserve and Mnandi's authentic Italian restaurant, Kommetjie Road, have buffalo, springbok and all sorts of creatures around their waterhole (tel: 021 785 1992). Right opposite is Two Oceans Craft & Culture Centre, with Saturday morning Afrobics, Sunday Afro-Jazz and stall holders selling locals wares from Masiphumelele Township. Tour around this informal settlement (see Masiphumelele paragraph under Township Tours). A little further along is Imhoff Farm, offering camel rides, snake park and amazing craft from waste at KEAG Environmental Centre (see Eco Tourism).

Scarborough to Cape Point: Witness the incredible beauty of this coastline, then follow the road inland to amazing roadside sculpture galleries. Haggle for souvenirs here and at the informal market outside Cape Point entrance. Explore small side roads leading to stunning bays in the Cape of Good Hope Nature Reserve, before driving to the end of the earth at Cape Point.

Simon's Town: Drive along False Bay towards Simon's Town, but stop at (and swim with) the colony of African Penguins at Boulders Beach. Simon's Town main street and Waterfront are worth a lengthy stop (see Off The Beaten Track -Simon's Town for restaurant suggestions). Take children to scrabble for gems in the Mineral World Scratch Patch (signpost on main road after station).

Fish Hoek, Kalk Bay & Muizenberg: Fish Hoek beach is great for swimming, while Muizenberg is perfect for novice surfers. Between these two small towns is Kalk Bay, known for unusual antique shops, quirky cafes and restaurants, and a traditional fishing harbour. Arrive at lunchtime to see boats pull in and offload their catch.

Muizenberg to Cape Town: Inland back to Cape Town, perhaps via the Constantia wineries or Kirstenbosch Gardens, or save these for another day.

Chapman's Peak Drive

Chapman's Peak Drive took 6 years to build with the help of convict labour and opened in May 1922. This extraordinary piece of engineering became renowned as one of the worlds most scenic drives. After a fatal rock fall late in 1999, and then forest fires that cracked and loosened rocks and mud, Chapman's Peak Drive had to be closed. Drastic measures were needed to contain rocks, and wire mesh nets were erected and a roof was built over sections of the road. This magnificent road re-opened as a toll road in 2003.

Two Oceans

Cape Point is the south-western most tip of Africa at a latitude of 34° South. Some say this is where the two oceans meet (Atlantic and Indian), but satellite photographs show that the cold Benguela current and warm Mozambique current tend to converge off Cape Agulhas - Africa's southern most point.

Chapman's Peak Drive

Cape Wine Farm

Picker at Work

DRIVE THE CAPE WINELANDS

It's so easy to spend a day sipping wine surrounded by mountains and vineyards, but take your time, stay over and extend the pleasure . Three wine estate visits with lunch in between, and a wander around town, is more than enough for one day.

CONSTANTIA WINE ROUTE

Grand Cape Dutch homesteads lord over the ancient Constantia vineyards. Groot Constantia is a prime example, but old meets new here in their excellent Simon's Restaurant (tel: 021 794 1143).

Klein Constantia is renowned for its Vin de Constance, which the John Platter wine guide rates as "*Superlative*".

Buitenverwachting wine estate also receives plenty of accolades and is perfect for a refined picnic under the oaks. Constantia Wine Route: tel: 021 794 1810.

STELLENBOSCH

Almost a hundred wine estates in Stellenbosch offer tastings, some also have restaurants or picnic dining and cellar tours, or in the case of Spier; guided tastings, carriage rides, farm stall, horse riding and cheetah park.

Stellenbosch town has a rich history and stunning architecture, but its university students make sure it lives in the present rather than the past.

Stop at the one hundred year old curiosity shop, Oom Saamie se Winkle, in Dorp street, for an assortment of indescribable peculiarities. Stellenbosch Tourism tel: 021 883 3584, email: eikestad@iafrica.com.

PAARL

Paarl Wine Route is recognised for Shiraz, but also has some of the Cape's best Chardonnay - for both and more besides, visit Glen Carlou, Nederburg and Villiera. The Fairview estate offers a great selection of wine, plus a cheese tasting room specialising in cheese from their own goats housed in a castle turret. For internationally awarded haute cuisine, dine (or stay) at Grande Roche. Paarl Tourism tel: 021 872 3829, email: paarl@cis.co.za.

FRANSCHHOEK

Franschhoek is a top contender for a scenic winelands stayover. Superb restaurants in the main street and on wine estates are. But it would be remiss not to mention SA's top chef Margo Janse at Le Quartier Francais (tel: 021 876 2151), and the up and coming Reuben Riffel, in the self-named Reuben's Restaurant (021 876 3772). Try and get to Cabrière's Saturday morning cellar tour, where swashbuckling wine grower Achim von Arnim opens bubbly with his sabre (021 876 2630). Franschhoek Tourism tel: 021 876 3603, info@franschhoek.org.za.

FALSE BAY BY ROAD

Drive the entire length of False Bay (wonderful by motorbike or car), from Cape Point to Cape Hangklip and beyond to Hermanus. Or to make this scenic journey more manageable in one day, begin your excursion in Muizenberg.

Muizenberg to Strand

The R310 Baden Powell Drive at Muizenberg, runs within a stone's throw of some windswept False Bay beaches, where shoreline fisherman are the only lone figures. If you should see a throng of seagulls flapping excitedly along this stretch, it usually indicates the presence of trek fishermen hauling in their net by hand. Stop and watch this amazing feat and their bulging net, but if they have only just started pulling, it could take an hour. This old fashioned style of fishing is centuries old and worth photographing for posterity.

It is not advisable to stop on the rest of this deserted road, as it runs parallel to the Cape Flats - containing some of the poorest suburbs and townships. But proceed without fear and appreciate the wildness and beauty of this untouched part of False Bay. As the road bears inland turn right onto the N2 motorway - direction Somerset West. After 10km turn right to Strand and re-connect with the False Bay coast once again to Gordon's Bay.

GORDON'S BAY TO CAPE HANGKLIP

A small seaside promenade with gift shops and snack bars and a sandy beach next to the yacht club make for a short stop in Gordon's Bay. From here follow the R44 south to Cape Hangklip. This beautiful drive has a backdrop of green mountains mirroring the emerald ocean hues. You are almost guaranteed to see whales during the months of July to October and may spot dolphins and seals too.

HERMANUS

Continue around Cape Hangklip and out of False Bay to Hemanus - the whale watching capital of South Africa. This slow route to Hermanus will get you in the mood for a late lunch and a stroll in this old fishing town. Or take your time and stay overnight - there are some superb places here, (see Hermanus section).

HERMANUS TO CAPE TOWN

The quick route back to Cape Town is via the N2 freeway, which drops down onto the low-lying flats via the spectacular Sir Lowry's Pass - a rapid decent from 452m above sea level. This road leads you directly to the centre of Town.

Trek Fishing

In time old tradition, a fishing boat rows out a short distance and drops a net in a horseshoe shape, with either end of the net on the beach. Then all hands on the beach start pulling and slowly but surely over the next hour or so, the net fills with all sorts of fish and sea creatures. The nearer it gets to shore the more excited the seagulls become and people appear as if from nowhere, alerted by the gulls, children run off with small fish that have wriggled through the net and their parents buy buckets full of silvery little harders to feed their large families.

False Bay

False Bay Drive

Chapman's Peak Drive has phenomenal viewpoints - stop at them all!

N.B. Don't stand too close to the edge on a windy day.

Chapman's Peak Drive

Aerial View

Table Bay

Cape Town Harbour

SPECTACULAR VIEW POINTS

"Life is not measured by the breaths you take, but by the things that take your breath away."

If you haven't been to the Cape before, it's beauty could just take your breath away. The unusual combination of mountains and oceans so close together is quite awe-inspiring.

There are some special spots that put the cherry on the cake in terms of views and you will pass many of them on any tour of the Cape. Take time to stop and wonder at the magnificence around you and make sure you have plenty of film in your camera.

BOYES DRIVE: Take this high road from Muizenberg to Kalk Bay and stop often to appreciate the vast beauty of False Bay and the little fishing harbour of Kalk Bay.

BLOUBERG: Take the perfect Table Mountain snapshot across Table Bay from Blouberg's beaches.

CHAPMAN'S PEAK DRIVE - HOUT BAY TO NOORDHOEK: With some of the most phenomenal viewpoints in the Cape (if not the world)- we suggest you stop at them all! Highlights include; staring back at Hout Bay nestled between mountains and south towards the great expanse of Noordhoek's endless white beach.

HELICOPTER RIDE: Aerial views of the Cape by helicopter are outstanding. Take a cheaper-than-you-think spin (see Air Charters page).

LION'S HEAD: Greeting the full moon from Lion's Head is a Cape Town tradition, but it's a rocky clamber to the top and only for the sure-footed.

ROBBEN ISLAND: Views of Table Mountain must have been a sight for sore eyes to the prisoners of this island and a reminder of their incarceration. Take the perfect Table Mountain picture from here.

SIMON'S TOWN: Drive a short way up Red Hill (a turning off the coast road just before Simon's Town) and stop for superlative views over the Navy Port, yacht harbour and False Bay.

SIGNAL HILL: Drive to the top of Signal Hill for views over Cape Town to Robben Island and far out to sea. (But don't stick around if you are the only ones here).

SILVERMINE: Stop at the entrance to Silvermine Nature Reserve on Ou Kaapse Weg for an incredible panorama across the Cape Flats. Then as you twist and turn down the mountainside (direction Cape Town), the Constantia vineyards reveal themselves on the southern slopes of the Table Mountain range.

TABLE MOUNTAIN: Nothing apart from a helicopter ride, tops the expansive experience of the top of Table Mountain. The world spreads out beneath you and the globe curves into a watery horizon.

TABLE MOUNTAIN

…the expansive experience of the top of Table Mountain. The world spreads out beneath you and the globe curves into a watery horizon…

CHAPMAN'S PEAK

…staring back at Hout Bay nestled between mountains and seeing the great expanse of Noordhoek's endless white beach unfold before you from Chapman's Peak.

BOYES DRIVE

…stop often to appreciate the vast beauty of False Bay and the little fishing harbour of Kalk Bay…

SILVERMINE

… as you twist and turn down the mountainside, the Constantia Vineyards reveal themselves on the southern slopes of the Table Mountain range.

HELICOPTER RIDE

Take time to stop and wonder at the magnificence around you and make sure you have plenty of film in your camera…

ECO TOURISM

Eco Tour Operators

When deciding between Eco Tour Operators, you might like to ask them to clarify exactly what 'eco' means to them. If it satisfies some of the criteria on this page and your own requirements, then go and enjoy the beauty and nature of the Cape. But don't rush, allow yourself time to appreciate the small things.

Baboons of the Cape

Squirrel

Cape Fox

ECO FRIENDLY TOURISM

Eco Tourism is often used as a euphemism for marketing just about any excursion or activity that takes place outdoors. Unless it has any ECOological benefit, you might be on more of an Ego Tour than an Eco Tour!

Eco Tourism could cover any experience where nature is not damaged as a result of the encounter with humans, and where your understanding and appreciation of the environment is enhanced. But additional criteria should be to ensure that the environment benefits as a result of your visit. This could be by contributing time or money to a research programme, protection organisation or sustainable community development.

AMAZING PROJECTS

An example on the Cape south coast is KEAG, (Kommetjie Environmental Awareness Group). They facilitate many projects such as; waste recycling, coast care, education centres and baboon protection. Their office has become the HQ for an amazing 'Craft from Waste' initiative. Trendy colourful items are being crafted from the waste products picked up by the coast care workers on the beach. The products are really in demand. They are even starting to export, but go and visit them for yourself and buy direct from the workers. KEAG is at Imhoff Farm, Kommetjie Road, Kommetjie. Tel: 021 783 3433, email: keag@ct.lia.net.

The Baboon Monitoring Project, which endeavours to keep baboons away from the dangers of human habitation and aggressive dogs, run out of funding on a regular basis. For a taste of real Eco Tourism, go along on one of their Baboon Monitoring Tours - see Local Wildlife Section for contact details of 'Baboon Matters'.

DELICATE BALANCE

Low-impact and low-consumption should also be the aim of a true Eco Tour, adhering strictly to the principle, *"take only photographs, leave only footprints"*.

Cape Town has a great deal of delicately balanced flora and fauna that can be put under strain from misuse or overuse. Capetonians seem pretty aware of this and usually take good care of their environment. There are always exceptions of course, and you should not add to the thoughtless few who throw lighted cigarette ends out of a car window, and unwittingly start a veld or forest fire.

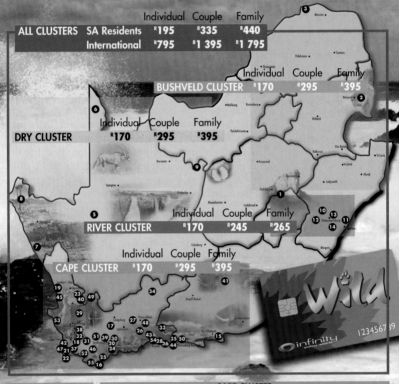

Creatures of Cape Point

The Cape of Good Hope Nature Reserve has diverse animals, birds and plants - many of which are found only in this little corner of the earth. While driving around, keep your eyes open for bontebok and eland antelopes, tortoise, baboon, mongoose and otter.

Boulder's Beach

Table Mountain

TABLE MOUNTAIN NATIONAL PARK

Table Mountain National Park (TMNP - previously Cape Peninsula N.P.), extends 60 kilometres from Signal Hill, all the way down the peninsula to Cape Point and consists of several separate reserves. Each reserve has its own particular needs and charges a different entry fee, but to simplify things, you can buy a WILD card allowing entry to all sections of TMNP.

TABLE MOUNTAIN

Cape Town's most prominent feature is of course Table Mountain, which stands 1087 metres high and rains its spiritual energy down upon the city. There are hundreds of hiking routes up Table Mountain, but none are considered easy. Even common routes such as, Platteklip Gorge, Nursery Ravine and Skeleton Gorge, are classified as 'strenuous'. A very rewarding option is to climb up one of the shorter routes, have lunch or supper at the top, then come down in the rotating cable car. The cable car is on a first come first serve basis and there can be a queue.

SILVERMINE

For splendid walks with spectacular views, visit Silvermine Nature Reserve off Ou Kaapse Weg (Old Cape Way). The reserve was misnamed after a pit was sunk in 1687 in the hope of finding silver. All they got was manganese, but the name stuck. Swimming in the large dam is truly wonderful and natural rock braai (barbeque) sites are discreetly positioned amongst the boulders. Circumnavigate the dam in 20 minutes on foot or wheelchair, on the beautiful new boardwalk. This is a little gem of a place that few visitors know about.

CAPE OF GOOD HOPE NATURE RESERVE & CAPE POINT

The Cape of Good Hope and Cape Point were important beacons for early explorers and myths that surround them are still told to day (see Ghosts & Legends section). Rocks at this south western-most tip of Africa remain treacherous and no sailor takes 'Rounding the Cape' lightly. Cool west coast waters meet the warmer Agulhas current from the east, which creates a wealth and variety of marine life around this part of the coast.

BOULDER'S BEACH PENGUINS

You can't come to Cape Town's South Peninsula without visiting the penguins - they are too cute! Facilities have been smartened up and there is now an information centre and wheelchair friendly boardwalk. There are several beautiful coves where you can swim while penguins go about their business.

WEST COAST NATIONAL PARK

The West Coast is a bit wild and windy, with vast uninhabited stretches baked by a hot summer sun. In contrast, the Atlantic Ocean that washes this coastline, is positively freezing and west coast bathers normally head for the warmer shallow waters of Langebaan lagoon.

BLUE LAGOON

There are only two roads in the West Coast National Park reserve, both of which skirt around the edge of the ridiculously azure waters of Langebaan lagoon. The soft sandy shores on the west of the lagoon become populated with locals on hot summer weekends, but are virtually empty during the week. Pull into the small parking area at Churchaven and have a picnic on the water's edge. The area remains peaceful and undisturbed here because although windsurfers and small sailing boats are allowed, motorised watersports are restricted to an area at the mouth of the lagoon.

While you sit in this beautiful spot, take time to think about a young woman who walked down the dunes to this lagoon 17,000 years ago. Her footprints were discovered in solidified sand here, and 'Eve', as she became known, found fame around the world because she represents modern man's closest relative and helps to validate the 'Out of Africa' theory of evolution.

HOUSE BOAT FOR HIRE

The only National Parks accommodation is a remote inland hikers cottage called Abrahamskraal, costing approx. R100 per person inc. bedding, plus R15 pp conservation fee, and the recently renovated, fully equipped Joanne's, overlooking the lagoon sleeping eight - prices to be confirmed. Enquire from the park office, tel: 022 772 2144/2799, website: www.parks-sa.co.za. There are camping and hostel facilities for youth groups.

Another attractive option within the park is a 6-bedded houseboat, but book early for this basic but desirable option (tel: 021 552 0008). There are also some privately owned cottages by the lagoon that are sometimes available for hire - contact Langebaan Tourism (number below). There is plenty of accommodation in Langebaan town, outside the park to the east of the lagoon. Contact Langebaan Tourism Bureau, tel: 022 722 1515, email: lbninfo@mweb.co.za, website: www.langebaaninfo.com

BIRD HIDES

Near the Geelbek Visitor's Centre at the base of the lagoon, are a couple of bird hides overlooking salt marshes and mudflats. These are home to thousands of wading birds who migrate here in April from Siberia, Greenland and northern Europe. Twitchers (dedicated bird watchers), come here for rare sightings of godwits, dunlins and sandpipers. Flamingoes are best seen here during the winter.

West Coast National Park - Facts

Opening Times:

1st April - 30th September 7am to 7.30pm

1st October - 31st March 6am to 8pm

Postberg Peninsula (a separate section at the far western end of the park)

Only open 9am to 5pm during spring flower season (approximately June to September)

Contact Details:

tel: 022 772 2144, website: www.parks-sa.co.za.

Langebaan Lagoon

The Langebaan lagoon is part of the West Coast National Park, which is located 100km north of Cape Town. This is a haven of pristine nature with a choice of coastal walks or lagoon swims and a variety of accommodation in and around the park.

Langebaan Lagoon

Club Mykonos

Canola Fields

CAPE FLORAL KINGDOM

The Western Cape has its very own Cape Floral Kingdom called Fynbos, born out of the effort to survive and diversify in the nitrogen-poor, rocky and sandy soil. Of the 8,600 species, 5,800 are endemic (found only here).

To put these figures into perspective compare this with the British Isles, which is three times larger and has only 1,500 plant species, of which fewer than 20 are endemic. Table Mountain contains more than this!

ILLEGAL ALIENS

Capetonians are well aware how lucky they are to have such unique and beautiful flora, and great efforts have been made recently to clear the hillsides of alien vegetation. Port Jackson wattle brought from Australia in the 1850's, has been a particular problem, as it overwhelms the natural vegetation and uses too much precious water. It is now illegal to have this and several other non-indigenous species on your property.

FIRE

Fire is the lifeblood of fynbos. Heat and smoke triggers seeds into sprouting and encourages shrubs to burst into blooms, swamping the area with seeds. Ants who cannot resist a fluid in these seeds, carry them underground where they remain until the next fire.

SPRING FLOWERS

Spring rain and a rise in temperature, create an incredible natural phenomenon along the Namaqualand, Cape west coast and to a lesser extent over the Western Cape. From July to September, millions of little flowers burst out of the barren countryside in vast colourful swathes. Their heads follow the sun throughout the day and sometimes you don't get the full colour impact until you look behind you. Call the Spring Flower telephone line for information on what is flowering where and when, tel: 083 910 1028. Failing that contact West Coast Tourism, tel: 022 433 8505, or email them on email: tourism@wcdm.co.za, website: www.capewestcoast.org.

Fynbos

KING PROTEA

The King Protea is best known Protea and is prized worldwide as a magnificent cut flower. It is honoured in South Africa as the national flower. Large plants produce between six and forty flower heads on one plant. The colour varies from a creamy white to a deep crimson, but the soft pale pink bracts with a silvery sheen are the most prized.

RED DISA

The emblem of the Western Cape, this famous red orchid appears in shades of red, pink and yellow, and is strictly protected. Flowers bloom in the summer months from December to March with a peak flowering period during mid-February.

STRELITZIA REGINA

Indigenous to South Africa where it grows wild and flowers in autumn, winter and spring this must be one of the most well-known plants in the world. Its fascinating brilliant orange and bright blue blooms are sold as cut flowers. Two of the blue petals are joined together to form an arrow-like nectary.

PINCUSHION PROTEA

Indigenous to South Africa, groups of Pincushion Proteas provide vivid splashes of orange and red between July and November. It is a popular garden plant as well as a much-used cut flower. An added attraction of these plants is the numerous birds found near them.

ALOE

The bitter aloe is most famous for its medicinal qualities. There are usually between five and eight branches, each carrying a spike-like head of many flowers. Flower colour varies from yellowy-orange to bright red appearing between May and August. This aloe forms a beautiful display and attracts many bird species

Best Bird Watching Locations

- West Coast National Park (Geelbeck and Salt-marsh hides)

- Rietvlei Nature Reserve, northern suburbs of Cape Town

- Bird Island, Lambert's Bay, West Coast

- Cape of Good Hope Nature Reserve

- Kommetjie shoreline, South Peninsula

- Boulder's Beach Penguin Colony, near Simon's Town, South Peninsula

- Rondevlei Nature Reserve, near Grassy Park, South Peninsula

- Kirstenbosch National Botanic Gardens, 15 minutes drive south of Cape Town

- Paarl Bird Sanctuary, Winelands

Sun Bird

Weaver

Ostrich Riding

BIRD WATCHER'S DELIGHT

With variety and numbers of birds at an all time low in Europe, it is a pleasure to see the many different colours, shapes and sizes of South Africa's prolific bird life.

ENDANGERED BIRDS

Several endangered species are quite common in the Cape; only a few thousand African Black Oystercatchers exist, and are easily identified with black bodies and a distinctive red bill. A rare land-based colony of African Penguins live at Boulder's Beach. See them from a wheelchair-friendly boardwalk, or swim amongst them in the small coves. See Table Mountain National Park for details.

CAPE SPECIALS

Some birds favour Fynbos nectar and dip their long beaks into delicate Erica flowers and robust Protea heads. The lesser and greater doublecollared sunbirds display a shimmering red chest and iridescent green back, while the Cape Sugarbird is brown but sports a lovely long tail.

SPECTACULAR IN FLIGHT

Pelicans in-flight are far more elegant than on land, and they inhabit the numerous vleis (lakes) and dams around the Cape, and can be seen circling in thermals. The Cape is also blessed with many raptors, particularly Buzzards, Kites, Sparrowhawks, Harriers, and Goshawks.

SEABIRDS

Beautiful little terns fly into Cape Town from the Arctic and Antarctic, to spend summer and winter respectively. When disturbed, they fly up in a beautiful confetti clouds of white. Often seen in Cape Point Reserve, along the shoreline at Kommetjie and the lagoon at Noordhoek Beach. Also look out for spoonbills, kelp gulls and cormorants. View a large and lively breeding colony of Cape gannets from a glass-fronted bird hide at Bird Island, Lambert's Bay. Open 7am-6pm, tel: 027 432 1000.

OSTRICHES

Ostriches run wild in nature reserves, but thousands are bred for their soft durable leather and cholesterol-free meat. There are several ostrich show farms in Oudtshoorn (Garden Route), and one at the entrance to Cape Point and another along the West Coast.

JACKASS PENGUIN

A rare land-based colony of African Penguins live at Boulder's Beach…

CAPE GANNET

View a large and lively breeding colony of Cape gannets from a glass-fronted bird hide at Bird Island,…

BLUE CRANE

The Blue Crane is the national bird of South Africa and is endemic to southern Africa. Due to its rapid decline, the species is classified Critically Endangered.

DOUBLE COLLARED SUNBIRD

The lesser and greater double collared sunbirds display a shimmering red chest and iridescent green back,…

CAPE SUGAR BIRD

…while the Cape Sugarbird is brown but sports a lovely long tail.

Great White Shark

Whale Watching

CREATURES OF THE CAPE

The Cape has lots of indigenous wildlife, and little effort is needed to see them. The last lion and elephant are long gone, but there are other creatures as fierce and as large.

GREAT WHITE SHARK

Cage diving for a face to face encounter with a Great White Shark, is now a very popular activity, but remains contentious. There are experts on both side of the argument that 'chumming' - baiting to attract sharks - increases shark attacks on humans. You are highly unlikely to encounter a Great White while swimming or surfing, but take your lead from locals whose approach is, *"It's either your time or it isn't bro."* For cage diving operators see 'What To Do In and Around Hermanus', as well as White Shark Projects tel: 021 552 9794.

DOLPHINS & WHALES

Dusky, Common and Bottlenose dolphins inhabit the Cape waters, but are often hard to see. However, at times there are several hundred in False Bay or along the Atlantic coast, indulging in an amazing feeding frenzy.

Look out for Humpback, Southern Right and lesser-seen Bryde's whales, anytime from June to November. They come very close to shore in Fish Hoek Bay and along the coast to Simon's Town.

CAPE FUR SEALS

In fishing harbours and the V&A Waterfront, you find some huge Cape Fur Seals, who loll around with flippers and feet in the air looking really cute.

BABOONS

Close proximity with humans does not bode well for the Chacma Baboons of the South Peninsula. Tourists have their handbags stolen or picnics pinched, and residents receive impolite house guests. Unfortunately the Baboon Monitors, whose task is to steer them away from human habitations, regularly run out of funding. Good news is that they are raising funds with baboon-watching trips. Contact Baboon Matters, tel: 021 783 3882 or 072 291 5479, email: nprm@netactive.co.za.

DASSIES

Think of the most unlikely creature to be directly related to an elephant, and you might choose the 'Dassie'. This local name refers to the Rock Hyrax, which resembles an overgrown guinea pig with a short temper. It is found on all rocky outcrops around the Cape.

SOUTHERN RIGHT WHALE

Look out for Humpback, Southern Right and lesser-seen Bryde's whales, anytime from June to November. They come very close to shore…

BOTTLE NOSE DOLPHIN

Bottlenose dolphins inhabit the Cape waters, but are often hard to see. However, at times there are several hundred in False Bay…

GREAT WHITE SHARK

You are highly unlikely to encounter a Great White while swimming or surfing, … a face to face encounter with a Great White Shark, is now a very popular activity, but remains contentious…

CAPE FUR SEAL

…and the V&A Waterfront, you find some huge Cape Fur Seals, who loll around with flippers and feet in the air looking really cute…

BABOON

Tourists have their handbags stolen or picnics pinched, and residents receive impolite house guests…

ACCOMMODATION

ACCOMMODATION

The range and quality of Cape Town accommodation can be overwhelming. There are fantastic hotels, guest houses, B&B's, country lodges, self catering options, backpackers and camping and caravan sites. It is so hard to decide which establishment to choose, that we have selected excellent representatives in each category, to assist you in your decision.

HOLIDAY SEASONS

There are literally thousands of beds available in and around Cape Town, but during peak holiday seasons it is sometimes hard to get a room in the accommodation you want. Summer school holidays (mid December to mid January) and Easter, are the main holiday months for South Africans, many of whom converge on Cape Town and the Garden Route from Johannesburg. November, December and February are top months for international tourists.

When booking accommodation, it should be noted that rates are usually quoted per person, and not per room. You should also check what, if any, meals are included.

GRADING

The Tourism Grading Council introduced a voluntary grading system in 2001, with ratings from one to five stars. Properties are rated according to the standards of furnishings, service and guest care, rather than the range of facilities. Up to date listings and descriptions of graded establishments can be found on: www.tourismgrading.co.za.

HEALTH & WELLNESS

For a rejuvenating holiday to boost your body and soul, try one of Cape Town's health and wellness spas. All sorts of mainstream and esoteric therapies are on offer and you can lie back and relax to a hot rock massage, sea salt exfoliation, mud bath or one of many treatments.

The Place On The Bay

The Cape Milner

WHAT TO EXPECT FROM YOUR ACCOMMODATION

BACKPACKER LODGES

Backpackers are particularly well catered for in Cape Town and you can choose one in a quiet but central suburban street or downtown in the thick of things. Beachfront property is scarce, so most of the backpack lodges are a little way from the beach. Many have swimming pools and activities rooms and all offer information, tours and the opportunity for adventure. They provide dormitories, and often have a few double rooms for those wanting a bit more privacy at an additional cost.

CAMPING AND CARAVANS PARKS

Cape Town and the peninsula are not known for extensive camping and caravan facilities, but further afield they are numerous and often very scenic. Those found around the Cape Peninsula, are stunningly situated with wonderful views of mountains or ocean.

GUEST HOUSES & B&B's

Cape Town is renowned for its hospitable B&B's and guesthouses, which are usually owner run. Sometimes you feel like a family guest, while other places offer more privacy and luxury. Breakfasts are often extensive buffets with homemade breads and jams and naturally ripened fresh seasonal fruits (the flavour of which will remind you what fruit should taste like).

SELF-CATERING

Self-catering chalets, cottages, apartments and bungalows are mostly found outside the city, and offer a delightful do-it-yourself style holiday. You can find anything from studios to large family chalets in extensive grounds. You are almost guaranteed a view of something rather splendid, from a well-tended garden, to an endless horizon over the ocean, or towering mountains. You won't be short of good food either as Cape Town's deli's and farm stalls offer tempting morsels. Fish is as fresh is it gets, meat is tender and excellent quality, and seasonal fruit and vegetables are full of flavour.

HOTELS

Cape Town is a very artistic city with bold and talented designers who are not afraid to experiment. As such there are quite a number of smaller upmarket hotels each with their own unique style. Classical and African décor themes are also to be found, but many are more creative, ranging from the extremes of minimalism to high kitsch and everything you couldn't possibly imagine in between. There are of course large hotel chains, in which you can feel safe in the knowledge of what to expect.

Think Pink

Cape Town has a large, loud and fun loving gay population and some accommodation establishments catering exclusively for this clientele. Many are not concerned which way you swing and welcome you whatever your inclination. See 'Painting the Town Pink' section.

Backpacker Lodge

Winchester Mansions Hotel

Bantry Bay Apartments

The Metropole Hotel

CRAIGROWNIE

GUEST · HOUSE

Nestled in a quiet cul-de sac at the foot of Lion's Head in Bantry Bay, ten minutes from the heart of the Mother City, you'll find a haven of tranquility. Here our guest house manager will pamper and delight you and ensure that your stay at Craigownie House will be the first of many. The luxuriously furnished and fully equipped five en-suite bedrooms each have their own balcony offering spectacular views of the Atlantic Ocean and Lion's Head, as well as all the modern conveniences required by the sophisticated traveller.

COLLECTIONS FROM AND TO THE AIRPORT, AS WELL AS ANY ONE OF MANY TOURS IN AND AROUND CAPE TOWN CAN BE ARRANGED FOR YOU.

Tel: +27 (0) 21 439 5688
10 Graigrownie Rd, Bantry Bay
www.gopassport.com

BRENWIN GUEST HOUSE

TOURISM GRADING COUNCIL

AA

Formerly the Port Captain's residence, and recently completely renovated, Brenwin Guesthouse has combined its history with all the modern comforts, to create a warm and memorable ambience. Situated in cosmopolitan Green Point, it is close to the city centre and the International Convention Centre, and only a short walk to the V&A Waterfront.

Tel: +27 (0) 21 434 0220
1 Thornhill Rd, Greenpoint
www.gopassport.com

Glen Avon Lodge
★★★★
No. 1 Strawberry Lane, Constantia
Tel +27 (0) 794 1418 Fax +27 21 794 1419
E-Mail: info@glenavon.co.za
www.glenavon.co.za

Nestled in the heart of the Constantia Valley winelands, "Glen Avon Lodge" is ideally situated to Cape Town, The Waterfront, beaches and wine farms. Tastefully furnished en-suite bedrooms, with luxury amenities. Personal attention to detail ensures a warm and pleasurable stay with fine cuisine provided by their own cordon bleu chef.

Tel: +27 (0) 21 794 1418
1 Strawberry Lane, Constantia
www.gopassport.com

Your Home Away From Home

DUNEDIN GUEST HOUSE

A warm relaxed ambience with an emphasis on comfort, luxurious accommodation, tranquil garden setting, patio and pool all contribute to making guests feel at home. Situated in the heart of the beautiful Constantia Valley this guest house also offers en-suite bathrooms with wonderfully large showers, hearty or continental breakfast and pub within minutes from city centre and beaches.

Tel: +27 (0) 21 712 0514
12 Tudor Road, Tokai
www.gopassport.com

Cha'Mel
· GUEST HOUSE ·

The 8 recently decorated en suite rooms with a true African theme have sea views over looking the Waterfront.. English breakfast is served in the dining room, or on the sun deck overlooking the pool with sea views in a beautiful garden. At night the colourful lights turn the garden into a tranquil oasis. Walking distance to V & A Waterfront and new Convention Centre.

Tel: +27 (0) 21 433 2006
13 Upper Portswood Road, Green Point
www.gopassport.com

Monkey Valley Resort
BEACH NATURE RESORT CAPE TOWN

Monkey Valley is set in a milkwood forest overllooking and with direct access onto an 8km unspoilt beach. Luxury thatched self catering cottages, superb seaview B&Bs, a la carte restaurant with log fireplaces and sundeck overlooking the sea, quaint Treetop pub with tree growing through – it is paradise.

Tel: +27 (0) 21 789 1391
Mountain Road, Noordhoek
www.gopassport.com

Hedge House

Hedge House is located in a peaceful pocket of Newlands, Sunnybrae. Four en-suite rooms, each with separate entrance, are extremely comfortable and are furnished with luxury beds and cotton linen. Breakfasts with homemade fare are served outside, in the dining room or in your room, should you prefer. The garden has beautiful mountain views, a salt water pool, trampoline and swing. Children are welcome.

Tel: +27 (0) 21 689 6431
12 Argyle Road, Newlands
www.gopassport.com

Afton Grove

Afton Grove is conveniently located in the beautiful Noordhoek valley on the Chapman's Peak Drive (M6), only a short drive from the city and all "must-see", Cape attractions. Nine charming "Cape-Style" cottages & an executive suite are set in a 2 acre bird-filled garden with mountain views and overlook a sparkling pool. 4 Star Graded. COUNTRY HOUSE & AA ACCOMMODATION AWARDS FINALIST 2002 & 2004

Tel: +27 (0) 785 2992
Chapman's Peak Drive, Noordhoek
www.gopassport.com

Boulders Beach
Lodge and Restaurant

www.bouldersbeach.co.za

Eat, Sleep, Swim ....with Penguins!

- 12 attractive en-suite rooms.
- Penguin Point Restaurant.
- Penguin Place Function House.
- Wellness Centre.
- Curious Penguin gift and curio shop.

Tel: (021) 786 1758
E.mail: boulders@iafrica.com

Rose dene
GUEST HOUSE

Warm welcome and relaxed, homely atmosphere always received • Perched high above Table Bay • Views of Table Mountain, Lion's Head, bustling city and harbour lights • Every room is individually furnished with exquisite hand-crafted Balinese furniture and artifacts • Hearty and delicious breakfasts are served inside or outside on the patio under a shady leafy old Oak tree • 2 minutes to TM cable station, 5 minutes to famous Camps Bay and Clifton Beaches, walking distance to restaurants • General facilities include suntan patio, pool, barbeque place, computer with internet access and fireplace

Room facilities: all en-suite, DSTV, direct dial telephone, tea and coffee tray, ADSL internet line, shower and/or bath, bar fridge

Tel:+27 (0) 21 424 3290 Fax: +27 (0) 21 424 3481
28 Upper Kloof Street, Higgovale
www.gopassport.com

This beautiful, modern 4 star guest house is uniquely situated on the slopes of Table Mountain with breathtaking views of the 12 Apostles and the Atlantic Ocean only minutes by car from beaches, V&A Waterfront, trendy bars and restaurants. The 7 African themed bedrooms overlook mountains, garden or the ocean. Also enjoy sumptuous breakfasts, amazing pool deck, well-stocked cellar and Finnish sauna.

Tel: +27 (0) 21 438 1344
Hely Hitchinson Avenue, Camps Bay
www.gopassport.com

Beluga of Constantia, the perfect place to enjoy your holiday. Offering breakfast lunch and dinner, en-suite king size rooms including TV, DVD, Hi-Fi's, and Mini-Bars. The ideal setting with landscaped gardens, beach effect swimming pool, fountain courtyard & pure relaxing, pampered, attentive and personal service. Recently renovated and upgraded we aim to make your stay a memory never to be forgotten.

Tel: +27 (0) 21 794 4594
5 Connor Close, Constantia
www.gopassport.com

The Place on the Bay offers a sophisticated, relaxed atmosphere for visitors to unwind. Choose between one or two bedroom suites and studio's, all luxuriously furnished with tranquil terraces and panoramic sea views; private pool or Jacuzzi. Enjoy the benefit of room service or dine in the Some Vino's Restaurant on the property.

Tel: +27 (0) 21 438 7060
Victoria Road, Camps Bay
www.gopassport.com

Casablanca

Casablanca Guest House in the windfree seafront suburb of Fresnaye is set on a mountain slope and enjoys spectacularsea views and African sunsets. Stylish decor combines antiques with African & Indonesian pieces. Relaxing massageson request. Close to the city , V&A Waterfront and famous beaches. Restaurants nearby.

Tel: +27 (0) 21 434 1385
7 Avenue Fontainbleau, Cape Town
www.gopassport.com

Jambo Guest House

This multi-award winning guest house has uniquely decorated luxurious double rooms, all with en-suite bathrooms and fitted with every conceivable extra make for a memorable stay. Relax in a hot Jacuzzi spa set in a lush, leafy garden or Barry's exclusive bar. Winner of the AA Travel Guides Accommodation Awards in 2000,2001&2002 and Hall of Fame 2003. SA Tourism Grading Council 5 Star Guest House.

Tel: +27 (0) 21 439 4219
1 Grove Road, Green Point
www.gopassport.com

All the themed rooms in this luxury guest house is situated in a private, quiet area with magnificent view of Table Mountain, 5 minutes from Camps Bay Beach, exclusive restaurants and nightlife, boast many comforts. A large garden with swimming pool, gazebo and sun loungers await you on the warm Cape Town nights.

Tel: +27 (0) 21 438 2729
21 First Crescent, Camps Bay
www.gopassport.com

Ocean View
H O U S E
★ ★ ★ ★

Ocean View House is nestled between Camps Bay and Bakoven. All Luxury Rooms and Suites are en-suite with some of the finest views of the Atlantic Ocean. Our unique combination of warm hospitality and highly personalized service ensures hotel standards with a "guest house" intimacy.

Tel: +27 (0) 21 4381982
33 Victoria Road, Bakoven
www.gopassport.com

ZEANOR
ALL-SUITE APARTMENTS
SEA POINT

Zeanor's 20 luxury, 3 star suites are conveniently located in the wind-free Bantry Bay end of Sea Point and are serviced daily. Just minutes from the V&A Waterfront, City Centre, Mountain, Clifton and Camps Bay. Breakfast overlooking a sparkling Pool and landscaped garden available on request. Off street parking available.

Tel: +27 (0) 21 434 4970
13 Queens Road, Sea Point
www.gopassport.com

Distinctive and unique villa, nestled against the famous Table Mountain Nature Reserve and ruggedly beautiful Twelve Apostles Mountain Range, capturing the ultimate in sea views , spectacular natural splendour and tranquillity! Magnificent heated pool, sundeck, stylish and elegantly appointed accommodation ensures superior comfort and a quality experience. TGSA 4 Star.

Tel: +27 (0) 21 438 2347
77 Theresa Avenue, Camps Bay
www.augergeducap.co.za

Harfield Guest Villa
★★★★

A unique hideaway where tranquility, comfort and professionalism are paramount. Private entrances lead to intimate havens, stylishly decorated with thoughtful touches. Candelit Victorian baths, beds hugged by cotton linen, farm-style breakfasts, home-baked breads, log fires, classical music, poolside patios with lovely views of Table Mountain. Cavendish, Newlands cricket and rugby grounds, Kirstenbosch, UCT, golf nearby. Waterfront, city, beaches, airport 15 minutes. All credit cards. Proudly South African. TGCSA 4-star guest house.

Tel: +27 (0) 21 683 7376
26 First Avenue, Harfield Village
www.gopassport.com

BIG BAY BEACH CLUB

Modern, fully furnished 1 and 2 bedroom apartments and 3 bedroom houses. Pool and braai area. Secure complex with parking, TV with M-Net. Walk to Big Bay Beach. Daily, weekly and monthly rates on request. Self Catering

Tel: +27 (0) 21 556 8626 Fax: +27 (0) 21 556 0790
Cell: +27 (0) 82 895 7784
www.gopassport.com

TWO OCEANS GUEST HOUSE

Situated on the slopes of Fish Hoek mountain with panoramic views, taking up to 14 guests but can be split into 2 units each sleeping 6 or 8. Upmarket finishes with pool, all the mod-cons, DSTV, telephone etc. All your transport needs may be met by our sister company, CABS Car Hire. Tours can be arranged to suit your specific requirements.

Tel: +27 (0) 21 788 7307
4 Rissi Road, Fish Hoek
www.gopassport.com

Cape Pillars
luxury apartments
★ ★ ★ ★

CAPE TOWN – DURBANVILLE
EXECUTIVE LUXURY APARTMENTS
Leisure/Business/Relocations

Fully equipped self-catering apartments/B&B nestled in upmarket suburb of Cape Town. Sunny en-suite bedrooms, large open-plan lounge, diningroom/kitchen. Private entrance/intercom/swimming pool/secure off-street parking with remote access. BBQ/DSTV.

Tel: +27 (0) 21 976 2170 Mobile : +27 (0) 83 441 8887
Email: info@capepillars.co.za
capepillars.co.za

Capsol
Tourism & Property Solutions

Capsol Property and Tourism Solutions has since 1996 successfully provided various associated services to our valued local and international clients. Our services are unique in that for the convenience of our clients we facilitate various related and associated services from one liaison/contact office.

Tel: +27 (0) 21 422 3521
www.capsol.co.za
www.gopassport.com

Whale Watcher's
Private Luxury Apartments
★ ★ ★ ★

4 Self-catering studio, garden and family apartments overlooking Fish Hoek beach. All with sea-facing balconies, hammocks and barbeques. Access to Table Mountain National Park - 500 metres. Boulders' Beach penquins, Cape point, Simon's Town and Constantia wine route 15 mins away.

Cell: 084 460 5987 E-mail: info@whalewatchers.co.za Website: www.whalewatchers.co.za

Echo Bay Villa offers up to 4 guests spacious yet affordable luxury, panoramic sea views, a modern fully equipped kitchen, lounge and dining area, two spacious bedrooms with en-suite bathrooms and a swimming pool. Echo Bay is a 5-minute stroll from the powdery Fish Hoek beach with its warm waters.

Tel: +27 (0) 21 782 1902
10 Echo Rd, Sunny Cove, Fish Hoek
www.gopassport.com

Opposite Saunders Rock Beach in wind free Bantry Bay with dramatic sea views, picture-perfect sunsets, and the ocean at your doorstep - the scene is set for a luxury stay. The self-catering apartments are modern and sophisticated with an African, colonial ambience. The penthouse has a private pool on the top deck with stunning views. Close to the Waterfront, Clifton beaches, Camps Bay and many shops and restaurants.

Tel: +27 (0) 21 434 0211
15 Craigrownie Road, Bantry Bay
www.gopassport.com

The Place on the Bay offers a sophisticated, relaxed atmosphere for visitors to unwind. Choose between one or two bedroom suites and studio's, all luxuriously furnished with tranquil terraces and panoramic sea views; private pool or Jacuzzi. Enjoy the benefit of room service or dine in the Some Vino's Restaurant on the property.

Tel: **+27 (0) 21 438 7060**
Victoria Road, Camps Bay
www.gopassport.com

Welcome to the Gardens Centre Holiday Apartments where we combine stunning views with comfort and great value! Our apartments are fully furnished and serviced and boast spectacular views of Cape Town and Table Mountain. Ideally located within the Gardens Centre shopping complex with supermarkets, banks, restaurants, coffee shops, boutiques and much more. The whole city is on your doorstep and everything is within easy reach – the V&A Waterfront, the beaches and Table Mountain. The city centre is just a 10 minute walk away. We offer great value with prices ranging from R280 to R600 per apartment per night, sleeping two.

Tel: +27 (0) 21 461 8000
Gardens Centre, Mill Street, Gardens, Cape Town
gardens@global.co.za • www.gardensapartments.co.za
www.gopassport.com

THE TWELVE APOSTLES HOTEL & SPA

This luxurious yet intimate five star hotel with its 46 Deluxe guest rooms and 24 spacious suites, lies in a stunning location where earth, sea and sky meet, poised above Atlantic rollers and flanked by the majestic Table Mountain and her Twelve Apostles mountain range. Exceptional standard of service and relaxed Cape hospitality provide the perfect counterpoint to this dramatic backdrop. All barely ten minutes from the bustling heart of Cape Town, with nearby attractions including prime diving spots, nature trails, and seals, dolphins, whales and penguins.

Set in four secluded wings linked to the public areas via airy walkways, all rooms are decorated with understated elegance and feature as standard a wide range of amenities, including 24 hour room service, individual air-conditioning, entertainment centres with DVD, and plush bathrobes and slippers.

You will never be bored with the wealth of activities on offer both within the hotel and in the beautiful natural surroundings. We can organise everything from helicopter tours to scuba diving. We also offer a well equipped fitness room, two breathtaking swimming pools and a croquet lawn for your leisure use, or simply relax on the hammocks scattered throughout our beautiful gardens.

We specialise in catering for families and have plenty on offer to keep the kids occupied where we will gladly help organise outings for them including picnic baskets, beach visits long walks as well as a host of amenities for babies and children including special menus and goodie bags!

Savour the finest indigenous and international cuisine on offer in our Azure Restaurant. The Head Chef is on hand to create a variety of exquisite meat, seafood and vegetarian dishes. Open seven days a week for breakfast, lunch and dinner as well as a Sunday brunch, taken on our stunning terrace overlooking the ocean and magnificent sunset!

The 24 hour Café is an al fresco styled eaterie offering a casual and relaxed dining experience while enjoying fabulous sweeping views of the mountain. Its flexible menu and 24 hour access means you can enjoy a California styled menu at any hour, including a breakfast if you are still functioning in a different time zone.

The Leopard Room Bar & Lounge is the perfect place to relax whilst enjoying live entertainment every night. We offer a fully stocked bar featuring some 72 varieties of Martini,s, a selection of cognacs, 75 ports and a wide selection of cocktails. The Leopard Room is also a great spot to enjoy ""Tea by the Sea"' something of an institution with the locals.

We operate Cine 12, a small 16 seater intimate cinema/screening room available to both guests and non guests with it also being available for exclusive private hire with movies screened five times a day.

In the Sanctuary Spa we have embraced the healing energies of earth, air and water to rejuvenate the mind, body and soul where the focal point is the indoor Hydro Pool, flanked by a Brine Pool, a hot and cold Plunge Pool and flowing outwards from this area is the spa's Health Bar.

A member of The Leading Small Hotels of the World. On Conde Nast Traveller Magazine's 2003 Hotlist of The 80 Best New Hotels in The World. One of the 15 hotels to watch world-wide as published in Travel and Leisure Magazine's 2003 List of the World's Best Awards. Voted GQ Magazine as the Hotel with the Best View in the World

THE TWELVE APOSTLES
HOTEL AND SPA

Perched at the edge of the Atlantic Ocean, with spectacular mountain views, minutes away from Cape Town's nightlife, melting –pot culture and world acclaimed waterfront lies this luxurious Hotel & Spa. Its 70 rooms & suites offer an exceptional array of facilities including a rock pool, a 16-seat Cinema, a wellness center and inspiring cuisine. A member of The Leading Hotels of the World, it prides itself on exceptional hospitality ensuring discreet attention to detail.

Victoria Road, Camps Bay
Tel: 021 437 9000   Fax: 021 437 9055
Email: bookta@rchmail.com
www.12apostleshotel.com

THE COMMODORE & PORTSWOOD HOTELS

The Commodore Hotel and Portswood Hotel are situated very close to each other, within a short stroll of Cape Town's most famous harbour, shopping and entertainment centre - the V&A Waterfront.

THE COMMODORE HOTEL

They call Cape Town the fairest city of all, with a vivid historical past and rousing natural splendour where the mountains meet the sea. At the base of Table Mountain, within a short walk of the Atlantic Ocean and just around the corner from the V&A Waterfront, is The Commodore Hotel.

The nautical theme of The Commodore comes to life throughout the 236 rooms, which provide individual space and serenity in a peaceful and secure environment. The stylish rooms are equipped for business too, with modem lines and Hot Spot Wireless facilities in the public areas. There is also state-of-the-art conference facilities.

WELLNESS CENTRE

Relaxation is encouraged in the well equipped gym overlooking the pool, with personal trainers on hand and a sauna and steam room. Afterwards, the remedial results of massive therapy and treatments in the S.K.I.N wellness center, which will restore fatigued limbs and minds.

Located in The Commodore, the Clipper Restaurant and its Executive Chef, Rob Creaser, showcases a natural passion for food. Creaser adds, "We use the freshest ingredients and keep it simple with varied influences from Asia and Africa. We create ideas that are new and different, and everything just works. "

THE PORTSWOOD HOTEL

The Portswood Hotel offers its guests superlative accommodation, stunning cuisine and world-class service in a beautifully restored National Monument. More intimate than its neighbour, there are 59 twin rooms, 35 double rooms and 9 suites, all decorated with a fresh marine theme.

PRIME LOCATION

The Portswood Hotel owes part of its success to its prime location, right at the Victoria and Alfred Waterfront. Almost every visitor to Cape Town, spends time at the Waterfront, and when staying at The Portswood, you are already there! Although The Portswood is so close to this busy centre full of entertainment, shopping and restaurants, the hotel is set back in a secure and tranquil environment. On sweltering Cape Town days, get out of the hustle and bustle and revive in The Portwood's sparkling swimming pool.

Business Facilities

Business users are catered for, with modem lines in the rooms, and also Hot Spot Wireless internet facilities in the hotel.

The Quarterdeck Restaurant is a relaxed yet elegant venue, housed in what used to be the Cape Colony's convict station. No prison was ever this comfortable, or served such wonderful food! With its rich history, the Quarterdeck is the perfect setting to savour the best Cape Malay cuisine. Chef Craig Paulse says, "There is no love more sincere than the love of food… my best being what is on the menu – enjoy !"

The Commodore Hotel

The Portswood Restaurant

LEGACY
HOTELS & RESORTS
INTERNATIONAL

The Portswood Hotel offers its guests superlative accommodation, stunning cuisine and world-class service.

This Premier hotel's success has been due to its location, situated away from the working part of the harbour, yet conveniently close to a variety of shopping and entertainment options in a secure and tranquil environment.

Apart from its amazing natural and cultural surroundings, The Portswood is also an ideal choice for the business traveler, with all the most sophisticated facilities he or she might need.

+27 21 418 3281

THE PortsWood

★ ★ ★ ★

Known as 'the fairest Cape in all the world', South Africa's Mother City is charming and friendly and continuously welcomes visitors from all corners of the globe.

Conveniently located in the trendy Victoria & Alfred Waterfront in Cape Town – which is regarded as one of the most popular tourism developments in the world – The Commodore offers stylish accommodation, state-of-the-art conference facilities, attention to detail, service excellence and splendid views of the city in a peaceful and secure environment.

Enjoy fine cuisine on the terrace overlooking the pool, or more intimately in the elegant Clipper Restaurant.

The Commodore

★ ★ ★ ★ ★

+27 21 415 1000

Portswood Road, V&A Waterfront, Cape Town
www.legacyhotels.co.za

NEW BOUTIQUE HOTEL OPENS AT CENTURY CITY

The Island Club - a prestigious new residential development constructed on the North bank of the Grand Canal at Century City - incorporates a new luxurious boutique hotel that forms part of this new 35 hectare R400m complex.

The hotel was purchased by the Singer Group, a leading independent tourism company, and is operated by Protea Hotels, South Africa's leading hotel operator with a portfolio of more than 100 hotels.

The relationship between the Singer Group and Protea Hotels began in 1997 when the Singer Group purchased the Dolphin Beach Hotel in Bloubergstrand. And according to Brian Singer, this relationship has been highly successful. "The Dolphin Beach Hotel operates at the highest occupancy of all Protea's hotels" said Singer "and we plan to repeat this winning formula at the Island Club."

The luxurious hotel suites at the Island Club are spacious and are furnished and finished with top-of-the-range interiors and appliances, to a four-star deluxe standard. The hotel is ideal for business travellers – considering its close proximity to the numerous offices developments within Century City. And the leisure traveller will have a host of facilities available to ensure an unforgettable holiday.

Apart from the 25m indoor heated swimming and the fitness centre, hotel guests can enjoy the hotel's own "island" – a private bathing area surrounded by water and covered with palm trees. Hotel guests can also stroll along the promenade level and walk across a footbridge to Africa's largest shopping centre – Canal Walk. With a choice of more than 35 restaurants, unlimited entertainment and the ultimate shopping experience, hotel guests will have every opportunity to enjoy themselves.

The developers of Century City, which is 10 minutes drive from Cape Town's CBD, have incorporated careful attention to details such as security, environmental preservation and design guidelines, so that hotel guests can be assured of a safe lifestyle in attractive surroundings. The entire Century City complex enjoys the protection of a 24-hour ground patrol and surveillance cameras, as well as permanently manned access control at all roads into the complex. Hotel guests can also enjoy the tranquillity of the nearby 14 hectare wetlands area, which has been created within the development, including a bird sanctuary.

For further details contact the Singer Group on telephone (021) 424 2288 or refer to www.singergroup.co.za

Island Club Hotel

SINGER GROUP OF COMPANIES

The Singer Group of companies comprises several businesses in the travel, tourism, hospitality and property industries in South Africa, and is owned and managed by the Singer family.

The founder of the group, Barney Singer, purchased a small travel agency in 1973. His wife, Esther, began working as a travel consultant and over the years assisted building Embassy Travel into one of the largest travel agencies in Cape Town. Sons, Leon and Brian joined the family business, and assisted by their sister Jill – a practising attorney - used this base to rapidly expand the group by acquiring and initiating a variety of businesses.

Today, the Singer Group of companies is regarded as the leading independent tourism business in South Africa.

EMBASSY TRAVEL

Based in the Cape Town CBD, Embassy Travel is a retail travel agency that specialises in Leisure and corporate travel.

GARDENS CENTRE HOLIDAY APARTMENTS

Fully furnished, equipped and serviced, the Gardens Centre Apartments offers affordable accommodation in a safe and secure environment.

44 Studio apartments conveniently located in the tower block of the Gardens Shopping Centre – "the whole city is on your doorstep"

DOLPHIN BEACH HOTEL

Located on the beach in Bloubergstrand, Dolphin Beach Hotel enjoys the most beautiful view of Table Mountain across the Atlantic Ocean.

Operated by Protea Hotels, this four-star property comprises 32 apartments and offers discerning guests spacious and luxurious accommodation.

BLOWFISH RESTAURANT

Located in the Dolphin Beach Hotel, Blowfish Restaurant is rated as one of the top fish, seafood and sushi restaurants in Cape Town.

Patrons can make their selection from an appetising display of fresh fish and seafood consisting of local, imported, exotic and deep sea game fish.

CONFINITIVE

An outstanding team of professional conference organisers and incentive travel planners.

SURE YOUTH TRAVEL

With branches located in Johannesburg, Pretoria and Cape Town, Sure Youth travel is a one-stop travel shop specialising in student, youth and independent travel. The company arranges working holidays and overseas job placements.

DOLPHIN TOURS

A Destination Management Company that specialises in in-bound travel for individuals and groups.

TRAVEL-LOTTO.CO.ZA

An on-line game where players can win dream holidays to fantastic destinations. Log on to www.travel-lotto.co.za – it's free, it's easy!

ISLAND CLUB HOTEL

Located on the Grand Canal in Century City, the Island Club Hotel comprises 23 luxury hotel suites. (Commencing business on 15 October 2004).

For further information telephone (021) 424 2288 or log-on to www.singergroup.co.za. Head Office: 17 Wale Street, Cape Town.

PROTEA HOTEL
DOLPHIN BEACH

...is located on Blouberg beach with beautiful views of Table Mountain and Robben Island across the Atlantic Ocean.

TOURISM GRADING COUNCIL
OF SOUTH AFRICA
★ ★ ★ ★

Premier
PROTEA HOTELS

Tel: +27 (0) 21 557 8140

Marine Drive, Bloubergstrand, 7441, Cape Town
dolphinbeach@icon.co.za
www.visitdolphinbeach.com

HIPPO BOUTIQUE HOTEL

Find yourself in the hub of Cape Town. Situated on the lip of the city bowl, close to Cape Town's buzziest strip, Kloof Street, which is lined with restaurants and renowned for its café culture, the recently opened Hippo is a hip, fresh, up-market hotel concept which smoulders with urban energy.

Ideally located for business travellers with high-speed Internet PC's in all rooms with 24 hour complimentary ADSL internet access, as well as the media and fashion industry, the semi-minimalist aesthetic and impeccable service of this ultra-modern twenty -room establishment has already made it a trendy insider destination.

Centrally located within a 5 minute walk from the heart of the business district, minutes from the two main motorways that traverse the Western Cape and a 15 – 20 minute drive from Cape Town International Airport. Many of the Cape's most famous landmarks such as the Table Mountain cableway, the V&A Waterfront and Nelson Mandela's old island jail, Robben Island are only a stone's throw from your door.

Only 5 minutes away from Camps Bay and Clifton, two of the Cape's world-renowned bikini beaches, 15 minutes drive to the local winelands, and 10 minutes from Kirstenbosch National Botanical Gardens.

The décor of the open-plan interiors combine industrial materials like chrome, stone and polished cement with leather couches, cherry wood floors and furniture and giant paintings as headboards reflect Hippo's character.

The bedrooms offer king size beds and decor is neutral but delights in designer details with modern furniture Haldane Martin and the sleek fittings including DSTV, CD- and DVD-player. All rooms are air-conditioned, have under floor heating as well as electronic safes, fully stocked mini-bars. Extra treats include rooibos body products and 'flight packs' stuffed with goodies.

Whilst each room has a fully equipped kitchen with complimentary tea and filter coffee, its location places you close to a plethora of restaurants and cafes to suit any palate all within walking distance. Breakfasts are offered as an optional extra.

Meeting and conference needs are catered for by the club-style lounge accommodating up to ten people.

Guests have access to the nearby gym and secure parking, and each room is kitted out with a hi-tech multimedia centre that includes ADSL internet access. The hotel also offers secure parking and guests have access to the gym situated in the neighbouring shopping centre.

Daily laundry service is also provided.

The staff is super-friendly and will organise everything for you including private tours, a personal chaperone or even that much-needed facial or hair-cut.

Airport transfer by arrangement.

The Hippo Lobby

Get *Comfortable*

Only unstinting quality and attention to detail can shift a place from being merely conveniet to seriously comfortable. Details like fine cotton linen, king size beds, leather couches, cherry-wood floors and interior design that lets you breathe a little deeper.

HIPPO

BOUTIQUE HOTEL

Get *Connected*

Complimentary 24-Hour Internet access. High speed dedicated ADSL computers in all rooms.

Home entertainment centre in each room: DSTV, DVD player, music system.

All bathrooms have underfloor heating.

Fully equipped kitchen units with complimentary tea and filter coffee.

Electronic safes accommodate laptop computers.

Fully stocked mini-bars.

+27 (0) 21 423 600
info@hippotique.co.za
5-9 Park Road, Gardens, Cape Town, South Africa

Overlooking the Atlantic, this gracious Hotel with 76 luxurious rooms and suites invites you to enjoy understated elegance & personalised service. The Waterfront and the city are minutes away making this the perfect location. Harveys restaurant, terraces, courtyard & bar, is designed to look after your culinary requirements, whilst the Ginkgo Spa at the Mansions looks after all wellness aspects.

Tel: +27 (0) 21 434 2351
221 Beach Road, Sea Point
www.gopassport.com

Ikhaya, Cape Town's unique African style guest lodge and conference centre, is located on Dunckley Square in the Gardens, below Table Mountain. We offer rooms equipped with en-suite bathrooms, self-catering options, secure parking, conference facilities and many restaurants and places of interest within walking distance.

Tel: +27 (0) 21 461 8880
Dunkley Square, Wandel Street, Gardens
www.gopassport.com

The Lodge is situated on the fringe of the CBD, 1.5km from the Convention Centre. The 114 spacious, luxurious rooms with all-round views of the Mother City offer a variety of services and facilities. Enjoy cocktails on the pool deck, a meal in our award winning restaurant with premier wines. Conference facilities available.

Tel: +27 (0) 21 422 0030
10 Buitengracht Street, Cape Town
www.gopassport.com

 the cape milner

This hotel is situated at the foot of Table Mountain and offers modern contemporary comfort, with the highest levels of service. Minutes from the arty CBD, popular V&A Waterfront and pristine white beaches. Visit the 2 on Milner Restaurant, Cigar Lounge Bar and Terrace Cocktail Bar.

Tel: +27 (0) 21 426 1101
2a Milner Road, Tamboerskloof
www.gopassport.com

Hôtel Le Vendôme

Hôtel Le Vendôme is an exciting new arrival to Cape Town's fold of luxury boutique hotels, blending French old-world charm with new millennium technology. Renowned South African hospitality completes the ideal formula for discerning travellers wishing to relax in style or explore the Mother City and the Cape Peninsula.

Tel: +27 (0) 21 430 1200
20 London Road, Sea Point, Cape Town
www.gopassport.com

RESTAURANTS

Spice of Life

All types of local and international food are available, such as Sushi which has reached a peak of popularity in Cape Town. Thai food is also favoured, but Indian curries are not as frequently seen on menus as sweet and subtly spiced Cape Malay dishes. With so many in?uences, a creative fusion of ?avours can result in some stunning combinations.

Traditional African Food

A typical African dish found across Southern and East Africa, consists predominantly of a high carbohydrate staple, which in Cape Town is called 'pap'. This is maize meal ?our cooked into a stiff porridge and served with tomato and onion relish or wild spinach (imi?no or merogo), and perhaps a meat stew or tripe. Don't expect too much of this kind of food in Cape Town's lively African restaurants, as they usually offer a much more tempting selection of dishes from around the African continent.

Vegetarians

Vegetarians are very well catered for, with some innovative meat-free dishes found on virtually every menu.

Sushi as served at Blowfish

RESTAURANTS

You are in for such a treat! Capetonians love to eat out, and as a result there are literally thousands of restaurants to choose from. Some rival the most sophisticated in the world, others are simply good value for great food. All are in a position to offer amazing quality, and we feature a number of reputable restaurants that should not disappoint you.

Freshness is one reason the food tastes so good in Cape Town, the other is because the ingredients are almost always seasonal. If it doesn't grow at that time of year, it isn't served. Do your tastebuds a favour and sink your teeth into the tastiest fruit and vegetables you have sampled in a long time.

CHOOSING A RESTAURANT

Look for restaurants patronised by locals, because Capetonians can be pretty choosy and if a restaurant doesn't make the grade, they just won't go there. They also object to being overcharged, but do not mind digging deep for a seriously good meal. Kloof Street is popular for its variety of food establishments and the V&A Waterfront has plenty of every persuasion. The suburbs and most of the South Peninsula villages have one or more particularly notable restaurants, worth driving some distance for.

LOCAL CUISINE

Cape cuisine is truly multicultural, influenced as it is by the different races that have made their mark on the Cape over centuries. Cape Malay food is renowned for perking up savoury dishes with fruits and spices, such as Bobotie - a traditional lightly curried mince under savoury custard.

All South Africans love a good braai (coal or wood barbeque), on which you will almost always find boerewors (thick spiced farm sausage) and chops, and perhaps sosaties (spiced minced meat kebabs).

FOOD FEASTS

SEAFOOD

Cape Town is renowned for serving fish straight from the sea and crayfish (rock lobster), takes pride of place at the head of the most desirable list.

Crayfish are available fresh during the open season (November to January - but this changes), and frozen at other times. So much of Cape Town's crayfish - (dubbed 'red gold')- is exported, that local prices have rocketed, although it is still affordable for a treat.

Large mussels and gentle-flavoured oysters are local, but prawns and langoustines usually come from the warmer waters of neighbouring Mozambique.

Cold water sea fish such as cape salmon, yellowtail and kingklip, are prepared as 'daily specials' or 'linefish' , and tuna steaks are on the menu when the tunny is running. These giants of the sea are usually landed at Hout Bay - centre of the tuna and crayfishing industry, and popular waterfront complex. Large thin silvery Snoek (of the barracuda family), must be eaten the day they are caught or they go a bit 'pap' (soft). A delicious traditional recipe is to poach the fish in garlic butter and apricot jam.

Kalk Bay harbour is a small fishing port on False Bay, and if you turn up around lunchtime, you may see the fishing boats offloading their catch. You can barter for your supper, but watch your back as the fish are thrown by hand from boat to jetty, and they don't stop if you happen to be in the way.

Meat

If your meat is in the slightest bit tough send it back. You can expect and demand really tender steaks, whether beef, ostrich or game meat like springbok or kudu. Once you have savoured these more unusual meats you will probably be coming back for more. Ostrich is a particularly healthy option as it is naturally cholesterol free.

RESTAURANT PROTOCOL

Booking & Paying

Good restaurants get booked up, not just at weekends, but during the week too, so reservations are advisable. Wednesday is a traditional mid-week big night out and is dubbed 'klein Saterdag ('little Saturday'). Most major credit cards are accepted, but cheques are often not.

Smoking in Public Places

Thanks to an avid anti-smoking Health Minister, South Africa now has strict laws against smoking in public places. What's more surprising is that most establishments adhere to them. There is no smoking in public buildings, and restaurants must either be smoke-free or provide a separate area for smokers.

Tipping Unless you are in a group of around ten or more, a service charge is not usually added to the bill. Waitrons get paid abominably and rely on your generosity to earn a living. They usually provide very good service and for that they hope you will tip them 10-15%.

BYO Wine

Capetonians have access to such excellent wines and with over 300 wine estates in close proximity, they can be picky about which label they prefer. They therefore often choose to bring their own wine and many restaurants do not mind and just charge a small corkage fee.

CAPE FOOD & WINE FESTIVALS

February - Harvest Festival of the Sea - Saldanha, West Coast

March - Franschhoek Harvest Festival Gourmet Fair

April - SA Cheese Festival, Franschhoek

May - Cape Town Gourmet Festival and Restaurant Week, Riebeek Valley Olive Festival, Cape Town Coffee Route

June - Swartland Food & Wine Festival, Malmesbury

July - Knysna Oyster Festival, Garden Route, Bastille Festival, Franschhoek, Calitsdorp Port Festival, Klien Karoo

August - Velddrif Food and Culture Festival, West Coast, Stellenbosch Wine Festival, McGregor Country Food & Wine Festival, Hermanus Food & Wine Fair

October - October Fest at Wilderer's Distillery, Stellenbosch, Strawberry Festival

For more information see Cape Town Events website: www.capetownevents.co.za

Springbok as served at Kennedy's

Dessert as served at Seaforth Restaurant

Mama offers warm, friendly hospitality in a totally relaxed way. She loves happiness, laughter, joy and the satisfaction that goes with a full belly and "Quality, not time is important to her". Leave all pressure and stress behind and enjoy her unique warmth and vibe. With her live African bands nightly, she ensures an African experience never to be forgotten !!

"Come to Mama's, she's cookin !"

Tel: +27 (0) 21 426 1017
178 Long Street, Cape Town
www.gopassport.com

Bloemendal
Restaurant & Cellar

Elegantly poised upon one of the tallest hills in the Northern Suburbs on the Durbanville Wine Route, Bloemendal Restaurant offers a 270° panoramic view of the Cape Peninsula. Serving a 'must have' traditional cape buffet, Bloemendal is also perfect for business meetings (cigar bar), functions, dinner dances or weddings!

Tel: +27 (0) 21 975 7575
M13, Racecourse Road, Bloemendal Estate, Durbanville
www.gopassport.com

Khaya-Nyama (house of meat) is set in a mock rural cave and is the only specialist game restaurant in Cape Town. Game is our forte with delicious dishes such as eland, warthog, gemsbok, springbok and ostrich served in a truly South African fashion, in a unique, relaxed atmosphere and prides itself in cuisine of an exceptionally high standard. Open 7 days a week for lunch and dinner.

Tel: +27 (0) 21 424 2917
267 Long Street, Cape Town
www.gopassport.com

KOPANONG B&B

This restaurant and B&B provides the taste of open-heart hospitality of South Africa. It's the all in one township cultural experience. A place to relax in comfort while you experience and learn the township life in the heartbeat of Africa. We provide accommodation, delectable traditional dishes, drinks and stories of South African's checkered history and do township tours for our guests on request.

Tel: +27 (0) 21 361 2084
C329 Velani Crescent, Khayelitsha
www.gopassport.com

The QUARTERDECK
Restaurant

No prison was ever this comfortable, or served such wonderful food ! Located in the exclusive Portswood Hotel; at the V&A Waterfront, the Quarterdeck Restaurant is a relaxed yet elegant venue, housed in what used to the Cape Colony's convict station. This beautifully restored National Monument with its rich history, is the perfect setting in which to savour the best of Cape Malay Cuisine, Patrons can sample a wide seleection of mouthwatering local dishes at lunch and dinner.

Tel: +27 (0) 21 418 3281
Portswood Hotel, V&A Waterfront, CT
www.gopassport.com

Out of Asia is situated on Victoria Road, Camps Bay. We offer a variety of Asian dishes such as Thai, chinese, Japanese and Vietnamese food. Your lunch and dinner is prepared when you request it. This ensures the best taste and quality in the unique flavour of Asian cuisine.

Tel: +27 (0) 21 438 1926
The Promenade, 79 Victoria Road, Camps Bay
www.gopassport.com

Jewel of India
EXQUISITE INDIAN RESTAURANT

Jewel of India revive and maintain the glorious culinary traditions of old in an ambience best suited for today's world. The warmth of the decor, the note of hospitality and the sheer culinary skills, make Jewel of India an unforgettable experience.

Tel: +27 (0) 21 419 8397
Shop 6264, V&A Waterfront, Cape Town
www.gopassport.com

Asu-Ma's

Asu-ma's Sushi Bar and Restaurant is situated in a beautiful seaside setting en-route to Chapman's Peak Drive. With reasonable prices, excellent service and delicious food, it's no wonder that it is being touted as one of the country's top Sushi restaurants.

Tel: +27 (0) 21 424 9530
Unit 1, By the Sea, Main Road, Hout Bay
www.gopassport.com

Gaylords

Savour the tantalizing exquisite dishes from North and South India. Relaxed Indian charm in rustic cottagey surrounds with fireplace. Extensive menu offering authentic seafood, meat and vegetarian varieties including a curried prawn speciality. Special uncurried meals are available on request. Separate function room available.

Tel: +27 (0) 21 788 5470
65 Main Road, Muizenberg
www.gopassport.com

同樂 TONG LOK
CHINESE RESTAURANT

"Tong Lok" directly translated from Chinese means "together in happiness" and we pride ourselves in the ancient art of Cantonese cooking. Each dish is skillfully prepared in the traditional and age-old wok using only choice authentic ingredients, ensuring the true taste of China in every dish.

Tel: +27 (0) 21 421 5055
9 Somerset Road, Green Point
www.gopassport.com

Whether you choose to join us for lunch or dinner, the elegant, intimate warmth of Saffron's Restaurant offers the perfect ambiance for an unforgettable experience. The emphasis is on superior presentation and service excellence which is reflected in every meal prepared and served by the highly competent team.

Tel: +27 (021) 424 3757
9 Orphan Street, Cape Town
www.gopassport.com

The beach, palm trees, the bay surround you on arrival. Over one hundred exotic cocktails to choose from. An a la carte menu incorporating numerous international flavours. Service excellence and quality. Dine and dance seven days a week to the elite of Capetonian musicians – If your mantra for life is to live it with passion – then this is the ultimate experience.

Tel: +27 (021) 438 3174
The Promenade, Victoria Rd, Camps Bay
www.gopassport.com

Leinster Hall was built in 1850 and today still survives as one of the four manor houses of Cape Town. This historic monument is known for its beautiful verandah, gardens and stunning interior. Award winning combine continental cuisine with award winning wine lists offering a dining experience difficult to surpass.

Tel: +27 (021) 424 1836
7 Weltevreden Road, Gardens
www.gopassport.com

Situated away from the city in rural Constantia with leafy vistas, Greens offers 'cafe au lait' decor with a comfortable and relaxed ambiance. With a roaring fire place for chilly winter months, there is also a sunny outdoor terrace. From the open style kitchen theatre, a wide selection of lunch and dinner options, woodfired pizzas, breakfasts served all day and freshly baked breads and muffins. Free parking. Fully licensed.

Tel: +27 (021) 794 3843
Shop 7 High Constantia, Main Rd, Constantia
www.gopassport.com

The Veranda Restaurant, on the 1st floor of the Metropole Hotel, offers uninterrupted views of Long Street. It is the perfect setting for a meal, with an interior that utilises clean lines, juxtaposed with contrasting colours. The menu is hearty and unpretentious and has been described as "comfort food with a twist"

Tel: +27 (021) 424 7247
Metropole Luxury Boutique Hotel
38 Long Street, Cape Town
www.gopassport.com

GREENS

Smack bang in the middle of the Kloof Street hot spot, the new Greens in Park Road, delivers the same stylish ecclectic offerings as it sister shop in Constantia, with an added Wine bar & lounge, extensive wine list, woodfired pizzas, espresso & fresh daily special from the open style kitchen theatre, Greens on Park offers an all round food experience. Breakfast is served all day. Fully licensed.

Tel: +27 (021) 422 4415
5-9 Park Road, Gardens
www.gopassport.com

Emily's

The Premier Restaurant for South African Cuisine
* Top 10 Restaurant
* Coffee & Wine Bar
* Champagne Room
* Wedding Chapel
* Brandy Bar

Tel: +27 (021) 421 1133
202, Upper Level, The Clock Tower Centre,
V&A Waterfront
www.gopassport.com

jakes
CAFÉ · RESTAURANT · BAR

Come on into Jakes where we are more than delicious food and drinks to suit your mood – we're also about atmosphere and an experience not soon to be forgotten. Whenever you visit us, whether it's for lunch, dinner or a couple of drinks, you can be sure that we'll create the perfect setting for you to relax and let stress and tension melt away. Of course you'll also find an interesting and tempting menu, but that goes without saying…

Tel: +27 (021) 701 3272
Steenberg Village, Steenberg Rd, Constantia
www.gopassport.com

Rive Gauche

Hôtel Le Vendôme's fine dining restaurant, Rive Gauche, conjures up exceptional meals, complemented with superb international and local wines, and served in equally tasteful surroundings.

Tel: +27 (021) 430 1200
20 London Road, Sea Point, Cape Town
www.gopassport.com

SAVOY CABBAGE
RESTAURANT &
CHAMPAGNE BAR

Exciting contemporary cuisine in a setting where glass concrete and four centuries of exposed brick combine to make a visually exciting venue. Vegetarians and carnivores enjoy a menu that changes daily, using the freshest local produce. The origin of the food spans continents. Gracious dining without excessive formality, high standards of cooking and service remain uncompromised. Airconditioned. Secure day and night time parking. CNN's "Hot Spot" for Cape Town. 3 top awards and Wine Magazine's top 100 for 5 years.

Tel: +27 (021) 424 2626
101 Hout Street, Cape Town
www.gopassport.com

Peddlars

Peddlars on the Bend's décor and diverse menu create a venue that is both casual and yet elegant, modern yet steeped in rich tradition. The summer terrace provides the ideal spot for aficionados of alfresco dining. Peddlars has a comprehensive winelist which also boasts an impressive selection of 'Grand Marque' Champagnes at extremely reasonable prices. Diners Club Winelist Award for the past fiveyears & 2003 Platinum Award.

Tel: +27 (021) 794 7747
Spaanschemat River Road, Constantia
www.gopassport.com

MOJA

Retro-safari in the land of Moja! A unique dining concept; Moja offers global cuisine - from Easy Food (food cooked for you by our chefs) to lava stones and fondue, which you cook yourself at the table. Play with your food and be sure to sample Moja's legendary urban cocktails too.

Tel: +27 (021) 423 4989
Heritage Square, 98 Shortmarket Street,
Cape Town
www.gopassport.com

The Clipper Restaurant

Enjoy the finest and freshest seafood, compliments of the nearby Atlantic Ocean combining it with the aromatic curry spices for which the Cape Malay cuisine is so well known! The Clipper Restaurant offers you an extensive à la menu of fine cuisine includes a variety of seafood specialities with some of the finest South African wines which you can enjoy outdoors on the terrace overlooking the sparkling pool, or more intimately indoors.

Tel: +27 (021) 415 1000
The Commodore Hotel, Portswood Road, V&A
Waterfront, Cape Town
www.gopassport.com

Zevenwacht RESTAURANT

Located in the historic Manor House of the wine farm and surrounded by vineyards, the restaurant serves contemporary continental cuisine. A selection of picnic baskets are available to be enjoyed on the tree-shaded lawn on the shores of the lake. Zevenwacht boasts ideal settings for banquets, gala dinners, weddings and parties. Open 7 days a week for lunch and dinner.

Tel: +27 (021) 903 5123
Langverwacht Rd, Off R102, Kuilsriver
www.gopassport.com

HARVEYS
at the Mansions
RESTAURANT • BAR • COURTYARD & TERRACES

Harveys restaurant, terraces, courtyard & bar, created for the love of good food, great wines and good company. Our executive chef prides himself in creating delectable dishes with international appeal and African influences. With stunning sea views or in the central courtyard, Harveys will hit your taste buds, guaranteed. Bon appetit!

Tel: +27 (021) 434 2351
221 Beach Road, Sea Point
www.gopassport.com

Simon's
at Groot Constantia

Nestled in the breathtaking Constantia Valley on South Africas oldest wine farm, Groot Constantia, you will find Simon's restaurant. A beautiful setting for light, outdoor, casual lunches, or in the evening enjoy a wonderful dining experience with a varied and enticing menu. Open 7 days a week. Lunch from 12pm and dinner from 6pm.

Tel: +27 (021) 794 1143
Groot Constantia Wine Estate,
Groot Constantia Road, Constantia
www.gopassport.com

aubergine
RESTAURANT

Aubergine Restaurant offers continental cuisine with Asian influences, of which game, seafood and vegetarian dishes are specialties. Our exciting, seasonally inspired menu is complemented by our extensive wine list – which boasts 250 positions from all regions in the Cape.

Tel: +27 (021) 465 4909
39 Barnet Street, Gardens, Cape Town
www.gopassport.com

The Paulaner Bräuhaus is a vibrant microbrewery and restaurant providing a touch of Bavaria blended with Cape cuisine and frothy freshly brewed beer. Situated in the Clocktower Precinct of the world-renowned V&A Waterfront, Paulaner is the only brewery in the world with its fermentation and maturation cellar below sea level.

Tel: +27 (021) 418 9999
Clocktower Precinct, V&A Waterfront, CT
www.gopassport.com

STREGA
ristorante

A bustling bistro serving Italian board of fare in a relaxed urban environment, Strega is the perfect venue for large gatherings or dinner for two. Pizza, pasta and the Mediterranean Chefs recommendations provide an ample selection to suit every palette. The wine list is locally priced and the courtyard seating goes first!

Tel: +27 (021) 423 4889
Heritage Square, 100 Shortmarket Street
www.gopassport.com

Situated in Green Point zero932 prides themselves on beautifully presented and delicious to eat meals that flirts with Belgian tradition, of international standard served by accomplished waiters chosen for their individual flare and élan. An impressive beer list of up to 24 Belgian imported beers, each served in its own branded glass is available or enjoy a cocktail in MONK, the upstairs bar.

Tel: +27 (021) 439 6314
Exhibition Bldg., 79 Main Rd, Green Point
www.gopassport.com

Morton's on the Wharf is an elegant yet informal restaurant where great attention has been paid to detail, ensuring that the menu, decor and ambiance are all typical of a New Orleans restaurant. Great steaks, superb seafood, gumbos and foot tapping jazz.

Tel: +27 (021) 418 3633
V & A Waterfront
www.gopassport.com

Piazza Trevi is has an exciting wine list and its menu offers pizzas, pasta, grills, seafood and house specialities. We also run weekly specials that concentrate on good homely cooking with a tendency towards fusion cooking. The ambiance is warm, friendly and definitely caters for the whole family, so bring the little ones as they are also very welcome.

Tel: +27 (0) 21 794 5817
Constantia Village Shopping Centre, Constantia Rd, Constantia
www.gopassport.com

Diva is situated in the heart of Bohemian Cape Town and besides the best pizzas, we serve a varied selection of homemade pastas and great lasagna. Add the most stunning interiors you'll ever come across and you will know why we are so popular. See you there !

Tel: +27 (021) 447 0098
88 Lower Main Road, Observatory
www.gopassport.com

Styled on the New Orleans jazz scene with a rhythm all its own we aim to provide you with a unique experience of spicy Cajun culinary delights and intriguing cocktails mixed with a vibe that will make your next social event truly unforgettable. JB Sushi is the new addition where our highly experienced sushi chef prepares the finest examples of sushi dishes. Open for lunch and dinner only.

Tel: +27 (021) 683 0840   Fax: +27 (021) 683 0841
Shop 630, Cavendish Square, Claremont
www.gopassport.com

The Lookout Deck is situated on the water in the stunning Hout Bay Harbour, offering unsurpassed views, in a setting rivalling those only found in Monaco. The extensive menu caters for all tastes and preferences, with an emphasis on freshness, flavours and presentation. Relax in your shorts or bikini on The Deck, or feel the sophistication of the Dining Room, whatever you prefer.

Tel: +27 (021) 790 0900
Harbour Rd, Hout Bay Harbour
www.gopassport.com

TWO OCEANS
Restaurant • Cape Point

Since 1995 Two Oceans Restaurant, with interior and exterior seating, has served visitors from near and far. Guests indulge in a mouth watering feast while overlooking the entire False Bay area, a view that you will remember for life. Explore Mediterranean-South African cuisine with fresh seafood a house specialty although vegetarians, meat lovers and little ones are also catered for.

Tel: +27 (021) 780 9200
Cape Point Nature Reserve
www.gopassport.com

PANAMA JACK'S

From humble beginnings circa 1989 this former boat yard became a household name. Well known throughout South Africa and indeed internationally for its live seafood, Panama Jacks is host to a 30 000l seawater tank from which you may select your own live lobster or abalone, mussels and Namibian oysters!

Tel: +27 (021) 447 3992
Royal Cape Yacht Club, Table Bay Harbour
www.gopassport.com

Blowfish

With a prime beachfront position in the Dolphin Beach Hotel, Bloubergstrand, and a breathtaking view of Table Bay and Table Mountain, Blowfish Restaurant is renowned for its delicious spread of seafood and sushi.

It offers an upmarket dining experience in a relaxed atmosphere. Its seafood counter boasts an appetising array of the finest fare from fresh prawns, langoustines, calamari and oysters to game fish, kingklip, kabeljou and sole.

Blowfish Restaurant also offers a selection of mouthwatering Asian dishes and serves a variety of exotic cocktails.

Tel: +27 (021) 556 5464
Dolphin Beach Hotel, 1 Marine Drive, Bloubergstrand
blowfish@mweb.co.za • www.blowfishrestaurant.co.za
www.gopassport.com

MUSICAL CAPE TOWN

More than one third of music bought by South Africans is generated in South Africa. Whatever shakes you up or gets you groovin', Cape Town has it all. Rhythm and blues, the pantsula or kwasa kwasa, gospel, rap and brass bands. Township jive, hip-hop, trip-hop, pop, rap, gangsta rap, spoken word or Afro-jazz. Rock and gospel, drum 'n bass, electro, techno, kwaito and a fair bit of classical stuff to boot!

LIVE GIGS

Green Dolphin Restaurant (V&A Waterfront, tel: 021 421 7471) and Marimba's at the Convention Centre (tel: 021 418 3366) remain steadfast jazz faithfuls, with regular live music. Jazz and rhythm & blues lovers will drive as far as necessary when Judith Sephuma, Errol Dyers, or Virtual Jazz Reality are in town.

The Independent Armchair Theatre (Lower Main Road, Observatory, tel: 021 447 1514), is rated highly for live gigs, and if contemporary trend-setters Freshly Ground should be playing, don't walk by. Plain old pop is always good too, of which Semisane is a fine example, and the band continues to improve with each new CD that tops the local charts.

Don't be too hasty to dismiss Afrikaans rock music, because baby it's come a long way since its accordion-pumping days. Be sure to get your fix of the 'Mystic Boer' (a.k.a Valiant Swart), when he drops by Stellenbosch's Dorp Street Theatre Café (tel: 021 886 6107).

Recapture your varsity days at Stellenbosch's University-student-cum-budding-rock-star crazed pubs. While you're there, track down the U2-meets-Soweto-String-Quartet inspired DNA Strings, which serves up what can best be described as an Afro-Celtic rhythm.

BIG OVERSEAS

Some South African bands have made it big across the water, like Vusi Mahlasela, and rock sensation Just Jinger continues to create waves in the USA, playing alongside the likes of Counting Crows.

AMANDLA!

See the movie Amandla!, which tells the story of black South African freedom music and the role it played in the battle against apartheid (www.amandla.com).

Kwaito

Kwaito is the unofficial mouthpiece of the townships – can best be explained as a slowed-down version of House music. It is even hipper than House because its street savvy comes straight from the dusty South African backstreets. There's nothing flat coming out of the Cape Flats either, with the likes of hip-hop biggies Black Noise, Brasse Vannie Kaap, and Prophets of Da City firmly at the helm.

Where to Buy

Show your support for the city's ever-emerging groundswell of talent and pick up something local to take home. Musica and Look 'n Listen (stores country-wide), stock a wide selection of music, as does the independent store Downstairs Music, in Greenmarket Square. The V & A Waterfront's Compact Disc Wherehouse (tel: 021 425 6300), is a good spot to raid the racks for the sounds of jazz icon Abdullah Ibrahim or sexy local all-girl string quartet Muse. Or try the sounds of rockers Krushed 'n Sorted or the harder lines of all-female Cape Flats rap group Godessa? If you drop on a Saturday afternoon, you'll be lucky enough to catch a live gig.

Live music at Marimba

An opulent venue, offering a traditional cigar bar and award winning resturant, whose international chefs have created a menu fusing Eurpoean, Califonian and African elements. After dinner relax and enjoy a drink in our Piano Lounge or downstairs on plush sofas while you sample our vast range of imported cigars, cognacs, single malt and whiskies to the sound of Cape Towns finest live musicians.

Tel: +27 (021) 4241212
251 Long Street, Cape Town
www.gopassport.com

Manenberg's Jazz Café - A place in Africa

Enjoy good food and wine, plus our balcony offers panoramic views of the Waterfront. Live sundowner bands every weekend, and South Africa's foremost musicians present live jazz and African music 7 nights a week. Open from 11h00 daily.

Tel: +27 (021) 421 5639
Clock Tower Centre, V&A Waterfront
www.gopassport.com

THE ALABAMA PRESENTS THE SEAHORSE CAFE

Cape Town's only floating Seafood Restaurant offering a Seafood Buffet and a la carte Menu with the freshest fare the Cape coast has to offer. Join us for an unforgettable cruise with magnificent views of Table Mountain while sipping cocktails on the deck.

Tel: +27 (021) 419 3122
Shop 6, Quay 5, V&A Waterfront
Info or Reservations : info@alabama.co.za
www.gopassport.com

Since 1990 The Green Dolphin has invited Capetonians and visitors to enjoy a heady combination of fine international cuisine and magical music by serving up a delicious live jazz every single night, showcasing top local and international artists, and contributing to the development of the Cape's jazz tradition. Open every day from 12 lunch to 12 @ night.

Tel: +27 (021) 421 7471
V&A Arcade, Pierhead, V&A Waterfront
www.gopassport.com

A TOUCH OF MADNESS

The Free House where time stood still. Beautiful decor, Regally elegant and rich. Fully stocked pub, with a whiskey selection the Isles would be proud of. The cuisine as wonderful as the ambience. Music from a bygone era. A perfect place to relax and enjoy a late night cap.

Tel: +27 (021) 448 2266
12 Nuttall Road, Observatory
www.gopassport.com

LIVE MUSIC DINING

MARIMBA

Marimba restaurant merges African influences with the contemporary stylish elegance of the Cape. Marimba has drawn on some of the country's finest talent to create a world-class dining experience, which reflects our African origins as well as Cape Town's global energy. Dinner at Marimba is a celebration of fabulous food and exceptional music as Marimba features a sophisticated seven-night-a-week music programme, including Blues, Big Band, Contemporary African, Motown and Jazz. Open seven nights a week for dinner and from Monday to Friday for lunches.

RESTAURANT

Born in Europe, raised in Asia and celebrating his life in Africa, Executive Head Chef Gernot Bunke blends the finest African cuisine with global fusion flavours to bring about a cuisine concept, which combines his African, Asian and European experience. He regularly steps out of the kitchen to meet his guests and to create special dishes on request, along with consulting for group, function and feast menus. The menu goes back to the basics where the natural flavours of the dishes are enhanced, rather than disguised.

ENTERTAINMENT

Not only does the privately-owned Marimba restaurant boast a menu inspired by flavours of the world, they also pride themselves on a diverse sophisticated music menu with dancing encouraged. Their mix of renowned international and local musicians brings the ultimate dinner/dance Jazz & Blues experience to life in Cape Town. The Marimba Restaurant presents top local and international performers hosted by our resident marimba player, Bongani Sotshononda

CIGAR BAR

The refined style of Marimba is echoed in the exclusive adjoining Marimba Cigar Bar, where you can watch the latest music DVD 's on our state of the art plasma screen while enjoying Cuba's finest cigars complemented by Cape wines, award winning Calitzdorp ports, scotch whisky and Marimba's unique range of African Cocktails, which celebrate marula, Cape cognacs and more.

CAFE

The Marimba Café offers quality, quick and casual coffees, lunches and suppers. With backgammon and chess sets available and tournaments for beginners and masters, the all-weather café offers an African cosmopolitan atmosphere along with regular art and exhibitions.

FUNCTIONS

Are you looking for a new or alternative venue for a corporate event or office party? Cocktail parties in the Cigar Bar or terrace with Table Mountain as the backdrop, product launches, gala dinners, awards evenings and year end events at Marimba we are able to accommodate all special events whether you are four or 150 people.

For groups between 110 and 150 the restaurant can be privatised. For cocktail parties our capacity is 240 people.

Included in the hire costs you have access to our state of the art sound and lighting system. Go to "In-house Audio Visual Equipment" to view details. All our menus listed are samples of what Chef Gernot Bunke can put together. We are happy to create a menu to your specific requirements. Prices and items listed are subject to change.

For that unique and special flair try our highly successful Marimba Feast which breaks away from the traditional set menu or buffet. Special dietary requests are met on an individual basis. Where possible it is advisable to notify us in advance of any special requests.

nightly live music • african & global cuisine

corporate events/breakfasts and private functions

MARIMBA RESTAURANT

African and Continental Chefs blending local and global cuisine; live music nightly - **Blues, Big Band, Contemporary African, Motown, Jazz and much more.**

MARIMBA TERRACE

Enjoy coffee, sundowners or your meal on our out-door terrace, with the atmosphere of the historic Heerengracht and the backdrop of Table Mountain.

MARIMBA CIGAR BAR

A range of cigars along with a selected range of South African and imported wines, Whisky, Port and Liqueurs and cocktails. Our plasma screen shows music DVD's and special events on satellite TV.

MARIMBA CAFE

The Marimba Cafe offers light lunches from R35 and imported Italian Coffee from early to late.

m a r i m b a

music • food • cigar bar

ENTERTAINMENT

South Peninsula Theatres

The Kalk Bay Theatre is a popular alternative restaurant theatre with talented performers in well received original plays. Have your soup and starter before the show and dessert and coffee afterwards, all for as little as R150. 52 Main Rd, Kalk Bay, cell: 073 220 5430, tel: 021 788 6886, email: liz@new.co.za.

The Masque Theatre in Muizenberg rose from the ashes of a devastating fire to continue its dramatics with such recognisable plays as Agatha Christie who-dunnits, Noel Coward classics and various musicals. Main Road, Muizenberg, tel: 021 788 1898.

STAGE PRESENCE

KIRSTENBOSCH SUMMER CONCERTS

Don't miss the Sunday afternoon concerts in Kirstenbosch Botanic Gardens. About five thousand people turn up to enjoy al-fresco blues or Afro-jazz, big band sounds, carols by candlelight, string quartets, divine diva's and classical music. Concerts run November to April, starting at 5.30pm for about an hour. Come early with a picnic and blanket. Entry R30, tel: 021 799 8782.

DRESSED TO KILL!

Be entertained by hilarious Irit Noble - who says she's a drag queen trapped in a woman's body. Or Lilly Slapsilly, who really is one. Don't miss 'Mince' every Tuesday and Sunday. **On Broadway**, Corner Somerset Road and Dixon St. Greenpoint. Tel: 021 418 8338, www.onbroadway.co.za.

SPIER AMPHITHEATRE, STELLENBOSCH

This historic one-stop food, wine and entertainment estate, has a superb open-air theatre. Enjoy an African take on the classics, opera and international stage shows. Open September-March, with a capacity of just over one thousand. Tel: 021 809 1178/1158, www.spier.co.za.

MAYNARDVILLE OPEN AIR THEATRE

Shakespeare African-style is absolutely fantastic in this perfect glade-in-the-wood setting. Standing ovations are not uncommon. Open during the summer months (Jan-Feb). Take a jacket or blanket for cool evenings. Refreshments available. Booking advisable via Dial-a-seat tel: 021 421 7695.

OTHER MAJOR VENUES

Artscape (Cape Town's main theatre complex), Box Office enquiries tel: 021 421 7839, www.artscape.co.za.

The University of Cape Town's **Baxter Theatre**, offers pre-show dinner. Tel: 021 685 7880.

Theatre on the Bay in Camps Bay is an absolutely delightful privately owned venue staging top class theatre. Tel: 021 438 3300.

City Hall hosts concerts by the Cape Philharmonic Orchestra, www.capephilharmonic.org.za.

Oude Libertas in Stellenbosch, feature contemporary drama, dance and live music on Wednesdays to Sunday evenings from December to March, tel: 021 809 7473/4.

Belville Velodrome hosts international bands the likes of Simply Red and UB40, enquire at tel: 021 949 7450.

Ballet at the Maynardville Open Air Theatre

Theatre on the Bay

The Baxter Theatre Centre with its distinctively 70's architecture and glowing orange domes is a vibrant cultural hub pulsating with the finest in South African theatre. It provides an exciting forum for the celebration of life – the essence of live theatre, music and dance.

At the forefront of performing arts both as a popular venue and as a leading award-winning producer, the Baxter presents cutting edge works and masterpieces from local and international repertoires. Top directors work with a host of well-known and respected theatre, television and film actors to ensure a diverse and stimulating programme throughout the year.

The seating capacity for the Main Theatre is 665, the Concert Hall 638 and the studio 174. The in-house Baxter Restaurant is able to meet all catering requirements. Pre-show dinners and a fully licensed bar is available.

web: www.baxter.co.za

Main Road, Rondebosch
tel: +27 (0) 21 685 7880
fax: +27 (0) 21 689 1880

BAXTER THEATRE CENTRE
at the UNIVERSITY OF CAPE TOWN

ARTSCAPE

Artscape Theatre Centre is home to the Cape Town Opera , the Cape Town City Ballet, the Cape Philharmonic Orchestra and Jazzart Dance Studio. Close to the Central Business District, the new International Convention Centre and the V & A Waterfront, Artscape is ideally situated.

Tel: +27 (0) 21 410 9800
DF Malan Street, Foreshore
www.gopassport.com

Kalk Bay THEATRE

The Kalk Bay Kitchen is a 70-seater theatre and restaurant located on the main road in Kalk Bay. It is a joint venture by the Cooper and Ellenbogen families. The theatre resides in a church, a national monument that has been lovingly converted into an intimate 70-seater theatre with the restaurant on a mezzanine level. The Kalk Bay Theatre offers a unique night of entertainment. Dinner, theatre

Tel: +27 (0) 21 788 6886
52 Main Road, Sunny Cove
www.gopassport.com

THEATRE ON THE BAY
PIETER TOERIEN PRODUCTIONS

CAPE TOWN'S MOST BEAUTIFUL THEATRE.
HOME OF WORLD-CLASS LIVE ENTERTAINMENT.

Local and international drama, comedy, cabaret and music. The Act I Theatre Café, as well as the coffee bar and the theatre bar, Dietrich's, are open before each show.
MAKE A NIGHT OF IT!

Tel: +27 (0) 21 438 3301
1 Link Street, Beachfront, Camps Bay
www.gopassport.com

CAPE TOWN CITY BALLET

South Africa's Premier Ballet Company

Delivering unique world-class dance entertainment through integrity, creativity and excellence.

Cape Town City Ballet performs a broad repertory of popular ballets, from the traditional romantic classics to contemporary works, produced by talented local and international choreographers. Visit this diverse dance company, performing at the Artscape Theatre.

ticket reservations: www.computicket.com
schedules and info: www.capetowncityballet.org.za
www.gopassport.com/cape-town-city-ballet

Escape the city and enter the mystical North African world of Po Na Na. Spend a drowsy afternoon on the balcony overlooking the historic Heritage Square courtyard or sip after-work cocktails and avoid the rush hour. Then return for a night on the town and soak up the Souk!

Tel: +27 (0) 21 423 4889
Heritage Square, 100 Shortmarket Street
www.gopassport.com

FERRYMANS
TAVERN

The tavern has local and international draught beers on tap including the popular Ferrymans Ale, which is brewed exclusively for the tavern. In the summer months, Ferrymans beer garden opens where patrons can enjoy the warm weather under the shade of leafy trees and visitors can witness the buzz of the V&A Waterfront and the working harbour. A seven member jazz band plays outside every Sunday evening from November to April.

Tel: +27 (0) 21 419 7748
V&A Waterfront, Cape Town
www.gopassport.com

The best "beach bar" in South Africa, boasting awesome ocean views and the majestic backdrop of Lions Head and the 12 Apostles. La Med has music and dancing every night and serves great seafood, salads, burgers and gourmet pizzas. Join us on the deck to enjoy the sunset and one of our fantastic cocktails. Open seven days a week. Glen Country Club situated between Clifton and Camps Bay.

Tel: +27 (0) 21 438 5600
Glen Country Club, Victoria Road, Clifton
www.gopassport.com

M·BAR & LOUNGE

The elegant M-Bar & Lounge is situated on the 1st floor of the Metropole Hotel. The richly hued poppy-red lounge area offers intimate relaxation corners and features red ostrich leather chairs and subtle sophisticated upbeat background music. Comic wire bent figurines appear where heavy stuffed animal heads once hung. The reddish illumination and styling oozes an atmosphere of sex and decadence minus any pretence.

Tel: +27 (0) 21 424 7247
38 Long Street, Cape Town
www.gopassport.com

MITCHELL'S

SCOTTISH
ALE HOUSE

Our passion for perfection doesn't stop at the brewery we want you to have a perfect experience all the way around. That's why the Mitchell's Scottish Ale House staff is witty, competent, energetic and friendly – real people providing real service and really, really great beer !

Tel: +27 (0) 21 419 5074
East Pier Road, Victoria Wharf, V&A Waterfront
www.gopassport.com

Since opening it's doors 8 years ago, On Broadway has become known as the venue for polished, stylish, and high quality shows, - from traditional cabaret, comedy and drama, to jazz, rock and retro compilation shows. As well as hosting many International performers, On Broadway has given young, previously inexperienced local performers a platform to showcase the extraordinary talent.

Tel: +27 (0) 21 418-8338 or +27 (0) 421 6668
21 Somerset Road, Green Point
www.gopassport.com

Sumptuous interiors of Eastern-retro chic welcome you. Friendly bar staff, cocktail waitresses serving tables and the dj's relaxed grooves warm you up for the evening. Doors open at 9pm and close at 4am. Dance floor opens after 11 pm. No cover charge until 10 pm, thereafter a charge apply. Although cutting edge styles are welcomed, be sure to dress to impress as a door policy will be in place.

Tel: +27 (0) 21 422 4218
86 Loop Street, Cape Town
www.gopassport.com

Café Manhattan, the oldest and most popular meeting, eating and drinking venue in De Waterkant Village is open for breakfast, lunch and dinner seven days a week. The best burgers by far, Sunday roast, and live entertainment on Thursdays and Sundays are just part of the fun. To reserve a table for lunch or dinner.

Tel: +27 (0) 21 421-6666
74 Waterkant Street, De Waterkant
www.gopassport.com

Manenberg's Jazz Café - A place in Africa

Enjoy good food and wine, plus our balcony offers panoramic views of the Waterfront. Live sundowner bands every weekend, and South Africa's foremost musicians present live jazz and African music 7 nights a week. Open from 11h00 daily.

Tel: +27 (0) 21 421 5639
Clock Tower Centre, V&A Waterfront
www.gopassport.com

One of Cape Town's longest running nightclubs, The Fez is a thoroughly Capetonian club, playing fresh funky house to sexy party people Wednesday through to Saturday. North Africa meets Turkish Delight in plush velvets, pink satins and gentle lighting. The party is from 10 till dawn.

Tel: +27 (0) 21 423 1456
38 Hout Street, Cape Town
www.gopassport.com

70's 80's
Celebration
PARTY

EVERY
SATURDAY
NIGHT

R20
before 11 pm

•Dockside•

GAY CAPE TOWN

MCQP - BEST PARTY IN TOWN

The annual Mother City Queer Project fancy dress extravaganza is a wildly creative art form, where costume and partying take on an entirely new meaning. The 2003 'Kitsch Kitchen' theme inspired such costumes as; Earl Grey and the Tea Hags, Frigid and Unfrigid Magnets, Condom-Mints and several Naked Chefs! Many revellers say they preferred the alluring dark corners of Cape Town's Castle to the open-plan Convention Centre, but the project tends to try out a new venue each year.

Annual Gay Pride Parade

Annual Gay Pride Parade

PAINTING THE TOWN PINK

Cape Town is a whole lot more than merely the Gay Capital of Africa. The city ranks in the world's top five gay hotspots and in 1998 was voted the World's Best Gay Destination. Gay lifestyle demands a vibrant night life and Cape Town has come to the party…!

FUN AND FROLICS

Scrutinise www.gaynetcapetown.co.za and catch Pretty Young Things at nightspots such as Bronx (31 Somerset Road, Green Point, tel: 021 419 9216), Café Manhatten (74 de Waterkant Street, Green Point, tel: 021 421 6666), and Obsession (76 Church Street, Cape Town, tel: 021 424 8489). Your tour of pink Cape Town is not complete without seeing the 'Mince' drag artists such as Lilly Slapsilly, strut their feathery stuff at On Broadway, Greenpoint (21 Somerset Road, tel: 021 418 8338, www.onbroadway.co.za), See also Theatre, Opera and Stage page.

PARTY TIME - THE BEST GAY EVENTS

- South African Gay & Lesbian Film Festival - end Jan to early Feb, tel: 021 465 1927

- Annual Gay Pride Parade - February, tel: 083 268 0635, www.capetownpride.co.za

- Queers by Candlelight at Kirstenbosch National Botanical Gardens - December. Cape Town Tourism can assist with details closer to the time, tel: 021 426 4260 or 021 405 4500

- The Mother City Queer Project/MCQP- mid-December, tel: 021 426 5709.

IMPACT OF THE MCQP ON CAPE TOWN'S ECONOMY

"Queerness is not a cut-and-dried definition of one's sexual orientation. Queerness is an attitude." - MCQP (Mother City Queer Project) marketing material.

Cape Town takes the gay market seriously, and an events research organisation was hired to quantify MCQP's impact on the city's economy. They found that of the 6,500 revellers attending the 2003 party, 12% hailed from abroad, with

67% of party-goers specifically in town for this event. Research also revealed that pink travellers usually stay in Cape Town for more than a month.

DISCERNING CLIENTELE

Gay 'DINKIES' (double-income-no-kids), are alleged to spend an average of 4.5 times more than the non-gay traveller. Cape Town is happy to encourage this economic spin-off and provides plenty of accommodation to meets the needs of a discerning gay clientele. Gay-owned lodges and hotels are featured on the website www.pinkroute.co.za, which showcases many establishments.

WHAT AND WHERE

Pick up the Pink Map and Cape Town Gay Guide at Cape Town Tourism (corner Castle/Burg Street, tel: 021 426 4260). Other good information sources are publications such as OUTright, Exit, Rush, Women on Women, Womyn, and Gay Pages available from bookstores. Cape Etc. magazine and Time Out are also decent information sources.

There is the Gay and Lesbian Hotline (tel: 021 422 2500), or call the Triangle Project (tel: 021 422 2500) for gay-related information and counselling. The gay-owned Atlantic Tourist Information Centre (243 Main Road, Sea Point, tel: 021 434 2382) will show you where to find Rainbow Trade, who act as proud purveyors of gay paraphernalia (29 Somerset Road, Green Point, tel: 021 421 0877). Amiene van der Merwe is a feisty and especially passionate guide whose organisation, Wanderwomen (tel: 021 683 9215), caters admirably for the needs of the lesbian traveller. South African Man Holidays, (10 Buiten Street, Cape Town, tel: 021 422 2485) is sussed and sorted to keep the dudes busy.

Gay Rights

The abundance of distinctive gay flags and bumper stickers offers one a sense of the impact of gay rights arising out of the country's post-1994 constitution. The South African Constitutional Court for example, now upholds that same-sex couples in life partnerships are entitled to pension benefits and may jointly adopt children.

Evita Bezuidenhoud

Annual Gay Pride Parade

Annual Gay Pride Parade

SHOPPING

CRAFT MARKETS

Food, clothing, arts and crafts found in Cape Town's markets, reflect the many cultural influences on this city. There is however, no doubt you are in Africa, but you might not be sure exactly where in Africa.

Wooden masks usually come from Cameroon or Congo. Many soapstone carvings originate from Zimbabwe and safari curios in Kenya. There are also plenty of local arts and crafts too, such as intriguing wirework skilfully crafted into cars, helicopters and other amazing shapes.

RECYCLING

Africans are masters at re-cycling and nothing much goes to waste. Fizzy drink cans are turned into novel handbags or amazing sculptures. Labels from sardine cans and tinned tomatoes make colourful decorations for book covers and trinket boxes, and used bottles are cut and sanded into attractive wine and beer glasses. Plastic bags worked into hats and mats are becoming scarcer, since a law was passed to charge for supermarket bags, (which is no bad thing as plastic bags used to decorate every street corner and fence).

CLOTHING

Cape Town is a laid back kind of place and market clothing reflects the easy-going nature of its inhabitants and its sunny climate. Forget monotone black and grey and get some colour into your life with tie dyed dresses, pastel T-shirts, patterned board shorts and dangling jewellery. The 'earthy' feel goes down well the further south along the peninsula you go, while a more chic look suits the city.

MARKETS (most markets are open air).

Daily Markets

Greenmarket Square is a popular open-air city centre craft and clothes market.

The Waterfront Craft Market is under cover, and also houses the Holistic Living Centre offering on the spot massages and therapies.

Famous Weekly Markets

Hout Bay Market (Sunday) - Mostly locally made lifestyle goods

Green Point Stadium Flea Market (Sunday & Public Holidays)- Hundreds of small stalls selling African artefacts, and just about anything.

Fresh etc Market, Pinelands (Saturday) - families enjoy organic produce and craft stalls in this rural setting.

Monthly Markets

Holistic Lifestyle Fair, Observatory (first Sunday of the month) - an intriguing wholesome market with an esoteric bent attracting a sociable multiracial crowd.

Constantia Craft Market (first weekend and last Saturday of the month) - homely crafts in a suburban setting.

Kirstenbosch Craft Market (last Sunday of the month) - a genteel outdoor market selling local crafts and gifts.

WATERFRONT
CRAFTMARKET

From 9³⁰am – 6⁰⁰pm daily

ART & CRAFT
WELLNESS CENTRE

Situated between the Aquarium and CD Wherehouse

Tel: (021) 408-7842 • Fax: (021) 408-7845
www.waterfront.co.za

A WEALTH OF CREATION

ROCK ART GALLERY
AND FRAMERS

Roaming throughout Southern Africa for thousands of years, the San people left a legacy of some of the finest Rock Art ever created. Through building rock water features and inspired by the Rock Art of Southern Africa, Sean Caulfield started painting on a light-weight resin based rock surface. Professional and creative custom framing is offered.

Tel: +27 (021) 419 5072
Stall 8, Red Shed, V&A Waterfront
www.gopassport.com

african art factory
development trade house

The African Art Factory, housed in an empty hospital building close to the Victoria & Alfred Waterfront, is a centre for businesses in the ceramic or African arts & crafts industry which has evolved from the experience gained from funding start-up businesses in the townships and has become the workplace for 12 businesses.

Tel: +27 (021) 4211 1661   Fax: +27 (021) 421 1914
E-Block, Old City Hospital Complex,
2 Portswood Road, Waterfront
www.gopassport.com

a·v|a
ASSOCIATION FOR
VISUAL ARTS

AVA is the oldest non-profit exhibition space in Cape Town and are committed to promoting the visual arts and artists of South Africa, both emerging and established and promote and advance diversity and have exhibitions which change every 3 weeks.

Tel: +27 (021) 424 7436   Fax: +27 (021) 423 2637
35 Church Street, Cape Town
www.gopassport.com

The Pan African Market located in a national monument on Long Street, comprises 33 stores and stalls representing 14 African countries including art and crafts, hair dressing, tailoring, holistic healing and catering. The traders man their stalls and is so structured as to allow them to showcase the work they choose and in so doing, bring a beautiful and unrestricted multi-ethnicity to this space.

Tel: +27 (021) 426 4478
76 Long Street, Cape Town
www.gopassport.com

Cape Town Fashion Calendar

Strut your sartorial stuff at the J & B Metropolitan Horse Race (February), the Nederburg SA Designer Collections Autumn Winter (April), Cape Town Fashion Week (August), the Fair Lady Fashion Awards (November), and the Cape Town Fashion Festival (November or December). Another tip is to highlight the annual sales in your diary - guided by the magazine Shop! - then impress the pants off the fashionista slaves back home!

Married to the Mall

Tried-and-tested shopping malls rank in no particular order as follows:

V&A Waterfront: you know where or you're square. Tel: 021 408 7600

Cavendish Square: dominating the southern suburb of Claremont. Tel: 021 674 3050

Tygervalley: bordering the N1 motorway 20 minutes drive out of town. Tel: 021 914 0718

Canal Walk: 15 minutes drive up the N1 on the left. Tel: 021 555 3100

Somerset Mall: in Somerset West, 35 minutes along the N2. Tel: 021 852 7114

Spinner at Work

CAPE TOWN FASHION

Fashion is in the very bones of Capetonians and South Africa is the destination du jour for emerging fashion designers. The Western Cape is a major fashion exporter and the industry employs approximately 170,000 people (which by association feeds about 400,000 people in the Western Cape province).

DESIGNER CHIC

The rate of exchange can be your new best friend – so go mad and exploit it! Big name local designers the likes of Shakur Olla, Errol Arendz, Jenni Button, Juanita Pacheco, Catherine Moore, Malcolm Klûk, Gert van de Merwe, and Hip Hop have various studios dotted around the Peninsula. While clothing chain stores make it difficult to discern which country you're in, there are hidden depths in some home-grown chains like unisex giants Truworths, Woolworths, and Queenspark, and menswear manufacturer Markhams. These are confidently on a par with their more instantly recognisable overseas counterparts. Did you know that Hugo Boss suits paraded stylishly down London's streets are the proud product of Cape Town handiwork?

BUY LOCAL

When the Rand appreciates, Cape Town's favour in the international fashion limelight may be threatened. But a twinning initiative of the Western Cape with Florence and its Polimoda Fashion School is a step in the right direction. This is coupled with a recently-signed declaration among South African retailers, to wholeheartedly support local manufacturers, with what is proving to be a successful 'buy local' campaign. You will find less and less imported products on South Africa's fashion rails, which gives your purchases a more unique quality.

SHOPPING ESSENTIALS

You're well on your way to a shopping Nirvana with the following firmly under arm: Shop! - that savvy shoppers' magazine-cum-fashion-Bible. Equally indispensable is the Cape Town Fashion Map, available at all tourism bureaux. Don't forget the Factory Shops page in this guide, for the low down on real bargains. Or check out the Markets section so you can acquire ethnic gear such as Loxion Kulca – a township rags-to-riches tale that rejects Nike and proudly flaunts township-produced clothing. You may well find too, that a consultation with specialist shopping tour operators could result in more bang for your shopping buck. Contact Blue Buyou tel: 021 671 1763, or Cape Fashion Tours tel: 083 299 8728. Both organisations offer shopping tours and an item-sourcing service.

2 JACKETS FOR THE PRICE OF 1

Stockists of Genuine Leather at its Best

Leather jackets & Blazers
Waist coats & dungarees
Shorts & trenchcoats
Ladies Tailored jackets

Ladies undergarments
Padded biker jackets
Skirts & dress etc.

Leather garments made to order on premises within 0-4 hours

Alterations and repairs done while you wait

Shop 505, Canal Walk Shopping Centre
Tel: 021-552 8688

Shop 19 Lower Level Canal Walk Shopping Centre
Tel: 021-552 8987

Shop 87 Golden Acre Shopping Centre, Cape Town
Tel: 021- 425 1993

For enquiries please contact our head office
Mr Abbassi Cell: 072 124 0336
Tel/Fax: 011-485 3669

Web: www.leatherzone.co.za
Email: leatherzone@webmail.co.za
Branches in Johannesburg, Durban and Port Elizabeth

martine's
on the bay

Exclusive fashion boutique situated in the heart of Camps Bay. Stockists of local and imported ladieswear. Eight years of personalised service to an international clientele.

Tel: +27 (021) 438 2325
Shop 7, The Promenade, Victoria Rd, Camps Bay
www.gopassport.com

BELAFONTE

"Our on-site tailor and same day alteration service ensures that, as our business develops, we remain committed to providing that personal touch so lacking in today's retail environment" – Gavin Ross

Tel: +27 (021) 683 4459
Cavendish Close, Warwick Street, Claremont
Tel: +27 (021) 794 4610
Shop 41, Constantia Village, Constantia
www.gopassport.com

la liberte en *animale*

Since 1985 Animale design and manufacture their own exclusive fabrics and patterns resulting in innovative quality casual fashion for women, available through their upmarket boutiques. Animale meet international standards and trends, catering for the needs of the not so perfect body shape yet offering bright, colourful and sophisticated designs.

Tel: +27 (021) 555 4066
Shop 617, Canal Walk, Cape Town
Tel: +27 (021) 914 1540
Shop 589, Tygervalley Shopping Centre
www.gopassport.com

LORENZI.
CLASSIC ELEGANCE

SINCE 1962

Ostrich, buffalo, crocodile and calf creations for those who appreciate traditional Italian handcrafting at its finest.

www.lorenzi.co.za

Sandton City **011-783 6013** | Nelson Mandela Square at Sandton City **011-784 2501**
V & A Waterfront **021-419 0359** | Sun City **014-557 1168** | Tokyo, Japan **+81 03 3986 2990**

SENSE OF SHOPPING

Indulge all your senses at

The Constantia Village

shopping centre - home to

art galleries, antique dealers,

fashion boutiques, jewellery,

lifestyle and interior decor shops,

e-stores, adventure dealers,

travel agencies, fresh foodhalls,

soul stirring music and book

centres, beauty treatment salons,

restaurants and bands.

Constantia Village Shopping Centre
Constantia Road, Constantia
Tel: +27 21 794 5065

THE
CONSTANTIA
VILLAGE

THE FINEST IN EVERY SENSE

www.constantiavillage.com

CANAL WALK SHOPPING CENTRE

Welcome to Canal Walk Shopping Centre, the home of crème de la crème shopping.

In the shadow of Cape Town's magnificent Table Mountain, you'll discover Canal Walk Shopping Centre – Africa's shopping destination of choice. Since opening its doors in 2000, it has competed for attention as one of South Africa's most famous landmarks. Today, Canal Walk has evolved into one of the Cape's must-visit destinations, attracting thousands of international visitors every year.

With more than 400 speciality stores tempting your taste in fashion, homeware, gifts, jewellery, shoes and more, Canal Walk truly offers the most comprehensive and compelling lifestyle shopping experience in South Africa - all under one roof. You name it, they have it. What's more, Canal Walk offers extended trading hours till 9pm, which means you're free to roam. So indulge and shop all day and into the night.

Even though Canal Walk is famous for its shopping, it's also home to a delectable mix of more than 30 restaurants, cafés and coffee shops, serving a range of international delicacies. And for those who simply want to relax and re-engerise before continuing the shopping spree, visit the Skywalk Emporium or the spacious Food Court, for a fabulous range of fast food options.

INFORMATION IS AT HAND

Canal Walk also has a Visitors' Information Centre and two information desks, where a friendly representative will ensure that you enjoy every moment of your shopping experience. They offer information on shops, restaurants and entertainment, as well as general information about the Western Cape.

Canal Walk also plays host to a range of entertainment, with a never-ending diary of events and promotions. Canal Walk's Central Promotions Court, with full stage facilities and state-of-the-art sound and lighting infrastructure, is a popular venue for spectacular live entertainment and promotional activities. It's not surprising, since it's the most sophisticated and technologically advanced promotions court in South Africa.

This is merely a taste of what Canal Walk has to offer. So take your time and roam through the website, and then come and experience the luxury of Canal Walk for yourself.

AFRICA'S FASHION CAPITAL.
WELCOME TO ROAM.

ake your time, and savour every moment f your journey through Canal Walk's najestic aisles. As you marvel at the plendour of Canal Walk's stunning Classical nd Victorian décor, treat yourself to the inest cuisine and refreshments at any of our 30 restaurants and coffee shops. Or simply peruse our selection of more than 400 speciality stores, which are open till 9pm daily, and offer everything from international fashion labels to local arts and craft. Whatever you do, feel free to roam.

CANAL WALK
SHOPPING CENTRE
discover something new every day

www.canalwalk.co.za

THE VICTORIA & ALFRED WATERFRONT
WHERE THE WORLD MEETS AT THE WATER'S EDGE

22 million people visit the Victoria & Alfred Waterfront every year, because it has everything you could possibly want all in one waterside venue. The fusion of history and modern convenience, alongside a busy working harbour, makes for a vibrant atmosphere. Add to this the dramatic backdrop of Table Mountain and you have a dockside shopping destination unlike any other.

RETAIL THERAPY

The V&A Waterfront offers a shopping extravaganza with over 400 stores, wonderful for browsing or for serious retail therapy. Shop for fashion and jewellery, homeware, gifts, curios and novelties, books and stationery, audio-visual and electronic equipment, food, wine and flowers. There is something to suit everyone. All stores are open until 9pm seven days a week and there is plenty of open-air or underground parking.

The stylish **Victoria Wharf Shopping Centre** is the main retail space and this boasts over 240 unique retail outlets. Shop here for a mix of luxury items, designer brands, and local arts and crafts. For more traditional antiques, art and jewellery, the **Alfred Mall**, situated within the historic Pierhead, offers a selection of stores for the discerning shopper.

Stroll around the harbour and cross the Pierhead swing bridge, which opens to allow large yachts to pass through. Enormous Cape fur seals swim around this area to the delight of visitors. This bridge leads to the latest addition to the Waterfront's retail offering – **The Clock Tower Centre**. This combines top quality South African designs, crafts, arts and foods together under one roof, as well as the Waterfront Information Centre. The Clock Tower Centre is also where the famous high speed catamaran departs from the Nelson Mandela Gateway for Robben Island.

Traditional African arts and crafts have pride of place in two craft markets; **The Red Shed Craft Workshop** (adjoining the Victoria Wharf Shopping Centre) has an eclectic mix of handmade merchandise and art, and an opportunity to see crafters at work. Adjacent to the Two Oceans Aquarium is **The Waterfront Craft Market** - one of the largest and most vibrant indoor craft markets in Cape Town, open daily. This market represents the Waterfront's culture of entrepreneurship and small business development, and features a diverse assortment of innovative designs and traditional handcrafts, antiquities and holistic lifestyle accessories.

Contact: V&A Waterfront Information Tel: 021 408 7600,

email: info@waterfront.co.za, website: www.waterfront.co.za

The Victoria & Alfred Waterfront is the most visited tourist destination in the Southern Hemisphere.

SHOP TILL YOU DROP ANCHOR.

Set in a real working harbour, the V&A Waterfront lends

itself to a truly unique experience.

The setting provides a combination of easy access and

navigation with the chance to relax within a unique and

leisurely environment. Where else can you enjoy a vast

selection of entertainment, restaurants, shopping and

sightseeing before winding down by hopping aboard a cruise

boat and setting off for sundowners?

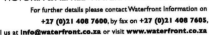

SOMERSET MALL

Situated in tranquil landscapes rich with natural splendour, Somerset Mall is conveniently placed next to major road routes. The Mall is surrounded by picturesque mountain scenery, hectares of the finest vineyards and white sand beaches. What better reason to escape the busy city Shopping Centres and relax with all your shopping on a single level?

FINE SHOPPING EXPERIENCE

Patrons can shop and dine in wide walkways that house items of luxury, like designer wear, imported garments and fashionable branded items offering the latest fashions.

Browse exclusive jewellery stores displaying Africa's finest carved pieces, or sample beauty products like oils and fragrances from the skincare and beauty houses. Gift shops give visitors the opportunity buy souvenirs of Africa and safari outfitters will advise you on what gear is most suitable for venturing into the African bush. While Somerset Mall's stylish home décor stores will give you the opportunity to furnish your home with touches of Africa.

The Official Tourism Kiosk inside Somerset Mall informs visitors of exciting things to do in Cape Town and can make bookings for tours and accommodation. Travel outlets will assist further with selecting destinations, co-ordinating travel arrangements and exchanging money to required currencies. Fashionable luggage purchased at our stores will make the travelling experience complete.

The technology retailers cater for all electronic requirements, cell phones, big screen televisions, digital camera's, DVD's, CD's and much more.

COFFEE, CAKES AND FINE FOOD

Visitors can enjoy scrumptious creamy cakes, with Lattés at cosy coffee corners. Dine on the finest cuisine, with traditional gourmet meals or light tantalising tastes of fresh seafood.

Somerset Mall is open seven days a week and offers a secure environment with 24-hour security, free parking, disabled facilities, baby rooms and more services for a memorable shopping experience.

For more information phone 021 852 7114 or visit the Somerset Mall website: www.somerset-mall.co.za.

Somerset Mall simply the most in shopping.

GOLD OF AFRICA MUSEUM

The Gold of Africa Museum houses thousands of years of legend, ritual and craftsmanship displayed in the world's most comprehensive collection of surviving artefacts, from the gold-rich kingdoms of Africa.

The power and wealth of these kingdoms is a little easier to comprehend once these exquisitely crafted objects have been viewed. But the collection goes a step beyond the aesthetic. The visitor takes away vital insights into the values of the people who created these objects through the symbolism surrounding each piece.

The collection was originally assembled by Swiss art lover, Josef Mueller, who collected African artworks and jewellery over a fifty-year period. Josef's daughter and son-in-law, continued to build the collection, which was displayed in Switzerland's Barbier-Mueller Museum until 2001 when it was returned to the African continent.

COLLECTION IN AN HISTORIC BUILDING

AngloGold-Ashanti (the world's largest gold mining company), took custody of the collection and restored one of the oldest colonial homes in South Africa, in which to house the collection. Built in 1783, Martin Melck House is believed to be the finest remaining example of original Cape Town domestic architecture. Its beginnings also coincide with the rise of the Akan Kingdoms that created many of the objects within the museum's collection.

The links between African royalty, gold and power first become apparent through colourful photographs and wall murals. Dominating the museum's hall is the image of a queen mother in gold finery, complete with gold mesh spectacles. Adoption of western-style glasses provided a novel solution to an age-old problem: how to prevent ordinary people looking directly into the eyes of royalty; dangerous since they might be blinded by the power of divinity beaming from the ruler's eyes.

Upstairs is one of the largest and most beautiful collections of African gold artefacts in the world.

The walls of an interleading room are covered by a time line first used in

---

Wine Cellar & Coffee Shop

The Gold of Africa Museum complex is home to a two hundred-year-old wine cellar that offers quality wines to visitors who can order a bite to eat at the coffee shop and relax in a tranquil garden courtyard.

Europe at the end of the 19th century. Below, a second line displays stories of gold and gold trade in Africa over thousands of years.

Leading from the map room, the visitor encounters a stone-laid wall: a reconstruction of the stonework found at Great Zimbabwe where an estimated 15 to 25 million ounces of gold were mined. This offers a mere glimpse of the majesty of these ancient cultures.

Perched above the collection is one of only a few surviving 'dakkammers' or attic rooms, now a lair for the golden lion; symbol of royal authority, courage and strength.

Goldsmiths at Work

A state-of-the-art gold jewellery workshop is the scene of courses and demonstrations. Here visitors can see local goldsmiths using South African gold to design and manufacture exquisite pieces of jewellery. Some of these pieces are sold in the museum shop that offers a variety of exclusive gifts crafted by local workers. After basking in the beauty of the gold collection, visitors may well wish to take a little of its magic away with them.

GOLD OF AFRICA
MUSEUM

The Gold of Africa Museum located in the historic Martin Melck House (built in 1783) is dedicated to the history & artistry of African gold.

Pangolin Night Tour • **Lion Walking Tour**
Jewellery Workshops & Courses • **Venue Hire**
Coffee Shop & Wine Cellar • **Museum Shop**

MARTIN MELCK HOUSE 96 STRAND STREET
CAPE TOWN 8001 SOUTH AFRICA
TEL 021 405 1540 FAX 021 405 1541
www.goldofafrica.com info@goldofafrica.com

MONDAYS TO SATURDAYS 09h30 to 17h00
PARKING AVAILABLE CNR STRAND & BUITENGRACHT STREETS

OLGA JEWELLERY DESIGN STUDIO

Jewellery has become an essential component of a woman's image. It is a powerful accessory, complementing a designer outfit and enhancing every-day clothes, giving a woman greater confidence.

Every woman would prefer to wear a piece of jewellery made especially for her, to reflect her personality and passion. Personalised jewellery is Olga's speciality and she spends quality time with each client, and according to personality, needs and budget, will design a perfectly fitting piece of jewellery, in every sense of the word.

Olga established her first jewellery design studio in 1977 and her philosophy is service and her passion is design. Olga takes personal pride in creating unique masterpieces for the individual, and her designs are handcrafted by her team of master goldsmiths. Jewellery runs in the family, as Olga's husband is one of South Africa's leading diamond jewellery manufacturers.

All Olga's jewellery is manufactured in her factory, and sold directly to the client. Her flagship store is in the V&A Waterfront, and there is also another outlet located in Cavendish Square, Claremont.

In order to stay ahead of overseas trends, Olga travels extensively and visits

Designing for Royals and Presidents

Olga's successes include a personal invitation to the Clinton Presidential Family and the Queen of England and Her entourage.

international jewellery design trade fairs. She likes to keep herself challenged and remain innovative. She likes to design pieces that can be worn with day and night-wear – that look even more thrilling the more you dress up. Her designs are always fresh and new, but they all have the same sensuality. Olga makes a woman feel and look sexy, without ever exceeding the boundaries of good taste.

When you buy a piece of Olga's jewellery, you are buying beauty. The value and significance of the piece is far beyond the monetary value.

Olga says: *"I have exacting standards and will not produce anything less than perfection. This applies to the design, manufacture, presentation, and follow up service to my clients."*

With each of Olga's purchases, you receive a printed valuation certificate with a full colour photograph of the piece.

Phone Olga for a private consultation at tel: 021 419 8016.

DESIGN ZERO3 050704

Olga

JEWELLERY
DESIGN STUDIO

Haute Couture of Fine Jewellery

Using De Beers diamonds, this outlet in the southern suburbs has their own diamond cutting factory. Enjoy watching your rough diamond being cut and polished before your eyes In-house designers and goldsmiths will design and manufacture your special piece of jewellery. Accredited by The Master Diamond Cutters Association and The Jewellery Council of South Africa.

Tel: +27 (021) 671 3815
Cavendish Place, Cavendish Street, Claremont
www.gopassport.com

We buy and sell diamonds and watches
Buy/Sell: Diamonds, gold, antique jewellery, Kruger Rands, watches: Rolex, Patek, Longine, Jaeger, Vacheron, Omega, Tag, IWC, Breitling (pre-owned) and pocket watches. Designer and manufacturing jewellers. Valuations. Watch batteries. Watch and jewellery repairs are guaranteed.

Tel: +27 (021) 423 2771
54, St. George's Mall, Cape Town
www.gopassport.com

You are invited to a remarkable diamond experience. See how cutters unlock the fire and brilliance of a rough diamond. Discover how diamonds and gemstones are graded and valued. Visit our design studio and see how goldsmiths create award-winning designs. Browse through our display rooms or be shown in private a stunning collection of diamonds and gemstones, without any obligation.

Tel: 27 (021) 422 1090
Huguenot House, c/o Hout & Loop Streets, Cape Town
www.gopassport.com

Custom made designer jewellery can be surprisingly affordable! Get the service of an award winning designer in this exclusive manufacturing studio in the heart of Cape Town. Choose from our signature pieces or get involved in designing your own jewellery assisted by a professional. Personal service is guaranteed.

Tel: 27 (021) 424 8621
7 United Building, 118 St Georges Mall, Cape Town
www.gopassport.com

World renowned for the beauty, daring of their unmatched designs and uncompromising quality, Köhler are without any doubt the jewel in the crown of our mother city, Cape Town. A visit to Köhler Master Goldsmiths and Jewellers, who specialise in individual designs and fine, hand crafted jewellery, is highly recommended.

Tel: +27 (021) 424 6968
64 St Georges Mall, Cape Town
www.gopassport.com

THE DIAMOND WORKS

DIAMOND CUTTING TOURS

JEWELLERY MANUFACTURING

HISTORY OF GOLD AND
DIAMOND MINING

WALL OF FAME

INTERNET CAFE

TANZANITE BOUTIQUE

AWARD WINNING DESIGNS

Hours of Operation
Monday to Sunday, 09h00 - 17h00. Extended hours on request
7 Coen Steytler Avenue, Cape Town, Tel: 27 21 425 1970,
Website: www.thediamondworks.co.za
e-mail: info@thediamondworks.co.za

Kalk Bay

Arty farty fishing village Kalk Bay, has a street full of art and antiques. Eclectic shop Cape to Cairo specialises in high kitch, such as an expertly painted fake Tretchikoff (King of Kitch). (100 Main Road, Kalk Bay, tel: 021 788 4571). Clementina Ceramics is in a class of its own with beautiful works by well-known ceramist Clementina van der Walt. (20 Main Rd, Kalk Bay, tel: 021 788 8718)

Carmel Art Galleries

In an arty corner of Claremont is Carmel Art Gallery - one of the largest contemporary galleries in Cape Town. Minimalist pastel landscapes by one of South Africa's most famous living artists - Pieter Van Der Westhuizen, are highly sought after here. Other important artists here include Gail Catlin, Robert Slingsby and Derris Van Rensburg. (Cnr. Vineyard/Cavendish Roads, Claremont, tel: 021 671 6601, carmel@global. co.za, www.carmel.co.za).

Carmel Art Gallery have another showroom in Constantia Village, with a selection of beautiful Cape landscapes. One of their signature artists is Andrew Cooper - quickly becoming famous for his photo realistic mountain scenes. (Constantia Village Centre, tel: 021 794 6262).

Noordhoek Art Route

Meet artists at work and buy direct from them on the Noordhoek Art Route, who open their studios to visitors on the first Sunday of every month (Nov-April). (Tel: 021 785 4600).

In the leafy lanes of Noordhoek is the Noordhoek Farm Village Werkswinkel (Workshop), where several artists paint and sell their work, including the talented Eatwell family (mother, daughter and son - tel: 789 2767).

FOR ARTS SAKE

Each Cape Town gallery has a different focus and signature artists. These descriptions should help you decide which galleries to visit (listed geographically from central Cape Town heading south).

Michael Stevenson Contemporary Art Gallery showcases some of South Africa's best contemporary artists e.g. William Kentridge, Norman Catherine and Robert Hodgins. (De Smidt Street, Greenpoint, tel: 021 421 2578).

Johans Borman Fine Art Gallery sells some of the best South African old masters; Irma Stern & Maggie Laubser, plus contemporary art. (Buitengracht St, tel: 021 423 6075, art@johansborrman.co.za).

The Cape Gallery has work reflecting the rich diversity of Cape culture, in paintings, sculpture, and bead work. (60 Church St, tel: 021 423 5309, cgallery@mweb.co.za, www.capegallery.co.za).

SA National Gallery has plenty of old masters, but is inspirational for their acquisition of African art. Government Ave - main entrance in Company Gardens. Tel: 021 467 4660. Open Tues-Sun 10am to 5pm. Entry R10 adults, R2 children, everyone free on Sundays.

Everard Read Gallery have been dealers in international art for years and have promoted several artists to internationally recognisable status. These include landscape artist John Meyer, and Dylan Lewis, specialising in life-size bronze wild cats. (3 Portswood Road, V&A Waterfront, tel: 021 418 4527)

Delightful Rossouw Gallery, showcases talented contemporary artists such as Tay Dall and Hugo Maritz. Life-sized glass encrusted cement mermaids perched on the wall outside, keep alive the legacy of Koos Malgas (of Nieu Bethesda Owl House fame). Portswood St, V&A Waterfront, Tel: 021 425 9806, website: www.art10.co.za.

Carrol Boyes transforms mundane cutlery into a fusion of form, function & fantasy with sensual sculptured items in pewter, stainless steel and aluminium. 43 Rose Street, tel: 021 424 8263, www.carrolboyes.co.za

Bell-Roberts Art Gallery represents established and emerging South African artists and has a coffee shop and bookstore selling art publications. 199 Loop St, tel: 021 422 1100, www.bell-roberts.com)

Watch the creative process taking place at the **Montebello Craft & Design Centre**. Witness ceramics, jewellery, metalwork and textile art take shape. (Newlands Avenue, Newlands, tel: 021 685 6445).

Simon's Town is home to the extraordinary **Bronze Age Sculpture House** - Foundry and Fine Art Gallery. (Albertyn's Stables, Simon's Town, tel: 021 786 1816, mwbronze@mweb.co.za).

BELL·ROBERTS

Bell-Roberts Gallery is an exciting contemporary space in South Africa. We exhibit monthly art exhibitions and a monthly experimental film screening entitled "Masjien". We publish exceptional artists books as well as quarterly magazines about contemporary culture, "ITCH" and the only award winning publication about South African art "Art South Africa".

Tel: +27 (0) 21 422 11 00
199 Loop Street Cape Town
www.gopassport.com

MICHAEL STEVENSON
contemporary

The Michael Stevenson contemporary gallery is an extension of Michael Stevenson Fine Art which was established in 1990. The gallery deals in nineteenth-century and twentieth-century South African art, and nineteenth-century African art from southern Africa. In addition to hosting many widely-acclaimed exhibitions, Michael Stevenson has published numerous books and catalogues.

Tel: +27 (0) 21 421 2575
Hill House, de Smidt Street, Green Point
www.gopassport.com

ROSS OUW GALLERY

The Rossouw Gallery is situated on Portswood Road, less than five minutes walk from the V&A Waterfront. The gallery specialises in modern contemporary art and hosts a number of established South African artists, of whom some have had significant international success. Artists on show include Tay Dall, Richard Scott, A.S. de Lange, Susan Mitchinson and Cobus van der Walt.

Tel: +27 (0) 21 425 9806
2 Portswood Road, Waterfront
www.gopassport.com

CARMEL ART

Carmel Art stocks the widest range of paintings by leading contemporary South African artists in a large variety of media and subjects. Our large air-conditioned gallery is a visual feast to art lovers and you are sure to find art that will interest and delight you. Join our many upcountry and overseas clients who visit us to view the latest works by some of South Africa's top artists.

Tel: +27 (0) 21 671 6601
66 Vineyard Rd, Claremont
Constantia Village Shopping Centre, Main Road, Constantia
www.gopassport.com

SPORT
&
ADVENTURE

GOLFING IN THE CAPE

South Africa has its very own golfing heroes in Gary Player, Ernie Els and Retief Goosen. Such talent has spawned lots of interest in the game and has given rise to some really top class courses. This has encouraged avid golfers to come to the Cape from all over the world.

CAPE TOWN & THE GARDEN ROUTE'S TOP GOLF COURSES

Royal Cape - Cape Town southern suburbs.

Set in parkland with Table Mountain views, this club has some snob value as it is the oldest in the country. Tel: 021 761 6551 bookings@royalcapegolf. co.za www.royalcapegolf.co.za

Steenberg - Tokai, 20 mins drive south of Cape Town. Set amongst vineyards with Table Mountain views, this course has large aprons around the greens and an enormous 72 metre green at the 14th hole. Upmarket Steenberg Hotel and Catharina's Restaurant are on the estate. Tel: 021 713 2233, mrussel@zsd.co.za

Westlake - Lakeside, South Peninsula.

This beautiful course has towering flat pines in lush parkland with sea and mountain views. Greens can be quick when freshly cut. The club has a good mix of male and female members give it a good atmosphere. Tel: 021 788 2020, wgc@weslakegolfclub.co.za, www.westlakegolfclub.co.za

Clovelly - near Fish Hoek, South Peninsula.

Set in a lush sheltered mountain valley with great sea views, the beautifully positioned clubhouse has peacocks wandering around it. Accurate tee shots are required for this narrow course. Tel: 021 782 1118, clubhouse@global.co.za, www.clovelly.co.za

Erinvale - Somerset West, 1 hour drive east of Cape Town.

This Gary Player designed Championship course, offers both flat and undulating scenic splendour with mountain views. A country course for serious golfers. Tel: 021 847 1144, clubhouse@erinvale.com, www.erinvale.com

Arabella - just outside Hermanus, 1½ hour's drive east of Cape Town. Overlooking the Bot River lagoon, close to coast and mountains, this award-winning golf estate, hotel and spa, sets the standards for others to follow. Tel: 028 284 9383, maree@w-capehotel.co.za, www.arabella.co.za

Reasons to Come

• All courses are playable year round.

• Courses are set amongst incredible scenery.

• Green fees are very reasonable.

• Access is easy.

• Club facilities are up there with the best.

• Accommodation is great value for money.

• Food is to die for!

Do you need any more persuading?

Golfing the Garden Route

Fancourt in George at the start of the Garden Route, hosted the President's Cup 2003. Four spacious 18-hole courses & three clubhouses are set amongst woods, wetlands and parkland, backed by mountains. Jack Nicklaus says it is the best inland links he has encountered. Tel: 044 804 0000, hotel@fancourt.co.za, www.fancourt.com

Pezula is in Knysna, the heart of the Garden Route. Varied and hilly indigenous bushland with dramatic cliff top scenery overlooking lagoon and ocean, make this a most spectacular golf course. Tel: 044 384 1222, golf@pezula.co.za, www.pezulaclub.com

Golfing in Milnerton

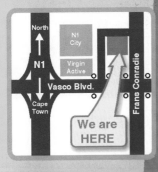

FANCOURT
Hotel and Country Club Estate

Fancourt Hotel and Country Club Estate, Africa's premier Golfing and Leisure Resort, has four golf courses, many recreational activities, a world-class Health and Beauty Spa, fabulous restaurants and superior accommodation, all in a stunning location.

Tel: +27 (0) 44 804 0000
Fancourt Hotel, Country Club Estate
www.gopassport.com

THE WESTERN CAPE
HOTEL & SPA

Tel: +27 (0) 28 284 0000
Arabella Country Estate, R44, Kleinmond
www.luxurycollection.com • www.altiraspa.com
www.gopassport.com

ATLANTIC BEACH
Golf Club   Cape Town

Atlantic Beach Golf Club boasts beautiful views of Table Mountain, the Atlantic Ocean and Robben Island. This Championship Links Course is a true test of golf, ensuring a challenging and exciting round of golf – a thinking golfers dream with every club in the bag getting a workout. The 12th, Par 3 is the signature hole for the course. The generous, 2 tier green is nestled amongst pristine fynbos with a backdrop of the Mother City at its best. Winner of the Compleat Golfer 5 Star Experience Award & host for The Open Championship International Qualifier for Africa, this course is a must to play

Tel: +27 (0) 21 553 2223
Unit 1, Birkenhead, Atlantic Beach, Melkbosstrand
www.gopassport.com

Founded in 1913 Club with its newly revamped clubhouse situated on the dunes overlooking the sea and unobstructed views of Table Mountain, provides an amenity and golfing experience unique to South Africa.

Tel: +27 (0) 21 552 1047
Milnerton Golf Club, Bridge Rd, Milnerton
www.gopassport.com

Royal Cape, South Africa's oldest club, established in Cape Town in 1885 – a prestigious championship course of flat parkland and an ideal introduction to golf in the Cape. Famous for its superb scenic beauty, but also known to be windy and difficult to play, although the ferocity of the wind is tempered slightly by the many trees that line the fairways.

Tel: +27 (0) 21 761 6551
174 Ottery Road Wynberg
www.gopassport.com

This 18-hole course established in 1911 is rated as a 'must-play' amongst golfers. Ten minutes from the city centre, and situated with magnificent views of Devil's Peak and Table Mountain from most holes, the course is a popular choice for local and foreign visitors.

Tel: +27 (0) 21 689 4176
Rondebosch Golf Club, Klipfontein Rd, Mowbray
www.gopassport.com

Established in 1932, and set against the slopes of the Silvermine mountains lies one of Cape Town's Premier Courses - Westlake. This easy to walk, 18 hole Par 72 golf course with towering trees lining many of its fairways has an interesting, yet user-friendly design and quite a few doglegs. Every step affords panoramic views of the surrounding mountains.

Tel: +27 (0) 21 788 2020
Westlake Golf Club, Westlake Ave, Lakeside
www.gopassport.com

Mowbray Golf Club was established in 1910. The club is recognized as being one of the best in the country and is set in a very central area - about 15 minutes from the Waterfront and Cape Town's International Airport - Mowbray is a parkland course, which provides an excellent test of golf. The terrain is flat, but plenty of trees and water features make for an interesting experience, with the beauty of the mountain and abundant wild life dominating the scenery.

Tel: +27 (0) 21 685 3018
Mowbray Golf Club, Alexander Rd, Pinelands
www.gopassport.com

This 18-hole golf course centrally situated in the Peninsula, within easy reach from all major access routes, the course is a must for all golfers. It is set in a sheltered valley of rolling hills with panoramic views of the Hottentots Holland mountains in the distance. The practice putting and chipping greens, and a limited practice area, are situated near the Clubhouse.

Tel: +27 (0) 21 913 3100
Jip de Jager Drive, Welgemoed
www.gopassport.com

Situated near Cape Town International Airport, this course has been the host of top golfing events over the years. The club is renowned for its fantastic atmosphere and great service. With its beautiful views and picturesque backdrop, this will be a great experience for any golfer.

Tel: +27 (0) 21 934 0365
Palotti Road, Ontana, Philippi
www.gopassport.com

Common Routes Up Table Mountain

- Platteklip Gorge (strenuous)
- Nursery Ravine (strenuous)
- Skeleton Gorge (strenuous)
- Kasteelspoort (strenuous)
- Constantia Corner (moderate)

Hiking Protocol

Ask advice before setting off as weather can change rapidly in the Cape.

Take a good route map.

Even for a short summer hike you need water, sunscreen, hat and jacket.

Do not light fires or remove any plants or animals.

Stick to the paths.

Stick to the paths

Hiking

TAKE A HIKE

If you are usually confined to an office or live in a city, hiking around Cape Town will liberate you. Horizons go on forever and you can almost see the world curve as you stare out to sea. Cape Town offers an amazing variety of walks, hikes and climbs in the most sensational scenery.

There are trails leading off into the mountains everywhere you go, but it is wise to pick up a good map or hiking book. Cape Town's walking fundi is undoubtedly Mike Lundy, and his guide books to the best local hiking trails will lead you on a journey of discovery.

TABLE TOP

A hike up Table Mountain represents everything that is best about walking in the Cape. The lower slopes are often lush and thick with indigenous protea bushes. The kloofs (ravines/valleys)have pockets of endemic flora and fauna such as the small Red Disa orchid, only found on Table Mountain. At the top, the most incredible views over Cape Town and the Atlantic Ocean views are revealed. The fulfilment at having climbed this magnificent mountain, is even better with the knowledge that you can take the cable car down (after lunch or dinner at the restaurant)!

THE TIP OF AFRICA

The Cape of Good Hope Nature Reserve offers a 2-day hiking trail staying overnight in a basic but comfortable hut. The trail undulates along the coast and through superb fynbos. Start on a Wednesday or Saturday only, tel: 021 780 9204. Check the weather forecast before booking, as gale force winds are not uncommon at this south-western tip of Africa.

AND MORE GREAT HIKES.....

Other exceptional walks are; to the caves of Kalk Bay; full moon at the top of Lion's Head; Tokai or Newlands Forests; Peers' Cave anthropological site in Fish Hoek; swim in the Silvermine Nature Reserve dam; the mountains all over the Cape Winelands. For more serious climbs contact The Mountain Club of South Africa Tel: 021 465 3412.

Hout Bay

THE ZEN OF HORSE & CAMEL RIDING

If you have always dreamed of cantering through the surf on a long white beach, then Noordhoek is the place for you. If you prefer the mountains and even a little tipple along the way, try Wine Tasting on Horseback for a ride with a difference!

Noordhoek & Kommetjie: The leafy South Peninsula suburb of Noordhoek epitomises everything horsey, with a long wide rideable beach, cross country course on the common and a horse in almost every back yard. Sleepy Hollow Stables (tel: 021 789 2341) offers lessons and morning or sunset beach rides for any level. But you can't get closer to the sand than The Dunes Racing Stables (tel: 021 789 1723), whose retired race horses are fine for beginners, but can show a turn of speed for the advanced rider. Dassenberg Stables (tel: 021 789 2011) along Noordhoek Main Road, also offers lessons and out rides. Imhoff Farm, Kommetjie (tel: 021 783 1168, www.horseriding.co.za) offers lessons, beach rides and bush rides, champagne breakfasts and sunset trail rides.

Winelands: Spier Equestrian Centre (R302 near Stellenbosch, tel: 083 627 2282), was sold out for its Johannesburg Spanish Riding School's Lippizaner show. Joe Public, on the other hand, will have to make do with trail or pony rides until he perfects his pirouettes. Sample the precarious art of horseback wine tasting at Zevenwacht Wine Estate (Kuils River, tel: 021 903 3662) and Mountain View Horse Trails (tel: 021 903 3662).

Several stables in the Franschhoek valley also offer wine tasting on horseback, which seems to improve ones riding capabilities no end! Contact Paradise Stables (Robertsvallei Farm, tel: 021 876 2160, Mont Rochelle (tel: 083 300 4368) and Steinmetz Arabians (tel: 083 782 7896, e-mail: steinmetz_arabian@deunet.co.za).

The horses at Paarl's Wine Valley Horse Trails (tel: 021 863 8687), grace many film shoots, but that doesn't stop you from enjoying a leisurely champagne breakfast, wine tasting or sundowner trail on these famous mounts.

Get on a horse at Wellington's Kontreikos in die Fynbos for a climb through vineyards to a wild olive tree-bedecked 'restaurant', where you are served typical Afrikaans country cuisine. If your nag should play up, hop on the tractor for the return trip. Obiqualand Tours (tel: 021 873 3398) handles bookings, and can also arrange an overnight at Diemersfontein Wine Estate (R44 outside Wellington), for more time to take in the region's historic wine estates, or a massage by the swimming pool to revive your weary legs.

Camel Riding

Camels have been described as 'horses designed by a committee', and if you want to try their peculiar lope, Imhoff Farm in Kommetjie have a few parked on the front lawn (tel: 021 789 1711). A camel's braking system can prove somewhat faulty – hence the Certificate of Bravery when you dismount!

Horseriding in the Suburbs

The Milnerton Riding Centre (tel: 021 557 3032) offers out rides, which can take you to Milnerton Beach where a gorgeous Table Mountain vista comes at no extra cost.

Horse Trail Safaris takes you through Ottery's dunes to lunch at Strandfontein Beach. (tel: 021 703 4396, website: www.horsetrailsafaris.com).

Hout Bay

A benefit of the Hout Bay Riding Centre (tel: 021 790 5286), is the kids horse camp which staves off school-holiday boredom. Bethel Farm is a short trot away and also offers lessons and hacks (tel: 021 790 1177). Horse Trail Safaris takes you through Ottery's dunes to lunch at Strandfontein Beach. (tel: 021 703 4396, website: www.horsetrailsafaris.com).

Ambient Landscape

Sun Coral

Anemone

Clown Fish

SCUBA DIVING & SNORKELLING

Scuba diving and snorkelling in Cape Town is very rewarding as long as you don't mind chilly water. The Atlantic is downright freezing (8-14°C) and False Bay (not quite Indian Ocean) is marginally warmer (11-20°C). A 5 millimetre Farmer John wetsuit with jacket (giving 10mm over your body) is the minimum requirement, 7mm is better for the Atlantic side and a dry suit tops the lot.

The benefit of the Cape Coastline is that you have two oceans to choose from, so if it is murky on one side, the other side should be clear. Another advantage is that most dive sites are easily accessible from coastal roads.

Diving in the Cape is not for wimps, and more so because of what's in these oceans. There are Great White and Ragged Tooth Sharks (rarely encountered), swirling kelp forests, plenty of shipwrecks indicating the strength of the storms, 15-metre whales (July to October), seals, dolphins, penguins and rich colourful reefs. Equipment can be hired and instructors are unfazable.

Cape Town is great for beginners or advanced divers, and if you learn to dive here, everywhere else will seem like child's play.

ATLANTIC DIVES

Oudekraal is the main dive-training area, well known for good marine life and colourful Justin's Caves, plus a 1670 wreck.

Nearby Coral Garden has vertical walls of stunning coral, often visited by seals.

The pinnacle of Vulcan Rock is a boat dive out of Hout Bay where all levels can enjoy the soft corals and sponges.

Another popular Hout Bay dive is on the Maori, sunk in 1909.

FALSE BAY DIVES

Boulder's is ideal for novices and snorkellers, as it offers easy shore entry and cute penguins.

Pietermartizburg ocean mine sweeper lying off Miller's Point (sunk for recreational diving in 1994) is a good wreck dive for all levels.

Several coves at Miller's Point are excellent for snorkelling, as is Simon's Town yacht harbour (for members and signed-in guests).

The 1914 wreck of SS Clan Stuart, is ideal for beginners as it lies very close to shore.

Smitswinkel Bay offers challenging wreck diving on five ships scuttled in the early 1970's.

Contact: Scuba Shack at 289 Long Street, Cape Town or Glencairn Heights Shopping Centre. Tel: 021 782 7358, email: info@scuba-shack. co.za, website: www.scuba-shack.co.za

CATCH YOURSELF A WHOPPER

The Western Cape boasts relatively un-fished freshwater, due not least to the remoteness of the terrain and the fact that many dams are farm-based, and belong to private individuals.

GUARANTEED CATCH

First-timers can hire a rod and sign up for lessons in the patient art of trout fishing in the well stocked ponds of Franschhoek's Dewdale Fly Fishery (tel: 021 876 2755, email: gareth@dewdale.com). Drive through the Huguenot Tunnel to cast your line in the trout dams at Du Kloof Estate (tel: 023 349 1151, manager@dukloofestate.co.za), where you are almost guaranteed to catch something. Local fly fishing aficionado Tim Rolston of Ultimate Angling (tel: 021 686 6877, email: rolston@iafrica.com), runs casting clinics to perfect your Figure of 8 Retrieve, and guided fishing trips to some of the best (and those lesser known) trout haunts.

WHERE TO CATCH YOUR FISH

Whether you prefer river or dam, it is wise to choose your location according to the fish you want to catch. Here is a selection of what to find where.....

Carp: Not far from Cape Town the lakes of Sandvlei, Princessvlei, and Zeekoevlei should deliver some carp. Brandvlei near Worcester, serves up carp and white fish, as does the middle and lower aspects of the Breede River.

Trout: The lovely mountain dam in Jonkershoek Nature Reserve, Stellenbosch has plenty of elusive trout and Steenbras Dam at the top of Sir Lowry's Pass, Somerset West has brown and rainbow trout. Rainbows are also to be found in Franschhoek's scenic Berg River and the Breede River's mountain tributaries, near Worcester and the Holsloot River near Rawsonville. Also in the Eerste and Lourens Rivers, in the sections above Stellenbosch and Somerset West and Lakenvlei near Ceres. Brown trout, on the other hand, dominate the Wellington-based upper Witte River.

Bass: The Winelands region of Paarl contains smallmouth bass and carp in its stake of Berg River. At the outer edge of the winelands the huge Theewaterskloof Dam near Villiersdorp's is a bass fisherman's haven. Their small-mouthed cousins, plus carp, are a specialty at Voëlvlei, between Wellington and Tulbagh. Travel up the west coast to Clanwilliam Dam for more small-mouth bass and indigenous Clanwilliam yellowfish (but mind the ever-present waterskiers)!

Other fish that might land up on then end of your line include Mozambique Tilapia and sharptooth catfish.

Knots in a Knot?

Learn to tie a decent knot with the able assistance of Dean Riphagen's The South African Fly Fishing Handbook (Struik New Holland Publishing).

Licence to Fish

Fishing on any inland water (apart from private land), requires a permit and catch and release is mandatory in conservation areas. To further complicate matters, fishing within State Forests also calls for a Forestry Licence. The following organisations service the various permits: Cape Nature Conservation (tel: 021 483 4051), Cape Piscatorial Society (tel: 021 424 7725), South African National Parks Board (tel: 021 422 2810).

Fishing Websites

Before committing to this addictive sport, trawl the following websites: www.safishing.co.za (the quintessential South African fishing pages, including a Ladies' page), the amusingly anecdotal fly fishing website www.smallstreams.com, and www.flyfishing.co.za, featuring fly tying tips for lesser patient mortals.

Trout Fishing

180° ADVENTURES

180° Adventures started in 1999 with a practicing civil engineer's decision, to pursue his dream of assisting people from all walks of life in the fulfilment of their passions for adventure.

BELIEVE IN DREAMS

The 180° vision is all about transforming fantastic dreams into unforgettable memories. The 180° team who make this happen, are all passionate people with a similar view on life. They believe in dreams. Some of them have made their own dreams a reality - the others are getting there. This is what we are about and that's what we want to share with you.

The 180° business has taken root across the length and breadth of sub-Saharan Africa. Professionals from Europe have joined the team and add substantial value to the 180° team. 180° have offices in Durban, Johannesburg and Cape Town, and all three centres have featured in local and international media for their exceptional tours and events.

In 2004, 180° launched a partnership with Logical golf, providing their client base with world-class golfing tuition, tours and events. Major corporate clients of 180° include, Barclays Bank, BMW, Deloitte, Gillette, Glaxo Smith Kline, Investec, Merrill Lynch, Pfizer, Shell and many more.

180° VISION

The people at 180° believe in living life to the maximum. 'We believe in putting everything we have into everything we do, and we want to be recognised as exactly this'. Whether it's Xavier winning the Camel Trophy in Tonga and Samoa, or Dwain perfecting his Sun Salutation in yoga, or Pierre sitting back and enjoying a fine glass of cape wine at the end of a golf day. We take care of every fine detail. This is how we live our lives and this is how we run our business.

We want you to have the confidence in us to handle all your corporate and adventure tourism experiences, events and related services, because you know that we are the recognised best. With us, you will know that we take care of every detail. 180° is proud of its reputation and we are looking to become the leading provider of these services not only in Southern Africa, but the world.

Contact 180° tel: 021 462 0992, email: lindsay@180.co.za,

website: www.180.co.za

The 180° Team

The 180° team includes adventure experts and elite athletes that have the benefit of substantial corporate grounding. This, combined with the organisational contribution of executives utilising global corporate management skills, provides a mix of talent, achievement and business expertise, that together afford 180° a competitive advantage that is both unique and unrivalled in its field.

Paragliding

Jet Skiing

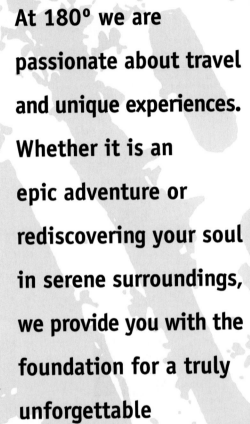

A touch of class, experience the good life…

Established in 1989, Wildthing Adventures is an Outdoor Adventure & Safari company that specialises in Southern Africa. Our field of expertise varies from soft adventures for all age groups (from 8 yr's and older) as well as fun, adrenaline pumping activities. Our certified guides come from interesting nature or conservation backgrounds. We practice a safety first approach to outdoor adventure and are proud of our safety record.

Tel: +27 (0) 21 423 5806
1 Vredenburg Lane, Cape Town
www.wildthing.co.za
Valley Road, Hout Bay
www.gopassport.com

CRUISE
SUB AQUA

Discover the thrill of floating weightless, make memorable encounters with seals and dolphins, or hover above the hallowed deck of a gigantic shipwreck Wedged between two mighty oceans, our waters have the a marine diversity second to none…whether from a boat or shore, Cruise Sub-Aqua will ensure you go home with INCREDIBLE scuba-diving memories.

Tel: +27 (0) 21 785 6994
Milkwood Park, Noordhoek
www.gopassport.com

DAD'S TOYS

Experience how to safely operate and fire handguns, shotguns and rifles. Challenge yourself and your friends (or your husband/wife?) to an adventure of control and concentration under simulated stress conditions, or just shoot for fun. If you're up to it, we will even give you a taste of what its like to operate in a SWAT team!

Tel: +27 (0) 83 297 8888
Shop 553, Canal Walk, Century City
www.gopassport.com

Your trip is not complete until we meet….
* Winelands Tours * Golf Tours & Events
* Cultural Interaction Tours- a taste of township living!
* Corporate Events / Teambuilding
* Custom Tours & Travel Centre

Tel: +27 (0) 21 421 1660
67 Dock Road, Waterfront
www.gopassport.com

Inkwazi Flyfishing Safaris (Previously Ultimate Angling), offer superb fully guided flyfishing around Cape Town. Crystal clear water, expert advice from a member of the South African National team, all permits and tackle supplied. We also run safaris for Orange River Yellowfish. See www.inkwaziflyfishing.co.za

Tel: +27 (0) 21 788 7611
10 Bluefin Ave, Marina Da Gama
www.gopassport.com

Join White Shark Projects for a real wildlife experience in the one and only real white shark Mecca of the world. 60000 Fur seals, penguins, whales and white shark cage diving and surface viewing. Meet the most amazing predator on earth. Let the most professional and experienced team in the world show you the White Sharks face to face.

Tel: +27 (0) 21 552 4080
Bookings : V&A Waterfront +27 (021) 405 4537
www.gopassport.com

Located a 1 hr drive (70 km) over Sir Lowry's Pass from Cape Town, a rare opportunity awaits you. 3 – 5 hr, full day or 2 day trails through forest & along the Koegelberg Nature Reserve with a professional field guide. Enjoy unique trails developed with Cape Nature Conservation, rare mountain fynbos and spectacular scenery. Max 6 in a group. Family prices. User friendly semi-automatic motorcycles and quads.

Tel: +27 (0) 21 859 1989
Mobile: + 27 (083) 461 4567
www.gopassport.com

PADI courses • Boat Charters • Guided • Shore • Dives
Full Gear Hire • Gear Sales & Services • Air Fills •
Career Development

Tel: +27(021) 424 9368
289 Long Street, Cape Town
Tel: +27 (0) 21 782 7358
Shop 3, Glencairn Shopping Centre, Glencairn
www.gopassport.com

ALPHA DIVE CENTRE

Enjoy an experience unique to Cape Town… that of diving in two oceans in one day. Accompany us to kelp forests of the Indian Ocean in False Bay and explore hidden shipwrecks of the Atlantic Ocean in Table Bay.

Situated in the fairest cape of them all and in the renowned False Bay, Alpha Dive Centre is a Pro Platinum Scuba Center catering for the "not yet diver", beginner diver and advanced diver. We offer a range of courses and qualifications starting with snorkel and scuba diver all the way through to Dive Master and Instructor certification.

We boast an air station and fully equipped dive shop offering top of the range scuba gear from leading manufacturers. We also pride ourselves on the high quality and availability of our rental gear and are able to provide divers with excellent equipment service and repair. For the adrenaline junkie there's great white cage diving or allow us to organize a dive in the Predator or Kelp Forest exhibitions in the Two Oceans Aquarium.

Tel: +27 (0) 21 854 3150/1   Mobile: +27 (0) 82 900 9163
96 Main Rd, Strand, Cape Town
www.gopassport.com

MIND, BODY & SOUL

ANNIQUE - AN ANCIENT REMEDY

Cloaking the slopes of the magical Cedarberg mountains in South Africa, is Rooibos. A natural herb unique to the Cedar Valley in the Western Cape.

Many centuries ago, this tea plant was well-known to the people of the indigenous Khoisan tribe; used by these ancient folk as a herbal brew.

A WONDER REDISCOVERED

After botanists discovered the plant in 1772, generations of South Africans simply enjoyed it for its sweet, refreshing taste; unaware of the startling powers this wonder of Nature possessed.

It was Annique Theron who rediscovered its magic. In 1968, this South African mother stumbled across its ability to soothe and calm her baby, relieving the infant of colic and insomnia. Amazed by its natural healing potential, Annique went on to investigate and document its health-promoting properties as a caffeine-free, low-in-tannin tea. Not just for babies, but allergies and ailments across a broad spectrum of age groups.

In the years since the publication of her book ("Allergies - an Amazing Discovery"), dr Theron's findings have been scientifically verified. And as the medical world has awoken to the healing powers of Rooibos, intensive research has begun to unearth the secrets locked in its leaves.

With each new revelation, the tea is enjoying increasing popularity among the health-conscious. Not only in its country of origin, but all across the world.

HEALTH AND SKINCARE

During the last three decades Annique has become synonymous with the innovative and revolutionary application of rooibos as an extract in a wide variety of products including skincare, vegicaps health supplements, baby skincare, teen skincare, herbal teas and slimming products.

SALONS

Treat yourself with a treatment that uses this unique South African herb.

Let our friendly and professional staff take care of your every need.

Annique salons offer treatments for men and woman, including facials, massages, waxing, manicures and pedicures and lymph drainage. Also on offer is aromatherapy for stress relief, reflexology, make-up and skin analysis.

You can also spoil a dear friend or family member with a gift voucher, available at salons.

Salon Annique Tygervalley is open every day of the week, including most Public Holidays and is conveniently located in Tygervalley Shopping Centre.

The salon received a 100% merit award from an independent pary claiming "a brilliant experience - a very tiny shop with service that made a huge impression".

Salon Annique Canal Walk trades during extended shopping hours and is located in one of South Africa's largest shopping malls, Canal Walk, situated only a few miles from Cape Town.

Salon Annique Bellville offers ample parking and a big reception area with a calm atmosphere. The running water will soothe your stresses away.

Annique products are sold nationally by professional independent distributors who are eagter to help. If you are interested in Annique's business opportunity, or would like to have a distributor of the product contact you, please phone 021 946 3780 for more information. You may also phone this number for product inquiries and all other general enquiries.

"At Annique your beauty care is in professional hands"

Experience the unique rejuvenating properties of Annique's rooibos products. Rooibos is a herb unique to the South African Cederberg Mountains. In 1968 Dr. Annique Theron discovered that rooibos could be beneficial in relieving allergies of the skin and body, and contains antioxidants to rejuvenate the body.

Today Annique Rooibos Health and Skincare provide skincare for all ages and skin types, with rooibos' antioxidant and anti-allergic properties.

Pamper your skin and body with a treatment from an Annique Salon. We offer treatments for men and woman, including facials, aromatic massages, depilation, manicures and pedicures, lymph drainage, and slimming. We also offer a personal, computerised health assessment for micronutrient therapy.

Annique Salons Cape Town:
- Salon Annique Tygervalley
  Entrance 7
  Tygervalley Shopping Centre
  Tel: +27 (0) 21 914 2020
- Salon Annique Canal Walk
  Entrance 6
  Canal Walk Shopping Centre
  Tel: +27 (0) 21 551 4577
- Salon Annique Claremont
  1st Floor
  The Link
  Tel: +27 (0) 21 671 6926
- Salon Annique Bellville
  C/o Voortrekker &
      Bill Bezuidenhout Ave
  Tel: +27 (0) 21946 3780
- Bellville Office
  C/o Voortrekker &
      Bill Bezuidenhout Ave
  Tel: +27 (0) 21 945 4356
  Fax: +27 (0) 21 946 1406

La Petite Parfumerie

La Petite Parfumerie, South Africa's first original store of its kind - we specialise in sourcing all original miniature fragrances. These little wonders are only manufactured once a year, once every two years or at times once off. Our miniature range changes on a monthly basis therefor giving the collector a wide variety to choose from.

Tel: +27 (0) 21 418 8927
Shop 145, Victoria Wharf, V&A Waterfront
www.gopassport.com

la prairie
SWITZERLAND

We offer the full range of luxurious La Prairie Art of Beauty salon treatments, as well as the NEW Five Star Spa Treatments. We offer the full range of La Prairie products for home care, and Body Spa Programs, Podiotherapy, Ayurvedic Massages, Permanent Make-up, Waxing, etc.

OPEN 6 DAYS A WEEK
Tel: +27 (0) 21 913 3455
Shop 5, Welgemoed Forum, Welgemoed
www.gopassport.com

Alfa BEAUTY

"Progressive therapy with a classical touch"

From traditional hand and foot treatments, massage and skin care to the more therapeutic aromatherapy, Le stone massage and Hydrotherapy. At Alfa, we offer the very best in beauty and therapeutic treatments. Along with our team of highly qualified therapists let us make your visit unsurpassable.

Tel: +27 (0) 21 761 1961
Claremont House, 8 Claremont Ave, Claremont
www.gopassport.com

sanctuary spa
at the twelve apostles hotel

Sanctuary Spa is situated a few metres from the Atlantic Ocean in an underground grotto on the slopes of Table Mountain. We believe the healing energies of nature combined with the expert choice of quality products and treatments are the best route to overall well-being. The heated jet & cold plunge pool provide the ideal relaxation spot, while the Brine flotation pool energises & restores. Our 7 latest technology treatment rooms offer Africa's inspiration through our full compliment of Moya body treatments that utilise essences of indigenous Fynbos. Unique treatments offered capture the energy of native crystals, tantalise the senses and restore body and mind. The outdoor treatment gazebo showcases Africa's beauty and the charming couple's treatment room is a must for two. Other facilities include the Dr. Kern's Tan Can, Hydrotherm hydro therapy facilities and the largest Rasul chamber in Cape Town.

Tel: +27 (0) 11 437 9000
www.12apostleshotel.com
www.gopassport.com

Carchele Spa

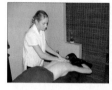  

Carchele Spa is the perfect retreat to restore mind, body and spirit. Situated in the magnificent grounds of the 5 star "Cellers Hohenort" Hotel, Carchele offers the perfect setting to indulge your senses. Stockists of Decleor and Pyhtomer. Carchele spa boasts a wide variety of specialized faceand body treatments as well as custom made packages with something to suit everyone! Local as well as overseas patrons are welcome.

Tel: +27 (0) 21 794 0349
Cellars-Hohenort Hotel, 93 Brommersvlei Rd, Constantia
www.gopassport.com

Spectacle World

WELCOME

So many things are important for your vision through spectacle lenses. The shape of your nose, how far apart your eyes are, the shape of your frame and how it fits. All these things make how you see and how you look unique. Just like you. We take your individuality into account. Your face shape, skin tone, personality, age, occupation, life style and prescription all play a vital role in the finished product.

High tech systems include a program that makes the possibility of pre-viewing your new spectacles a reality!

Our online optometrist can assist with information when you are too far away to come in, or before and after a visit.

We regularly service inter-continental clients and would be delighted to assist you in any way we possibly can. Complimentary delivery of new pre-fitted spectacles will be arranged to guest houses and hotels.

• Rodenstock German technology spectacle lenses.
• Contact lenses, spectacle frames & sunglasses - Polo, Hugo Boss, Rodenstock, Vogue, Rayban, Bausch and Lomb and more.
• Style and Image certified optometrists and eyewear consultants.
• We deliver

Tel: +27 (0) 21 595 3410, N1 Value Centre, Goodwood N1 Exit

www.gopassport.com

REDS HAIR DESIGN

Need to look groomed and gorgeous without any fuss? We'll make sure you leave feeling relaxed yet vitalized and vibrant! You can have a relaxing head massage before getting the designer cut that you want to get you looking and feeling sexy and elegant. Choose from endless possibilities of fashion haircuts and awesome colour. For hairstyles tailored to suit your lifestyle. Stockists of Kérastase.

Tel: +27 (0) 21 439 8658
Paramount Place 105, Main Rd, Green Point
www.gopassport.com

Yazo
tony martin HAIR

Tony Martin and Kevin Epstein, highly acclaimed hair artists, have won 10 International and national awards including SA Hairdresser & Avante Garde Stylist of The Year, are renowned for their talents and their popularity amongst celebrity clients including Jennifer Lopez, Kate Moss and Sophia Anderton. Their vast experience in advertising, editorial, commercial, TV and film is too great to list.

Tel: +27 (0) 21 424 4880
62 Kloofnek Road, Tamberskloof
www.gopassport.com

scar HAIR

shop 1
43 Kloor Str.
Tel. (021) 422 5900

from the sleek trim
to the complete street whack.
THIS IS THE ANSWER!

The Association of Plastic and Reconstructive Surgeons of South Africa (APRSSA) can be contacted on tel: 031 566 4100, website: www.plasticsurgeons.co.za

South Africa's Most Popular Surgery and Cosmetic Procedures

1. Botox Injections - paralyses nerves that create lines such as the frown and puckered lip

2. Breast augmentation and reduction - top cosmetic surgical procedures

3. Eye tucks - fat and excess skin are removed from the upper and/or lower eyelid

4. Laser Skin Resurfacing - a painful procedure that vaporises the top layer of skin

5. Liposuction - removal of fat deposits (should be recommended as a weight loss tool)

6. Tummy tucks - removing excess skin and fat from the abdomen area and tightening the abdominal wall muscles

7. Face Lift - lifting sagging skin and loose jowls

8. Ear correction - reducing 'bat ears' by setting them closer to the head

9. Nose jobs - cosmetic, functional or reconstructive

10. Brow or forehead lift - lifting the brow and removing frown lines

A CUT ABOVE THE REST

South Africa's medical expertise has been making headlines since the late Professor Christian Barnard first performed the world's first successful heart transplant in 1967. The country's reputation for performing highly skilled surgery at affordable rates has been growing rapidly over the last few years, and people now come from all over the world for this purpose.

They don't just come for cosmetic surgery, but for elective surgery which is either too expensive in their home country, or where their state hospital waiting list is just too long.

PAIN AND PLEASURE

Cape Town's biggest surgical draw-card these days is Cosmetic Surgery. There are no hard and fast figures to show the extent of South Africa's medical tourism boom, but Cosmetic Surgeons appear to be benefiting as a result. The Association of Plastic and Reconstructive Surgeons of South Africa, say that the industry continues to prosper several years after the country first started offering, 'Pain and Pleasure Packages'.

There are many companies dedicating themselves to facilitating the entire surgical process, from selecting the right surgeon, setting the date, making the hospital arrangements, arranging flights and accommodation and booking post-surgical recovery at a retreat or on safari. This service is proving to be highly popular with overseas visitors, as the fear factor is diminished and administration is taken care of.

A CUT ABOVE THE REST

If the undisputed talents and impeccable reputations of South Africa's surgeons don't immediately convince a potential client, then the state-of-the-art medical facilities ultimately do. If there is still any doubt, then the cost of the entire operation including a recuperation and rejuvenation holiday, will usually tip the balance. The combination of good exchange rates and lower prices make surgery in South Africa more affordable and much more pleasant than staying at home.

A sunny climate, exquisite health spas, country retreats, wine and golf estates, private beach houses and safari lodges, can make choosing recovery accommodation quite difficult. Quality food is a given, with fresh sea food, cholesterol-free ostrich steaks, and flavoursome fruits and vegetables.

Cosmetic surgery no longer holds a stigma, after all you only need look at most film stars, and you could come to South Africa as one person and go home as another!

MEDI-CLINIC PRIVATE HOSPITALS

The Medi-Clinic Private Hospital Group currently has more than 45 hospitals in South Africa and Namibia, six of which are situated in the Greater Cape Town area. These hospitals offer residents and visitors 24-hour emergency & trauma care, backed by multi-disciplinary services, facilities and associated medical practitioners.

WHO IS YOUR DOCTOR?

Medi-Clinic realise that in this information age, the needs of its patients have expanded to wanting information about the Doctors who will be treating them. As a result they provide a doctor search facility on their website, which enables prospective patients, as well as health care providers, to access comprehensive information regarding medical practitioners in various areas. Doctor's contact details are listed, as well as the Medi-Clinic hospitals in which they practice. See their website: www.mediclinic.co.za

MEDI-TRAVEL INTERNATIONAL

Should you require vaccinations for foreign travel or medical advice before travelling, you can visit Medi-Travel International. Medi-Clinic's travel clinic is in the Clock Tower Precinct of the V & A Waterfront. The clinic is open from 9am to 9pm, seven days a week. Visit the website www.meditravel.co.za

For patients requiring pre-hospitalisation services such as emergency medical transport, contact ER24 on 084 124.

 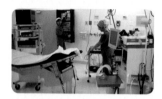

UCT PRIVATE ACADEMIC HOSPITAL – THE HOSPITAL WITH HEART

UCT Private Academic Hospital, an innovative joint venture between the University of Cape Town (UCT) and the private healthcare sector, is the only facility of its kind in the Western Cape.

Conveniently located in the heart of Cape Town, this superbly equipped new-generation hospital offers high quality medical expertise and services at extremely cost-effective rates. Their procedures are 10-20% cheaper on average than other private hospitals.

The hospital's superb medical expertise –professors and specialists from UCT Medical School – continues to attract patients from other cities throughout South Africa, the African continent and Europe.

Many of the specialists have developed their own individual areas of interest and are especially skilled in handling difficult or complex cases. That means you have access to some of the finest medical minds in South Africa.

With many of their doctors enjoying international recognition in their respective disciplines, they provide specialised services in more than 25 surgical and medical disciplines.

A cost effective approach and financial flexibility enable them to offer global (all inclusive) fees, special discounts for certain patient categories and assist patients with limited medical aid cover.

So whether you're considering elective surgery, are a Cape Town resident needing medical attention, or you become ill while visiting the Mother City as a tourist or holidaymaker, UCT Hospital is an excellent cost-effective option.

Contact 021 442 1800/09/14, or email: info@ucthospital.co.za.

Visit the website on: www.ucthospital.co.za for more information and a comprehensive list of our medical specialists.

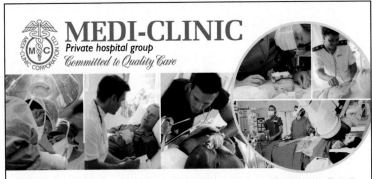

  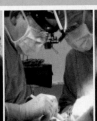 

WINERIES
&
BREWERIES

Steenberg Vineyards:

Steenberg Estate is the oldest farm in the Peninsula and wines were first produced in 1695. Since 1990 a number of cultivars, including its flagship cultivar Sauvignon Blanc, as well as Chardonnay, Merlot, Pinot Noir, Cabernet Sauvignon, Cabernet Franc, Shiraz and Nebbiolo have been produced in the state-of-the-art cellar. The cellar boasts a viniteque, where bottled wines can be kept under ideal conditions until ready to be enjoyed. The buildings have been declared national monuments. Steenberg is also home to a luxurious 24 suite country hotel, golf course and the top class restaurant, Catharina's. Tel: 713 2211

Constantia Uitsig:

Constantia Uitsig produces award winning wines including Sauvignon Blanc, Chardonnay, Semillon, Cabernet Sauvignon and Merlot. Although only producing wine for four years, accolades for the Constantia Uitsig Wines include Veritas Gold and Double Gold, Michelangela awards, a gold medal at the London International Wine Challenge, as well as listings on major airlines such as SAA and KLM.Constantia Uitsig Farm is also home to the gracious Constantia Uitsig Country Hotel, two top class, award- winning restaurants, and the Constantia Uitsig Wine Shop. Tel: 794 1810

Buitenverwachting:

At Buitenverwachting during the past five years, fifteen wines were selected by international airlines for their first and business class wine lists. Six double gold and twelve gold medals were awarded at the Veritas national Wine Shows. Buitenverwachting achieved the trophy for the best red (1994) and white (1991) wine on the South African Airways wine list and the Diners Club Winemaker of the Year Award was won for the 1991 Merlot. The restaurant is consistently rated amongst the top ten restaurants in the country, and is the winner of Business Day's Restaurant of 1996 and 1997. Tel: 794 5188

Klein Constantia:

This estate has played a major part in the re-establishment of the historic Constantia Valley as one of the finest wine-growing areas of the Cape. Klein Constantia is owned by Duggie Jooste, whose family has been involved in the South African wine industry for four generations. He bought the farm in 1980 and immediately initiated a restoration and replanting programme with his son, Lowell, handling the running of the farm. Klein Constantia specialises in Sauvignon Blanc, Chardonnay, Cabernet Sauvignon, Marlbrook and Vin de Constance, the re-creation of the legendary Constantia wine. Te; 794 5188

Groot Constantia:

Dating back to 1685, Groot Constantia has been producing a range of wines and has won numerous awards. The Manor House houses a cultural history museum portraying the early years of Groot Constantia. The original Cloete Cellar, dating back to 1791, houses a display of drinking vessels and wine making equipment. The tasting cellar offers wine tastings, sales ana a souvenir/gift shop. The estate is home to Simon's Restaurant, offering a variety of continental dishes and catering for larger functions as well as the graceful Jonkershuis Restaurant offering Cape Malay, classical and contemporary cuisine. Cellar tours and tasting takes place daily. Tel: 794 5128

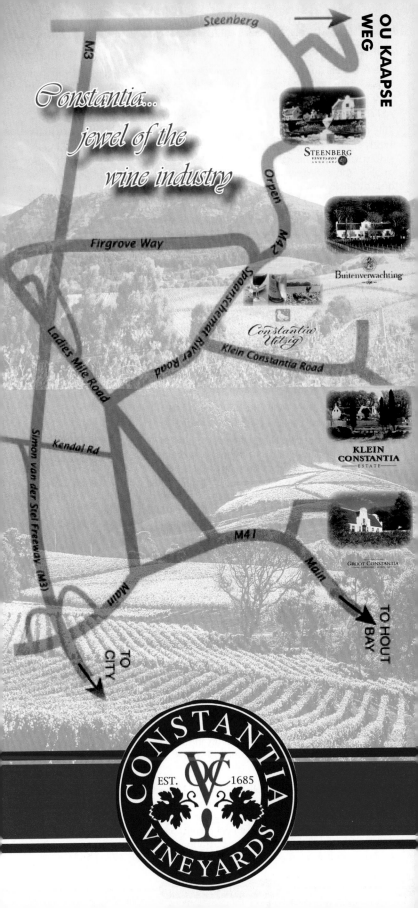

DURBANVILLE WINE ROUTE

"intense fruit driven wines from the Durbanville wine valley, as different to each other as the slopes that create them and the individual characters who craft them." Our cellars : Tel: 083 310-1228

ALTYDGEDACHT - where yesterday and today come together

This 300-year-old has been farmed for six generations by the Parkers. Today it is the biggest wine farm in the area. The rich variety of soils, slopes and elevations create perfect conditions to produce the highest quality noble grapes. In the cellar they aim to make subtle, complex and distinctive wines, using oak with care to complement Durbanville's beautiful fruit. Tel: 976-1295

BLOEMENDAL - walking with nature

Jackie Coetzee learnt his love and great instinct for the land as a child growing up on Bloemendal, which was purchased by his great-grandfather in the late 1980s. "I get a thrill transforming a wine I taste in the vineyard into reality, respecting the perfect flavours and balancing them to make a stunning wine. What an honour it is to turn nature into a product I can share." Tel: 976-2682

DIEMERSDAL - four generations, one passion

This 300-year-old estate has been farmed by the Louw family since 1885. Tienie Louw passed his passion and dedication on to his children, now the 5th generation to create wines of outstanding quality. "Our vineyards are the most important component in creating our wines. Breezes, sunshine, excellent soil, rain and mists also contribute to the quality of our grapes. In the cellar, minimum interference ensures that the natural attributes of the grapes are reflected in our wines." Tel: 976-3361

DURBANVILLE HILLS - breaking new ground

Grapes for Durbanville Hills' wines are grown by a group of neighbouring farmers who all share a common goal of producing the best possible grapes for world-class wines. Grapes are hand-picked and the innovative equipment in the state-of-the-art cellar ensures the gentlest handling with optimal extraction of colour, flavour and tannin. "Our methods are New World, whilst respecting of Old World values. The result is Future World wines in the spirit of the Old World, which are elegant with complex structure." Tel: 558-1300

MEERENDAL - rejuvenating a proud heritage

Meerendal, on the slopes of the Tygerberg, dates back to the early 1700s and boasts some of the country's more ancient vines, which stand alongside carefully selected modern clones. Dedicated to re-establishing Meerendal as a benchmark for quality in the SA wine industry, Meerendal can produce both white and red wines comparable with the best in the world. Its wonderful rich, red soils combine with perfectly moderated temperatures and airflow from the cool summer wines to yield grapes of great character. Tel: 975-1655

HILLCREST -renaissance

When Haw & Inglis relocated their offices to the exhausted quarry site in Durbanville, the property boasted a "groot gat in die grond", derelict "buildings" and 150 tonnes of scrap metal. They transformed this slope by getting expert advice, planting the best vineyard clones, and vowed to offer only the finest under their label, producing a 4½ star sauvignon blanc and one of the top rated olive oils in the country. Recent enhancements include a country kitchen and function venue. Tel: 975-2346

NITIDA - hand made wines

As the smallest farm in the Valley, with only 13 hectares of specially selected cultivars planted on a perfect slope, it is a privilege to grow grapes in this area where every vineyard repays us a hundred fold for our love. In the cellar, we handcraft these gems with the utmost respect for their individuality - infinite attention to detail for the fussy sauvignon blanc and uncompromising emphasis on elegance with complexity for our reds. Tel: 976-1467

DURBANVILLE
wine valley

ALTYDGEDACHT
BLOEMENDAL
DIEMERSDAL
DURBANVILLE HILLS
HILLCREST
MEERENDAL
NITIDA CELLARS

Long long ago
when the world
was young
Mother Nature set
out to create a beautiful valley

Enclosed by a hilly surround
with a patchwork of colourful
soils she further bestowed her kindness
by sending cold winds off the icy Atlantic
ocean and thick swirls of evening mist

For generations we have protected this small
enclave so that now we can offer you a taste
of these hills

Intense fruit driven wines as different to each
other as the slopes that create them and the
individual characters who craft them

natures vineyard

contact 083 310 1228

WINE VILLAGE

Wine Village is a South African company dedicated to creating a market acceptance for South African wines on a global basis. They endeavor to continually market, sell and distribute quality South African wines at the most reasonable price.

The Wine Village has the most comprehensive collection of internationally acclaimed white and red South African wines in the largest wine shop in South Africa. The elegant displays boast wines from more than 420 wine producers and cellars represented.

A selection of wine is opened daily for tasting. Friendly and knowledgeable staff will be happy to assist you. There is sure to be a wine to please the palate and respect the wallet.

RED WINES

Prepare for an exciting adventure! The impressive range, quality and affordability of South African red wines await your discovery. The style of South African reds includes the full spectrum, from new wave to robust, traditional stalwarts.

To assist you with your selection, please note that the most sought after red cultivars include the Nobles which are Cabernet Sauvignon, Merlot, Pinot Noir and the South African classic, Pinotage. Other varietals such as Cinsaut, Gamay Noir, Shiraz, Tinta Barocca, Zinfandel, Ruby Cab, Mourvèdre, Cabernet Franc, Pontac, Nebbiolo, Barbera and Malbec are available.

WHITE WINES

The rich diversity of wine styles, cultivars and quality to be found in South African white wines has established a love of wine in this country and a burgeoning market internationally.

To assist you with your selection, the most sought after white cultivars include the Nobles which are Chardonnay, Sauvignon Blanc, Gewurztraminer, Weisser Riesling, the most commonly planted and highly versatile Chenin Blanc (also known as Steen).

Others varietals include Bukettraube, Colombard, Muscadel, Muscat d'Alexandrie, Palomino, Pinot Gris, Cape Riesling, Sèmillon, Fernão Pires, Hàrslevelü, Sylvaner and Voignier.

Blended whites are referred to by many terms, often not in keeping with the definition used in other wine producing countries such as France. Among them are: Blanc de Blanc, Grand Cru, Blanc Fume, Fume Blanc, Late Harvest, Special Late Harvest, Noble Late Harvest.

Blended red wines are labelled by name rather than style — do not expect to find the words "Claret" or "Burgundy" used. (It is against the law here to use these terms outside their original area!) Discover the style of each blend the most exciting way — through your taste buds.

THE KEY TO OUR SUCCESS:

- Purchasing good value and consistent quality wines
- Exporting South African wines that appeal to the ever-changing palate
- Expanding lines of existing and new wineries/estates/vineyards
- Building long-term relationships with our wine producers and customers.
- Helping wine producers gain market awareness for South African wines.
- Delivering the product to consumers in a timely fashion.
- Updating information on new wine releases and developments.
- Offering wine appreciation evenings, for tasting and reviews of wines.
- Creating awareness of South African wines for consumers.
- Gaining press coverage in wine magazines and in various newspapers

WINE VILLAGE
HERMANUS
SOUTH AFRICA

For the Largest & Finest Selection of South African Wines

CAPE TOWN BEER ROUTE

In Cape Town new micro-breweries seem to pop up every other day and you are spoiled for choice on the Cape Town Beer Route.

START AT THE VICTORIA & ALFRED WATERFRONT

The Paulaner Brauhaus (tel: 021 418 9999, Clocktower Precinct, www.paulaner.co.za) gets its name from Munich's Paulaner monks, who stumbled onto a good thing back in 1634. Moving on to Mitchell's Scottish Ale House (tel: 021 418 2461, Victoria Wharf), this watering hole is the city's oldest brewery and you can down Forrester's Lager and Bosuns Bitter, as well as delightfully-named Old Wobbly Ale, Raven Stout, and Milk and Honey Ale – and we have not even got onto the 90 Shilling Spicy Ale yet! Imports include Newcastle Brown, Beamish, Irish Stout, Kronenbourg 1664, and John Smith's Extra Smooth. There is also plenty of that great Australian Outback thirst quencher on tap, Fosters.

Then make your way to Den Anker (tel: 021 419 0249, V & A Waterfront Pierhead, www.denanker.co.za). While not a brewery per se, the restaurant does nonetheless serve up an extensive range of imported Belgian beauties (beer that is)!

STAGGER TO THE SUBURBS

The legendary Zero932 (tel: 021 439 6306, 79 Main Road, Green Point) is a Belgian beer den. Get to grips with giant beer mugs brimming with anything from sour beers, to their more aromatic and fruity cousins, or the malty and carbonated pale ales that make for easy consumption.

The home of South African beer is South African Breweries in Newlands, (corner Main/Boundary Roads, tel: 021 658 7386, www.castlelager.co.za), which became the second largest brewing company in the world when they bought American giant Millers. Partake in their daily 10am and 2pm free tours, which only run with a minimum of ten participants and debate which of their four main brands is the outright leader: Castle, Lion, Carling Black Label or Amstel?.

TOWNSHIP BREWS

Traditional African beers are best savoured in the good company of township communities - but get your terminology right before heading out! You are now in the land of the 'wash down' (effectively the slang for swigging back a beer). This is no ordinary beer either... the home-brewed umqomboti is a maize and sorghum-based beer, with an unforgettable sour taste that you either instantly love or hate. For the best shebeens (township-based pubs), consult the Township Tours section of this book.

German Beerfest

Somerset West's Helderbrau is best known for its natural German beers (Mondeor Road, tel: 021 858 1309, website: www.malinowski.co.za), as is the Wilderer Distillery in the Winelands of Paarl (tel: 021 863 3555 website: www.wilderer.co.za), which celebrates with original Weissbier und Schnapps, fine German Bratwurst, Leberkäse, plus live Jazz.

World's Biggest Boozers

Czechoslovakians dominate world beer consumption with an average of 160 litres per capita per year.

Cape's First Brewery

A fitting end to a brewery tour is at Africa's first brewing estate in Stanford near Hermanus – the Birkenhead Brewery (tel: 028 341 0183) - where a brewery tour is followed by a beer and pub meal.

Testing Beer Quality

Beer Mad!

In New York, Ashrita Furman entered the record books for balancing 75 pint beer glasses on his chin for 10.6 seconds. Ashrita asserts that this feat helped him realise his inner spiritual resources.

The Paulaner Bräuhaus is a vibrant microbrewery and restaurant providing a touch of Bavaria blended with Cape cuisine and frothy freshly brewed beer. Situated in the Clocktower Precinct of the world-renowned V&A Waterfront, Paulaner is the only brewery in the world with its fermentation and maturation cellar below sea level.

Tel: +27 (0) 21 418 9999
Clocktower Precinct, V&A Waterfront, CT
www.gopassport.com

The tavern has local and international draught beers on tap including the popular Ferrymans Ale, which is brewed exclusively for the tavern. In the summer months, Ferrymans beer garden opens where patrons can enjoy the warm weather under the shade of leafy trees and visitors can witness the buzz of the V&A Waterfront and the working harbour. A seven member jazz band plays outside every Sunday evening from November to April.

Tel: +27 (0) 21 419 7748
V&A Waterfront, Cape Town
www.gopassport.com

Situated in Green Point zero932 prides themselves on beautifully presented and delicious to eat meals that flirts with Belgian tradition, of international standard served by accomplished waiters chosen for their individual flare and élan. An impressive beer list of up to 24 Belgian imported beers, each served in its own branded glass is available or enjoy a cocktail in MONK, the upstairs bar.

Tel: +27 (0) 21 439 6314
Exhibition Bldg., 79 Main Rd, Green Point
www.gopassport.com

A perfect opportunity to see the fascinating process by which talented brewmasters work the ancient magic of turning water, yeast, hops and barley into one of mankinds greatest pleasures : beer ! Mitchell's beers are made from scratch in a true micro-brewery, where everything is done with passion, by hand. Interesting and fun, a Mitchell's Brewery tour makes an unusual and enlightening mini-tour for friends, family gatherings and corporate outings. German language tours and other special arrangements can be booked in advance.

Tel: +27 (0) 21 419 5074 Fax: +27 (0) 21 425 4908
East Pier Road, Victoria Wharf, V&A Waterfront
www.gopassport.com

BUSINESS
&
INVESTMENT

Recent Big Spending

R500 million was spent on the Cape Town International Convention Centre, which is due for further development. R113 million went into upgrading Cape Town International Airport, but this is just the start of its expansion. Roggebaai Canal Precinct is an ongoing initiative linking the V&A Waterfront to the Convention Centre.

Film Industry

Don't underestimate the number of international film and television crews here either, taking advantage as they do of a host of gorgeous locations and great weather, not to mention a competitive exchange rate and professional local crew. They descend on the city to shoot documentaries, feature films, television and magazine advertisements and fashion pages.

Cape Town Business District

Cape Town International Convention Centre

BUSINESS MATTERS

"Jobs, jobs and jobs are the dividing line in many families between a decent life and a wretched existence." Nelson Mandela

EXPANDING INFRASTRUCTURE

The Government Information and Communication System's South Africa Yearbook 2002/3 rates the official unemployment figure at 18.4% - substantially lower than any of the other nine provinces. Yet set against the background where most wealth lies with the minority and increasing poverty of the majority, Cape Town's fathers are painfully aware of their responsibility to curb unemployment and create jobs. The city's scorecard is looking good – but the City of Cape Town is not about to rest on its laurels.

Viewpoints vary and some people see Cape Town as a value-for-money destination, while others may quote instances of being ripped-off. Opinions aside, you only have to stand in the CBD to observe the ever-expanding office developments and tourism infrastructures. Business in Cape Town is alive and kicking.

COMMERCIAL ADVICE

Cape Town's Regional Chamber of Commerce and Industry is a veritable one-stop shop for business information and advice. It is funded by more than 4,500 members, 70% of whom are small businesses. The Chamber is a private organisation and offers a host of networking opportunities, interactive website including a searchable database, local and overseas contacts and international trade information. Aside from being a reliable sounding board, the Chamber boasts a comprehensive library, events and exhibition management facilities, specialist advice in all business fields, and links with local, regional and central government. Find them at Cape Chamber House, 19 Louis Gradner Street, Foreshore, Cape Town, tel: 021 402 4300.

The Western Cape Trade, Investment and Promotion Organisation (WESGRO), situated in the NBS Waldorf Building, St George's Mall, tel: 021 402 8600, is the province's investment agency and another indispensable contact.

Pick up a copy of the free 'Cape of Good Hope Business Guide' from Cape Town Tourism (corner Castle/Burg St, tel: 021 426 4260). Its contains a list of, business associations, local financial institutions, property brokers, and costs, taxation, exchange control and asset swapping guidelines, to name a few. You will soon be ready to open for business in a region that has variously been termed the 'Lifestyle City', the 'Smart Cape,' and the 'Learning Cape.'

BUSINESS AND INVESTMENT

In terms of doing business in South Africa, a website link worth a visit is a government information site: http://www.gcis.gov.za/docs/publications/pocketguide.htm.

THE CAPE'S THE PLACE

Tourism, textiles, viticulture and agriculture are the Western Cape's lifeblood and the province contributes 14,21% to the GDP - the third highest provincial contribution and a healthy 3.1%, above the national average.

The tourism sector continues to be punted as a panacea for economic growth and job creation, but Cape Town is an increasingly desirable business location for local and offshore organisations, a number of which have relocated here. An interesting trend (one which many proprietary Capetonians find amusing), is the relocation to Cape Town of Johannesburg-based organisations. Historically Cape Town's cost of living and working is more expensive than Johannesburg, but the lure of a Cape lifestyle and its economic success is too much to resist.

BUSINESS HOT SPOT

Cape Town has traditionally been the country's clothing and textile capital (see Fashion section), with the likes of Wooltru headquartered here. The clothing and textile sector employs an estimated 170,000 people – the most significant industrial source of employment in the province. Another feather in Cape Town's cap is that the largest segment of South Africa's printing and publishing industry is based here.

Financial services power houses that have made Cape Town their home include insurance giants Old Mutual, Sanlam and Metropolitan Life. Another interesting business development is the country's first information technology cluster - 'Bandwidth Barn', 128 Strand Street.

The University of Cape Town's Graduate School of Business (situated at the V&A Waterfront's Breakwater Prison, tel: 021 406 1922 website: www.gsb.uct.ac.za, has done its fair share of coaxing overseas visitors to soak up an MBA at the same time as basking in glorious Cape sunshine.

On an entirely different tack, supermarket giants Pick 'n Pay and Shoprite-Checkers have also chosen Cape Town as their home base, as have oil giants Engen, Energy Africa and Soekor.

Black Economic Empowerment (BEE) organisations, are on the lips of city businessmen, and there is ever increasing pressure on organisations to tow the line regarding black empowerment and procurement policies. Affirmative Action policies, to place more previously disadvantaged South Africans into management positions, are a requirement of South African businesses.

Cape Town Foreshore

The bad and the ugly...

It's not all a bed of roses though. The country remains one of those with the greatest income inequality, second only to Brazil. A millennium estimate alluded to the shocking fact that half the population receives only 11% of the total income, while the wealthiest 7% receive 40% of total income! HIV/Aids is also making an increasing impact on the country's economy, from decreased productivity, sick leave, staff loss and increased medical costs.

... but the tide is turning

The disappearance of legal barriers to black participation in business, coupled with the rapid rise of black entrepreneurship, and a government enforced Affirmative Action and business empowerment policy, have played a major role in contributing to the ever-expanding black middle class.

Inside the Cape Town International Convention Centre

Zevenwacht Restaurant

University of Cape Town

LEARNING UNDER AFRICAN SKIES

Being able to converse in English is like owning an international currency. Since the 1994 tourism boom, Cape Town has tapped into the language school market with great success as well as more indulgent short courses on wine and food.

LANGUAGE SCHOOLS

Before signing on the dotted line, it would be wise to choose a language school that belongs to the English Language and Travel Association of South Africa (ELTASA) (tel: 021 419 0494 email: info@eltasa.com, www.eltasa.com). Also take a look at www.studyabroad.com, with information about studying in South Africa. You will need patience, because there is a significant amount of paperwork involved, all of which is detailed on: www.southafrica.net/tourism/formsf/visa.html.

As a guideline, some of the big boys in Teaching English as a Foreign Language include: Good Hope Studies (tel: 021 686 0060, www.geosct.co.za), Shane Global Village English Centres (tel: 021 419 8524, www.sgvenglish.com), One World Language School (tel: 021 423 1833, www.owls.co.za), Inlingua Language Training Centre (tel: 021 419 0494), Cape Communication Centre (tel: 021 439 7410, www.lalgroup.com), and GEOS (tel: 021 421 2860, www.geosct.co.za).

HOTEL & COOKERY SCHOOLS

Cape Town Hotel School (part of Cape Technicon), runs full time 3-year internationally recognised courses in Food & Beverage Management and Hospitality Management. Also short courses and stand alone sessions. Tel: 021 440 5700, email: pillay@ctech.ac.za, www.ctech.ac.za

South African Culinary Academy in Observatory, provides tomorrow's chefs with world-class training from two of the country's most well respected chefs. Accredited by South African THETA Authority & City & Guilds. Cell: 082 413 3001, email: info@saculinaryacademy.com.

The Silwood School of Cookery has thirty-five years of international recognition and a high reputation. Tel: 021 686 4894, cooking@silwood.co.za

The International Hotel School in Green Point offers full and part time courses for young people entering the hospitality industry, and the not quite so young to broaden their knowledge and improve promotion prospects. Tel: 021 421 5222, email: enquirecpt@hotelschool.co.za.

The Chef School offers prestigious internationally recognized British City of Guilds courses. Short courses for housewives and cookery enthusiasts are also available.

Tel: +27 (0) 21 906 1033
Langverwacht Road, Off 102, Kuils River
www.gopassport.com

SHANEGLOBAL
LANGUAGE CENTRES

Quality Tuition in a friendly international atmosphere
General, Academic and Business English

- Cambridge FCE, CAE & CPE Exams
- TOEFL & IELTS Preparation
- Individual Tuition
- University & Workplace Preparation
- Cambridge accredited Teacher Training (CELTA)
- Recruiting Teachers for placement in Asia.

Tel: +27 (0) 21 419 8524
Portswood Business Park, V&A Waterfront
www.gopassport.com

DAD'S TOYS

Experience how to safely operate and fire handguns, shotguns and rifles. Challenge yourself and your friends (or your husband/wife?) to an adventure of control and concentration under simulated stress conditions, or just shoot for fun. If you're up to it, we will even give you a taste of what its like to operate in a SWAT team!

Tel: +27 (0) 83 297 8888
Shop 553, Canal Walk, Century City
www.gopassport.com

OWLS

One World Language School in Cape Town provides high quality English courses so that you can learn English as a second language. The courses include General English, Business English and Exam Preparation and are presented by highly qualified English language teachers who give you personal attention in our small classes ensuring individual attention. We also offer TEFL Teacher Training

Our Cape Town location and the favourable exchange rate means that our English language courses and accommodation options are very competitively priced and cost effective. These benefits ensure that One World Language School is one of the leading language schools where you can learn English in Cape Town.

Accommodation and tours can be arranged.

Tel: +27 (0) 21 423 1833
37 Strand Street, Cape Town
www.gopassport.com

THE CAPE TOWN INTERNATIONAL CONVENTION CENTRE – FLEXIBILITY WITHOUT COMPROMISE

Cape Town's profile and reputation as a premier business destination was considerably heightened by the opening of the Cape Town International Convention Centre (CTICC) in July 2003. Located on Cape Town's northern foreshore, beneath Table Mountain and only a 20-minute drive from Cape Town's International Airport, the CTICC provides flexibility without compromise, as well as the most modern amenities and technology as mandatory ingredients.

The CTICC has been designed by an internationally experienced professional team, with its operating company being the Dutch RAI Group, which has extensive international experience in all facets of the facility's operation.

The centre is built to meet and fulfil the unique and varied needs of its delegates and visitors. Its sub-divisible multi-use convention facilities and dedicated exhibition space create a conducive environment for a variety of functions to occur simultaneously.

The CTICC offers 10 000m2 of dedicated exhibition and trade show space, two raked auditoria seating for 1 500 and 620 delegates, a 2 000m2 grand ballroom which can dine up to 1 500 people, one roof terrace meeting room with spectacular views of Table Mountain, as well as over 33 break-out rooms varying in capacity from 25 to 330 people each. It also has three different restaurant facilities, of which one is a la carte and open 365 days a year, while the other two are day restaurants used during events at the centre.

Other infrastructures that add up to the CTICC being a world-class facility are the highly sophisticated IT network with its fibre optic backbone with over 1 800 CAT5e data points located across the exhibition halls, meeting venues and public spaces and a wireless LAN in all the public galleries. The CTICC further has a catering division with internationally trained chefs and the largest and most advanced kitchen facilities in the Western Cape at its disposal.

Being located in the heart of Cape Town's city centre, the CTICC is within walking distance of the city's major hotels, providing over 3 500 rooms of three star quality and above, including the centre's integrated 483-room five-star ArabellaSheraton Grand Hotel.

There are more than 16 000 rooms in hotels, auberges, and guest houses in a 45-minute radius of the city centre, which has an efficient road network and good local transportation. Cape Town's leading recreational amenities, shopping areas and cultural attractions, among which is the internationally acclaimed Victoria and Alfred Waterfront, are also nearby.

With the construction of the Roggebaai Canal, which provides a water-taxi route between the CTICC and the V&A Waterfront, the Cape Town International Convention Centre assures delegates and visitors a memorable, richly rewarding visit to the city.

NOW YOU HAVE A BUSINESS EXCUSE TO COME TO CAPE TOWN.

The perfect holiday destination is now the perfect business destination because of the Cape Town International Convention Centre. Our state-of-the-art facilities boast two large auditoria, 33 meeting rooms holding from 25 to 300 guests, a grand ballroom that seats 1 500 guests, three restaurants offering delicious cuisine, 10 000m² of dedicated column-free exhibition space, and a roof terrace room with spectacular views to remind you that you're still in Cape Town. There goes the old saying of not mixing business and pleasure. The Cape Town International Convention Centre. Meet your greatest inspiration.

CAPE TOWN
International Convention Centre

BOOM OR BUBBLE?

At the time of writing (late 2004), the Cape Town property market is booming and has been so for a couple of years.

In some areas of Cape Town, prices have surprised everyone by just going up and up, out of all proportion to income and inflation. ABSA - the country's biggest supplier of home loans - recorded a 24% increase in house prices in the 12 months to April 2004, and Pam Golding Properties - the country's largest estate agency - reported record sales in the same period. So the million Rand question is, are we in a boom or a bubble?

GOING UP!

Noordhoek for instance, was a sleepy village 40 minutes drive south of the city, which many considered to be too far from Cape Town to commute. Not any more! You can barely get a patch of land there for less than a million Rand. Desirable areas closer to Cape Town, such as Clifton and Camp's Bay, are out the league of all but the very rich (in South African terms). Many foreigners still find the prices very attractive, and prime properties are often purchased by overseas owners. Buying a plot of land and building on it is a path many people choose, in order to possess their ideal home. Unlike many parts of Europe, there is still land available in South Africa to be able to do this. However, the real estate housing market is highly active and very competitive.

BUYING PROPERTY IN CAPE TOWN

An Offer to Purchase in RSA, is a legally binding, enforceable contract, but a 'cooling off period' will allow you be able to withdraw, with certain conditions attached. Other costs involved in buying property in RSA include transfer fees and transfer duty (according to set rates related to the purchase price), and mortgage bond registration fees (if relevant). Mortgage finance for overseas clients are based on a 50/50 structure - for every Rand in foreign currency brought into South Africa, an equal amount of borrowing will be allowed. Foreigners living and working in RSA can qualify for 50-90% mortgage loans. Completion of Form E is essential if you wish to register foreign currency brought into South Africa, so that you can take it out again at a later stage. The seller pays the estate agent's commission - usually around 5% + vat. There has been some talk of limiting overseas ownership of title deeds to land, because of the effect that locals can no longer afford homes, and you should check the current status with a real estate agent.

CAPE TOWN MAKEOVER

The New Face of Cape Town - a makeover of the city centre by Irish developers - made headline news in June 2004. Cape Town's historic heart, containing several grand buildings, will be transformed from a financial centre, into a thriving residential and retail hub. Such is the optimism, that in their first week, the agents sold over 100 apartments from plan - priced between 1.1 million and 5.5 million Rand. The development is expected to be completed by mid 2006.

This is much part of a broader urban renewal process, which will see pedestrianisation of streets close to the Company Gardens, changes to Thibault Square, Greenmarket Square and the main railway station, plus plans to put the 'Grand' back into the Grand Parade. Most people have little concept of the amazing transformations that Cape Town will see over the next few years.

Cape Town Property Bureau

The Cape Town Property Bureau assists foreign buyers in the process of finding a good property investment, through all the red tape, culminating in a successful purchase and transfer. Contact them on email: vip@capetownproperty.org, website: capetownproperty.org or Tel: 021 794 0646.

CAPE TOWN
PROPERTY BUREAU
www.capetownproperty.org

eside in
style...

ape Town Property Bureau offers the test and most innovative way for ternational buyers to find their peace f paradise not only in Cape Town but ll over South Africa due to our powerful etwork and partnerships of top class xury properties but also apartments, mily homes, luxury villas, commersial roperty and many more. Additionally e offer long and short term rentals.

ape Town Property Bureau welcomes OREIGN BUYERS & SOUTH AFRICAN ELLERS! We offer exclusive properties l over South Africa as well as APE TOWN apartments, long and nort term rentals!

P.O. BOX 415, Constantia 7848
Tel: 021 794 0646

www.capetownproperty.org

Send us your inquiry today online

Capsol
Tourism & Property Solutions

THE "ALL IN ONE" SERVICE PROVIDER TO THE PROPERTY AND TOURISM INDUSTRIES !

Capsol Property and Tourism Solutions has since 1996 successfully provided various associated services to our valued local and international clients. Our services are unique in that for the convenience of our clients we facilitate various related and associated services from one liaison/contact office.

Some of our associated services are :

- standard to exclusive upmarket holiday accommodation
- exclusive properties for sale
- property investment guidance
- property management service incl. decor/furnishing etc
- properties for locations eg fashion/film productions
- short/long term rentals
- safari/adventure/sport/ travel tours
- guesthouse/hotel bookings
- car rental/shuttles
- assistance with finance to facilitate property transactions
- comprehensive associated legal and financial services
- various holiday/tourism services for example sharkdiving/river rafting/winetours/deepsea fishing

- standard to exclusive upmarket holiday accommodation
- exclusive properties for sale
- property investment guidance
- property management service incl. decor/furnishing etc
- properties for locations eg fashion/film productions
- short/long term rentals
- safari/adventure/sport/ travel tours
- guesthouse/hotel bookings
- car rental/shuttles
- assistance with finance to facilitate property transactions
- comprehensive associated legal and financial services
- various holiday/tourism services for example sharkdiving/river rafting/winetours/deepsea fishing

Contact details :
E-mail: info@capsol.co.za
www.capsol.co.za   www.capsolsales.com
www.capsolelite.com   www.law.capsol.co.za
Tel: +27 21 422 3521   Fax: +27 21 422 3532

RELOCATION & IMMIGRATION

South Africa welcomes visitors, but for those wishing to come and live here as a permanent resident, it can be a long hard process.

TEMPORARY RESIDENCE PERMITS

VISITOR'S PERMITS.

South African Visitor's Permits are for holidaymakers or charitable volunteers working without remuneration. Most European passport holders do not require a visa prior to entry. A Visitor's Permit is issued at the airport or border immigration for a maximum stay of 3 months. You must be able to show a return ticket, or officials may march you to an airline counter to purchase a ticket back to your point of origin. You may extend a Visitor's Permit by another 3 months or longer (maximum 3 years), if you can prove a monthly income of R15,000 or if continuing unpaid volunteer or charitable work.

BUSINESS PERMITS

People investing in an existing business or conducting their own business may apply for a Business Permit for up to 2 years. You are supposed to prove that you have a minimum of R2.5 million to invest. However, this may be waived by Wesgro (an organisation involved in promoting businesses), or the Department of Trade and Industry, if your business plan proves it is not necessary.

STUDY PERMITS

A Study Permit may be granted to students attending educational institutions from Grade 1 (age 6) onwards for the duration of the studies.

RELATIVE PERMITS

If you have a Mother, Father, or dependent who is an SA Citizen or Permanent Resident, you can apply for a Relative Permit for up to 2 years.

RETIRED PERSON PERMITS

If you are retired and will not work in SA, and can prove a minimum monthly retirement income of R20,000, you may apply for a Retired Person Permit for up to 4 years.

WORK PERMITS

Application for a Work Permit must meet the criteria in one of three categories; General, Quota or Intra-company transfer.

Quota work permits apply if a prospective employer can justify that they require your services, and that this falls within Home Affairs quotas.

General work permits apply if the prospective employer advertised the position nationally and can indicate why candidates were not suitable.

Intra-company transfer work permits apply if a foreigner is employed outside SA and is being seconded, assigned or transferred to a branch inside South Africa.

Useful Information

You may change the condition of your existing permit whilst in SA.

If you want to extend or change a permit, documentation must be submitted to Home Affairs at least 30 days before the existing permit expires.

Most financial documentation must be certified by a Chartered Accountant.

Permanent Residence applications take approximately 1 year to be processed.

Work Permit Applications are usually completed in 30 days.

Working through a company specialising in Relocation and Immigration, can increase your chances of success and make your life a lot easier. Contact: Intaglio (021) 422 5313, email: francois@intaglio.co.za website: www.intaglio.co.za

Permanent Residence

The following foreigners qualify to apply for permanent residence in SA:

• Holders of business permits

• Retired persons

• First step of kinship (parent or dependent of SA citizen)

• Spouse or Life partner of SA citizen or permanent resident

• Workers who have been employed by the same company for a minimum of 5 years and/or who has been offered a permanent position

INTAGLIO

IMMIGRATION & FINANCIAL SERVICES

Since 2001 **INTAGLIO IMMIGRATION & FINANCIAL SERVICES** has, due to our experience and expertise, been in a position to offer you an even more personalised and effective service, as we are specialists in our respective fields.

INTAGLIO specialises in assisting foreign nationals with all their requirements pertaining to immigration and emigration to and from South Africa.

Due to the various immigration and taxation policies and regulations which are implemented and amended by the Ministers of Home Affairs and Finance, we at **INTAGLIO** specialize in providing a personalised service to suit the needs of our clients. **INTAGLIO** Immigration & Financial Services makes the tedious yet essential task of dealing with the Department of Home Affairs, S.A. Embassies, High Commissions and the Receiver of Revenue as easy as possible for the client. Thus saving our clients the frustration, time and expense of waiting for hours on end in long queues and otherwise having to deal with Departmental Officials.

OUR SERVICES INCLUDE:

IMMIGRATION:

- Assistance in obtaining work, business and accompanying permits;
- Extensions thereof;
- Study Permits;
- Visa Applications;
- Change of Purpose of existing permits;
- Permanent Residence Applications;
- Life Partnership Applications;
- Accompanying Spouse Applications;
- South African Citizenship Applications;
- Obtaining of Foreign Passport;
- and Appeals

RELOCATION:

- Accommodation (short and long term);
- Familiarization of the area;
- Schooling requirements;
- Import requirements for vehicles, pets, furniture, etc.;
- Au-pair; and
- Rental or Purchase of motor vehicle.

TAXATION:

- Consultations in respect of New Worldwide Taxation;
- Completion of local and international Income Tax Returns;
- Salary Structure;
- Setting up of Employment Contracts;
- Registration of Companies and Close Corporations;
- Registration of UIF and completion of monthly UIF returns;
- RSC Levies;
- PAYE;
- Skills Development Levies;
- VAT; and
- Payrolls

WITH A 100% SUCCESS RATE TO DATE, WE ACHIEVE AND MAINTAIN AN EXTREMELY HIGH STANDARD OF SERVICE AND RELIABILITY

Unit 5, 10 Pepper Street, Cape Town
Tel: +27 (0) 21 422 5313

EXCURSIONS

IN AND AROUND HERMANUS

Hermanus is one of those cute seaside towns that has realised its own potential and become a major attraction in its own right.

WORLD'S BEST LAND-BASED WHALE WATCHING

Hermanus was once a whaling station, and it is interesting how our consciousness has done a complete turnaround and we now shoot these animals with cameras instead of harpoons. Ever since this rustic fishing village achieved the accolade of being the "Best land-based whale watching in the world", it has been catapulted it into international limelight and seems to be revelling in it.

The annual visitation of Southern Right Whales, who come here from June to November to mate and calve, is celebrated in the arts and culture of Hermanus. Whale season activities culminate in September, with the Hermanus Whale Festival. Events, talks, films, exhibitions, flea markets and hopefully some attendant whales, are the focus for five days of celebration.

ACCLAIMED WINE

Nothing goes better with the local seafood than some fresh white wine, and the nearby Hemel-en-Aarde valley provides exactly that. Chardonnay is a speciality of the area, as well as award winning Pinot Noir. The quality is so exceptional that you can expect to pay top South African prices, (which is still good value for quality). See 'What to Do In and Around Hermanus' for more details of wine estates.

LOCAL COMMUNITY

Eight diverse communities make up Greater Hermanus, and this gives the visitor an opportunity to experience several different cultures. There are no regulations governing where people must live anymore, but each of the previously segregated areas reflect their own traditions. Contact Ubunti Township Tours tel: 028 312 2629 or 028 312 4334 or Hermanus Tourism Bureau Tel: 028 312 2629, infoburo@hermanus.co.za.

Nearby Hawston is one of the oldest settlements and was historically designated a 'coloured' area. It has some of the best sea views in the area - great for whale watching and surfing - and historic buildings.

Hermanus

Fishing Boats

Beach Cottages

WHALES OF HERMANUS

There are three types of whales usually seen along the Cape Coast; Southern Right, Humpbacks and Bryde's. The Southern Rights are the most common and were so named because they were the 'right' whale to catch. Very large, curious and passive, they made easy targets for whaling boats.

Southern Right Whales travel over 10,000 kilometres from feeding grounds in the Antarctic to arrive in Cape Town. Here they do without food while they concentrate on mating or giving birth. Sometimes a rare albino baby pops its head out of the water, and there is great celebration from adoring onlookers. Breaching, spyhopping, lobtailing and flipper slapping are also great crowd pullers.

BEST VANTAGE POINTS

The reason that Hermanus can rightly be called the 'best land-based whale watching in the world', is not only because of the amount of whales at close proximity to shore, but because cliff top observation provides the next best thing to aerial views. The best vantage points are along the cliff path and on the rocks overlooking the old harbour. You can see whales from the beaches too and swimmers and surfers should take care not to bump into them!

LAWS TO PROTECT WHALES

South African law does not allow any unlicensed craft to get closer than 300 metres to a whale. Whale watching boat licence holders may approach no closer than 50 metres. There are only two licensed whale-watching boats in Hermanus which operate in designated areas. Much of Walker Bay in front of Hermanus, is a protected whale sanctuary, and only sea kayaks may enter this area. See 'What To Do In And Around Hermanus', for boat-based whale watching and kayak tour details.

Southern Right Whale- Facts

• Size : Newborn 4.5 - 6 metres, Adult 11 - 18 metres long

• Weight: Birthweight around 1 tonne, Adult 30-80 tonnes

• Diet: krill or other small crustaceans

• Behaviour: curious, approachable, slow but acrobatic and playful

• Group size: generally 2 or 3 but more at feeding grounds

• Population: numbers visiting the Cape waters have increased by 9-10% per year for the past 30 years

Southern Right ID Checklist

• black with some white markings

• large head covered in sandy-coloured callosities

• strongly arched jawline

• large rotund body and broad back with no dorsal fin

• large paddle-shaped flippers

• broad black tail with distinctive heart-shaped centre

• slow lumbering swimmer

WHAT TO DO IN & AROUND HERMANUS

FISHING & WATERSPORTS

The New Harbour - west of town - is the hub of the local fishing industry and is where most water-based activities start. Charter a fishing boat from Tai-Pan Fishing Charters, tel: 028 314 1023. Scuba Africa Diving runs courses and pleasure dives, tel: 028 316 2362, Email: aron@scubaafrica.com, www.scubaafrica.com. Saltwater or freshwater fly-fishing is available from Hooked On Fly, tel: 082 555 8317, Email louis@hermanus.co.za. Sea Kayak amongst whales from the old harbour to the new harbour every morning during whale season. Contact Walker Bay Adventures tel: 028 314 0925, Email: wbadventures@hermanus.co.za

GREAT WHITE SHARK CAGE DIVING

Nearby Gans Bay is the centre for this controversial activity, but there are two renowned experienced operators based in Hermanus. Kim Maclean, Shark Lady Adventures tel: 028 312 3287, Email: sharklady@hermanus.co.za, Website: www.sharklady.co.za and Brian McFarlane, Great White Shark Tours, tel: 083 300 2138, Email: brian@sharkcagediving.net.

WHALE WATCHING

Only two operators have Hermanus whale-watching boat licences, departing from the new harbour. Hermanus Whale Cruises, tel: 082 750 7351, www.hermanus-whale-cruises.co.za and Southern Right Charters tel: 082 353 0550, seascapes@hermanus.co.za.

An exceptional whale watching location is in De Hoop Nature Reserve near Bredasdorp. This is the world's most important nursery for Southern Right Whales. Book very early to get a cottage during whale season. Email address: dehoopinfo@sdm.dorea.co.za, tel: 028 425 4020.

The world's only Whale Crier wanders around Hermanus with a kelp bugle, a sandwich board and a cellphone. Call him to find out where the whales are. Tel: 073 214 6949.

WALKING & BIRDING

Walker Bay has a stunning backdrop of mountains that provide excellent hiking. The Fernkloof Nature Reserve has over 50 kilometres of interconnecting paths through pristine mountain flora, with splendid mountain and sea views. Over one hundred species of birds have been recorded here. Tel: 028 313 8100, website: www.fernkloof.com

GOLF

The locality has gone up in the world of golf, with Arabella Country Estate in prime position on the Bot River lagoon just outside Hermanus. Non golfers are mollified by their spa facilities. Tel: 028 284 0000, reservations@w-capehotel.co.za, www.arabellasheraton.com/westerncape.

Wine Tasting

Chardonnay and Pinot Noir from the Hemel-en-Aarde valley are internationally acclaimed for their excellence. Visit award-winning wines estates such as, Bouchard Finlayson tel: 028 312 3515 and Hamilton Russell tel: 028 312 3595. Both are open for tastings all day Monday to Friday and Saturday mornings. For an amazing array of local wines at good prices, stop at Wine Village on the main road just before Hermanus. Tel: 028 316 3988.

Information Bureau

Hermanus Tourism Bureau in the Old Station Building, is very helpful. Email: infoburo@hermanus.co.za, Website: www.hermanus.co.za, Tel: 028 312 2629.

The Old Harbour

The Old Harbour's history seems ingrained in its cobblestones and its quirky little museum reflects its interesting past.

Hiking

Originally a fishing village, today's Hermanus has a wide variety of attractions for the holidaymaker. Regarded by many as the best land-based whale watching destination in the world.

From relaxing on pristine beaches, a sun worshipper's dream with their soft powdery white sands, to exploring the beautiful mountainside, there is no shortage of activities to keep the visitor busy. Fernkloof nature reserve boasts unrivalled birds-eye views of Walker Bay for those willing to put a little effort into their walking. For the less fit, there is the relatively flat cliff paths that trace the coastline of Hermanus from one end to the other.

GROTER HERMANUS VERENIGING VIR HANDEL EN TOERISME
GREATER HERMANUS ASSOCIATION FOR COMMERCE AND TOURISM

HERMANUS
TOURISM BUREAU

If you would like to know more about what Hermanus has to offer, contact the Hermanus Tourism Bureau, situated at The Old Station Building on corner of Mitchell & Lord Roberts Streets, PO Box 117, Hermanus, 7200.

(028) 312-2629 Fax 313 0305. E-mail: infoburo@hermanus.co.za

Website: www.hermanus.co.za/info

Hemel & Aarde Village
For a Heavenly Experience

Situated at the entrance to Hermanus
and the Hemel and Aarde Valley.

Art
Wine
Pottery
Interiors
Nursery
Glassware
Jewellery
Restaurants

Relax in our midst,

Refresh your mood

and Recharge your spirit.

For a Heavenly Experience

Situated at the entrance to Hermanus and the Hemel and Aarde Valley.

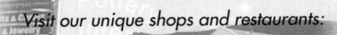

Visit our unique shops and restaurants:

- Wine Village • The Glasshouse • Ralph Walton Design
- Village Farm Stall • Walkerbay Nursery
- Southern Art Ceramics • WhaleHaven Winery
- Nico's Hair Studio • House of Persian Carpets
- B's Steakhouse • Incredible Fish Restaurant
- Meadows Coffee Shop • Gallery 64
- Hormbill House • Sylvia Smith Art Gallery
- Kate's Village Restaurant • Kai Ore
- Champagne Collection Holiday Home Rentals

Visit our exciting Hemel en Aarde Village and experience a lifestyle of classic wines, sumptuous foods, designer jewellery, various in' house artist and painters, stylish interior and exterior consultants and shops.

Date: Saturday 27th September to Saturday 4th October
Time: 9:00 to 17:00

Hemel-en-Aarde Village, at the Mian Road and Sandbaai intersection

For more information phone +27 (0) 28 316 2671

AMPLE FREE PARKING

CAPE WEST COAST

The West Coast of South Africa has a dry Mediterranean climate and a lack of natural fresh water. It has miles of empty white beaches and wild rocky shores, pounded by a chilly Atlantic Ocean. It can seem barren and inhospitable, but when the spring flowers bloom, this impression is replaced with one of abundance.

WHALES AND DOLPHINS

The Benguela Current is as nutrient-rich as it is cold and supports a wealth of marine life. There has been a good increase in the whale population in the last 30 years, and whales, dolphins, seals and penguins can be seen from land and boat. Hotspots are St. Helena Bay, Cape Columbine and Saldanha Bay. Contact West Coast Tourism tourism@capewestcoast.org, tel: 022 433 8400.

SEAFOOD

The West Coast is renowned for crayfish (lobster), fresh linefish, juicy mussels and delicate flavoured oysters. High plankton levels encourage growth and Saldanha mussels get to 60mm in four to six months. Sample these delights at legendary beachfront restaurants, some of which offer all you can eat!

Mullets

DRIED MULLET – AN ACQUIRED TASTE

One West Coast seafood delicacy that you may not find so palatable are bokkoms. These are dried and salted mullet, caught in a net pulled in by hand at the mouth of the Berg River at Velddrif. The slippery catch is immediately gutted, soaked for two days, then strung from rafters to dry for a couple of weeks, before being salted.

Locals say it helps to be born within the smell of drying bokkoms to truly appreciate them. Initiate yourself with a slice of thickly buttered bread topped with shaved slivers of bokkom, washed down with beer. Try this at the Velddrif Food and Culture Festival every August (Velddrif Tourism Bureau tel/fax: 022 783 1821)

SPRING FLOWERS

West Coast Flowers

The West Coast's real claim to fame lies in its springtime transformation from a monotone scrubland, into one literally exploding with colour.

Daisies, paper-thin vygies, orchids and lilies barely get their feet wet before bursting as if with joy, at the onset of rain. This occurs all along the entire West coast anytime from mid-July to mid-September and people come from all over the world to see this miracle of nature (see dedicated pages about Cape Floral Kingdom and West Coast National Park).

DARLING WHAT A DRAG!

The small town of Darling, hosts its own Wild Flower Show specialising in orchids, in the third week of September every year. For dates contact darlinginfo@mweb.co.za.

But that is not all Darling is famous for. One of South Africa's most famous stage satirists, Pieter Dirk Uys, displays schizophrenic tendencies as he transforms between male and female characters. One in his drag glad rags, becomes the outspoken middle-aged blonde Evita Bezuidenhout.

Pieter Dirk Uys's characters perform regularly in their own theatre at Darling Railway Station, www.evita.co.za, (and at 'On Broadway' in Cape Town - see Gay Cape Town section).

SPORT AND NATURE

The West Coast offers all sorts of other enticements to visit, most of which involve sport and nature and often a combination of both. For example, the deliciously inviting Langebaan Lagoon is partly surrounded by a nature reserve and has warm shallow aqua marine water, in which you just cannot resist a dip. Sporty types hare across the bay on hired wind surfers and hobie cats, while kite surfers search out a blustery corner with a good wave break and perform impressive acrobatics. Horseriding is also available around Langebaan.

PROPERTY DEVELOPMENT

Coastal housing developments have been popping up all along the West Coast and are proving popular. Fresh water is piped in to such enticing sounding locations as Pearly Beach and Shelly Point. The sweet old fishing village of Pater Noster, (Latin for Our Father as named by catholic Portuguese explorers in the 16th century), has new neighbours too, as another smart development rises out of the coastal dunes near Saldanha.

Long Distance Paragliding

Take an inland detour via Porterville, for a breath of mountain air. Paragliders favour this sleepy town at the foot of the Groot Winterhoek mountains, for long distance flights over the flat Swartland wheat fields. Spiralling thermals lift them to over 9 000 feet, enabling the paragliders to reach distances of over 100km.

Paternoster

Saldanha Bay

Glass-fronted Bird Hide

A lively and impressive colony of Cape Gannets is accessible for close up viewing in a glass-fronted bird hide, just beyond Lambert's Bay harbour. Packed tightly together, these large creamy coloured seabirds have exquisite black paint-by-number facial markings, blue eyeliner and fearsome beaks. It is an incredible sight with great opportunities for close up photography. Open 7am-6pm, entrance R10 per person. Tel: 027 432 1000.

West Coast Farming

Fruit Picking

WEST COAST NATIONAL PARK

Langebaan town may be a good base from which to enjoy the lagoon, but the surrounding hillside suburbs are dotted with a mishmash of housing styles and some dubious taste.

An exquisite contrast is found within the West Coast National Park, surrounding the southern portion of the lagoon. In this pristine wilderness you are likely to see ostrich, tortoises, antelopes, lots of birds of prey and visiting migrant birds, (50-70,000 of whom fly in from Russia to spend their summer here, and who can blame them)! Gate opening hours are: April to September 7am-7.30pm, October to March 6am to 8pm. There is a small entrance fee, more details on: www.parks-sa.co.za.

ANCIENT ANCESTORS

We know that our ancestors found Langebaan an amenable place to live, because in 1995, an ancient set of footprints was discovered solidified into the sand. Scientist and discoverer Dr David Roberts, has carbon dated 'Eve's Footprints' (as they are nicknamed), to 117,000 years old. He says they represent the first steps taken by the closest relative to modern man or woman ever found. This was so newsworthy that the discovery made worldwide headline news with substantial coverage in such magazines as National Geographic.

Thousands of fossil bones have been found along the West Coast, which are now housed in the West Coast Fossil Park. A fascinating range of extinct animals are displayed and you can become more involved by offering your services as a volunteer. Opening times 10am-4pm weekdays, 10-1pm Sat & Sun. Entry R20 adult, R10 Child. Tel: 022 766 1606, www.museums.org.za/wcfp

ORANGES AND LEMONS

Inland from the coastline running north to south, there is a monumental mountain range, at the base of which is fertile fruit growing area. Citrusdal is named for its citrus groves, and funnily enough even the soil around here is bright orange. Grapes are also grown and there are several wine estates and co-operative 'wynkelders', where you can simply turn up and sample wines for free.

ROOIBOS TEA

Further into the hills of the Cederberg Mountains, a special bush with fine, needle like leaves is harvested to make Rooibos (Red Bush) tea. It is now sold all over the world as a healthy caffeine-free alternative to normal leaf tea.

Either way...

CLUB•MYKONOS
LANGEBAAN

**...be it for a romantic getaway, an idyllic famliy holiday, a conference for 400 delegates, a business lunch or team building session or....
even a strike of luck at the Casino**

.......the legend lives on to celebrate the most fun under the West Coast sun...through all seasons!

For enquiries or bookings, contact 022 707 7000 during office hours, or 0800 226 770 tollfree.
E-mail: Resort bookings: thereta@clubmykonos.co.za
E-mail for Conference bookings: conferences@clubmykonos.co.za
Website: www.clubmykonos.co.za

No person under the age of 18 years allowed in the Casino. Licensed by the Western Cape
Gambling and Racing Board. Play with your head and not with your heart.
National Responsible Gambling Programme 0800 006 008

Pinotage

Pinotage is South Africa's national grape - a cross between Pinot Noir and Cinsaut (Hermitage) developed in the 1920's.

Wine Cork

Harvesting

Wine Tasting

WINE OF THE CAPE

The Cape's wine industry has come of age! It is better equipped than ever to compete confidently on the world wine stage. This is demonstrated by the increasing collection of medals and trophies from each subsequent International Wine Challenge.

Cape wine exports are growing in quantity and value and are earning greater respect from foreign palates. The UK remains the biggest recipient of South African wine, but other international markets are expanding.

BEST WINE GUIDE

Another award winner is the Platter South African Wine Guide - a bible to SA wine that is updated every year. This ever-enlarging pocket guide book tells you all you need to know about every wine estate in South Africa. Website: www.platterwineguide.co.za. This is no mean feat as there are more than 300 wine estates in the Western Cape, most of which you can visit personally!

FANCY A TIPPLE

You don't have to make an appointment at a wine estate. All you have to do is turn up, sometimes pay a small tasting fee, then choose any or all of the wines you would like to taste. Start off with white wines, then onto reds and lastly ports and brandies. A word of warning, the more wine estates you visit the better the wine tastes, until at the end of the day everything tastes just wonderful…hic!

It is said, "the poorer the soil, the better the grape," so many vineyards are situated on beautiful mountain slopes whose poor rocky soil produces fantastic wine. Historic estate manor houses in old Cape Dutch style with thatched roofs, whitewashed walls and intricate gables, are all part of the pleasure of a Cape wine tour.

WINE TASTING THE (SEMI) PROFESSIONAL WAY

Step 1 - Tilt the glass and look at the colour for clarity and depth.

Step 2 - Swirl the wine then stick your nose in the glass and give it a good sniff. Think what it reminds you of and don't worry if that includes old socks, mouldy cheese, grass cuttings, bananas or any other weird thing.

Step 3 - Look in Platter's wine guide to see if your impressions were correct.

Step 4 - Draw a small quantity of wine into your mouth and suck air through it, then swish it around your mouth. Spit it out (or better still drink it)!

Step 5 - Take a swig of water and repeat the process with the next bottle.

POPULAR CAPE WINE REGIONS

CONSTANTIA

Just 15 minutes south of central Cape Town is the oldest wine region in the country, with just a few estates forming a close-knit community. A bottle of 1791 Constantia wine was discovered in the UK some years ago, and was returned to South Africa for a ceremonial tasting. The sweet amber liquid scored an incredible 18.7 points out of 20, by the tasting panel!

DURBANVILLE

Just north of Cape Town, in the rolling Durbanville hills are some of the Cape's oldest farmlands under vines. Cooled by night mists they are particularly recognised for sauvignon blanc and merlot. Fine solo estates have emerged from a region previously known for bulk production.

FRANSCHHOEK

This enchanting village and millionaires playground is hemmed in by spectacular mountains. Literally translated to 'French Corner', this is where many Huguenots fled to in 1688. For a taste of France in Africa, you only have to visit such wine estates and restaurants as; Chamonix, Cabriere, La Petite Ferme, La Couronne, Le Quartier Francais and Haute Cabriere (to name a few of the best).

PAARL

Paarl offers a wide variety of wines in some delightful estates. It is home to KWV - the export-focussed winery who produce brands specifically for global palates. A smaller success story is New Beginnings Wines - the first black owned wine farm in SA, which started humbly in 1997 and now shows good potential.

ROBERTSON & WORCESTER

The Robertson valley of vines and roses produces fresh white wines with the occasional flash of red brilliance in shiraz and cabernet. Much of Worcester's production goes into brandy or directly to wholesale producers. Wines tend to be cheaper here (it is a couple of hour's drive from Cape Town) and offer excellent value for money.

STELLENBOSCH

Perhaps the best known wine area in South Africa, Stellenbosch has intensively cultivated undulating farmland between imposing mountain ranges. Known for its a red wines; cabernet sauvignon, merlot, pinotage and shiraz, it also turns out some premier league whites and bubbly.

WALKER BAY

Some sophisticated wines at fancy prices come out of this region, especially in the Hemel-en-Aarde valley close to Hermanus. Their secret is stony, clay-rich, shale-derived soil that produces exquisite chardonnay and pinot noir. (See What To Do In Hermanus section).

> ## Champagne vs Cap Classique
>
> South Africa's version of Champagne is called Cap Classique, and can compete admirably with its European rival.

Vineyards

The Vines

Winelands

FRANSCHHOEK SOUTH AFRICA'S FOOD AND WINE CAPITAL

Franschhoek has become known as the food and wine capital of the country. This is not surprising when eight of the top one hundred restaurants are located in the valley, including the Chef of the Year two years running. The talent in the valley continues to climb to new heights, with a number of past chefs being drawn back to the valley where they made their names to open up new temples of gastronomy.

Settled more than three hundred years ago by the French Huguenots, the Franschhoek Valley also produces some great wines.

Franschhoek complements the artistry of its chefs and winemakers with the breathtaking beauty, it lies on the banks of the Berg River against a backdrop of the towering Franschhoek and Drakenstein Mountains - a dramatic setting indeed for the town and its attendant vineyards.

You can taste and buy wine at most of the twenty-nine wine cellars, and there are some seventeen restaurants attached to wineries. For the adventurous you can explore the vineyards by mountain bike or you could even try some wine-tasting on horseback.

Franschhoek's charming main street is lined with shops and galleries providing a choice of antiques, art, crafts and bric-a-brac. Naturally, the gourmet is well-catered for, and here you will also find fromageries, a Chocolaterie and coffee shops serving delicious, freshly baked confections - a must when you're all shopped out and need to build up your strength.

With your energy restored, venture into the mountains for a walk or go to the Forestry Station for hiking, cycling, horse riding or flyfishing (some of the wine farms also have trout streams - check with the tourism bureau).

Or, to understand why Franschhoek is rich in French heritage - and for a glimpse at how life was lived way back when' - visit the Huguenot Memorial Museum. And if you're in the area on the weekend closest to Bastille Day (14 July), join the locals for their annual gourmet fair and celebration of the town's French heritage.

Of course, with all these attractions and culinary temptations, you'll want to stay more than two or three nights. It is increasingly becoming, because of its central location, a base from which to explore the wonderful pleasures of the Western Cape ~ from the winelands to whale-watching to exploring the mother city. Franschhoek offers a myriad of eclectic places to stay, for all budgets, from internationally acclaimed country lodges to intimate B&B's, charming country guest houses to comfortable self-catering cottages.

Recently described as one of South Africa's most beautiful spots with a picture-postcard village, 45 minutes from Cape Town. If you are going to choose one place as your base, Franschhoek should be it.

FRANSCHHOEK WINE VALLEY & TOURIST ASSOCIATION

Tel: 021 876 3603/2767   Fax: 021 876 2768

E-mail: info@franschhoek.org.za   Web: www.franschhoek.org.za

Wine tasting on horseback

eat sleep drink

FRANSCHHOEK

one village of relentless charm

eight of South Africa's leading restaurants

twenty nine extraordinary wine cellars

ninety nine eclectic places to stay

a plethora of galleries and shops

a lifetime of discoveries

FRANSCHHOEK WINE VALLEY

a single-minded choice

telephone +27 (0)21 876 3603
e.mail info@franschhoek.org.za
www.franschhoek.org.za
An inspirational leader in innovative and sustainable tourism.

STELLENBOSCH - "HEART OF THE WINELANDS"

As a premier tourist destination, Stellenbosch's history is reflected in neo-Dutch, Georgian and modern Victorian architecture. Oak trees bear witness to its proud and dignified heritage. The town on the banks of a river in the premier wine producing Jonkershoek Valley is encircled by majestic mountains.

WINE ROUTE

As one of the oldest wine routes in the country with 110 farms and cellars, it attracts wine-lovers and tourists from around the world. The wines are of a high standard and regularly win International awards. Many farms have beautifully maintained homes and gardens that are open to the public. Wine tours are a must for visitors.

ACADEMIC STELLENBOSCH

With roots going back to 1866 and a student population of 18 000, Stellenbosch University is one of the oldest universities in South Africa the finest academic institutions in Africa. The Boland College for Further Education & Training was started as a Technical College in 1918. Practical courses are offered mainly for the service industry and in particularly the hospitality industry.

ACTIVITIES

The magnificent hills surrounding the town offer unequalled opportunities for hiking, abseiling, mountaineering, cycling, off-road biking jogging hang-gliding, horse riding, camping, white water canoeing/ rafting, picnicing and other sports and recreational activities which can be arranged through the Bureau and members. Stellenbosch has three excellent golf courses and another six within a 30km radius.

STELLENBOSCH ON FOOT

Historic guided walks take place twice daily starting at Tourism Bureau in Market Street. Take this opportunity to explore the rich heritage of "The Village of the Oaks". In summer Twilight Walks and spine tingling Ghost Walks are offered by specially trained guides.

CULINARY DELIGHTS.

Every taste is catered for from local traditional to cordon bleu International. The side-walk cafes and friendly meet-&-eat pubs add to the relaxed pleasures of the town. Lists of Restaurants, side-walk cafes and the Wine Estate dining & picnic facilities are available from the Bureau and on this web site.

MUSEUMS

Stellenbosch is the home to several museums. Information on these are available from the Bureau.

SHOPPING

Stellenbosch boasts all the shops and malls of a large city including curio shops, antique shops and is host to regular street markets. At Oom Samie se Winkel one can purchase anything from sweets to alcohol, clothing and fruit. This shop is a true reflection of how locals use to trade 200 years ago.

TOWNSHIP EXPERIENCE

Offering excellent opportunities for the visitor looking for a cultural, or traditional experience Stellenbosch is home to Kayamandi, Cloetesville, Idas Valley and Jamestown, all vibrant townships, where food, crafts and genuine African hospitality can be experienced.

WELLNESS

Stellenbosch now has various options in this category and offers services ranging from complete release from stress and strain or for a healthier level of fitness. With the magnificent surroundings, excellent food and wine, its would be a natural extension to complete the overall Stellenbosch experience.

The Stellenbosch Tourism and Information Bureau provides maps, brochures of the town and surrounding Winelands and information on restaurants, theatre, films and attractions – see web site for updated information.

STELLENBOSCH
The heart of the winelands.

ACCOMMODATION   CONFERENCES   HISTORICAL TOURS
DAY-TRIPS   RESTAURANTS   WINE TASTING   THEATRE
FLY FISHING   GOLF COURSES   UNIVERSITY   SITE SEEING   WILD
LIFE   WINE SALES   OAK LINED STREETS   STRAWBERRIES   FINE
FOOD & WINE   PRESTINE SURROUNDINGS   HIKING   SHOPPING

For all your Accommodation, Conferences, Tours, Day-trips, Venues,
Restaurants and general enquiries.
Stellenbosch Information Centre • 36 Market Street, Stellenbosch, South Africa •
Tel: 021 883 3584 • Fax: 021 883 8017 • e-mail: info@stellenboschtourism.co.za
www.stellenboschtourism.co.za

The 'Big Five'

The 'Big Five' animals of Africa are leopard, lion, elephant, buffalo and rhino. They are so called not because of their size, but because they are the most dangerous animals to hunt. If injured, each one of these animals has a reputation for pursuing its attacker with intent to kill - the buffalo being the most persistent and dangerous.

Wildebeest

Big Cats

• A male lion's roar is audible up to 8km (5 miles) away, and if you are close by you can feel the ground vibrate.

• Cheetah are the fastest land mammal, reaching a top speed of up to 100 km per hour.

• Leopards are solitary and shy and use stalk and ambush tactics to pounce on prey before it can react.

Rhinos

SAFARI IN THE CAPE

Two hundred years after lions were last seen in the Cape, they are returning to some game reserves in the Western Cape (and particularly in the Eastern Cape). More and more private game reserves are opening to the public, most offering a somewhat 'softer' safari than you could expect in the wilds of Kruger.

Nevertheless, they have the advantage of being within reasonable driving distance from Cape Town and totally malaria free. This convenience means that more and more people are choosing to add a local safari element to a Cape Town holiday.

WHICH GAME TO WATCH

Many of the Western Cape's game lodges have big game like elephant, buffalo, rhino and giraffe, but usually only in small numbers. The more common species you will encounter are grazers like zebra, wildebeest, eland, springbok, bontebok, and small antelopes. Lions are still a rarity and leopards and caracal may be in them thar hills, but are secretive and tend to stay there.

In 1801 Lady Anne Barnard noted that lions were common near Cape Town. Only 40 years later, vast improvements to firearms led to more successful hunting and the extinction of lions in the Cape.

DRIVING…WALKING…HORSE RIDING… MOUNTAIN BIKING

The advantage of a 'soft' safari is that you are not restricted to bumping around on a game drive. You can get out and feel the African Earth under your feet. Bush walking brings Africa to life with sounds and smells that you miss in a vehicle. It also increases your appreciation of the small things like birds, beetles, flora and fauna.

A beautiful way to see game is from the saddle, as riding a horse somehow adds an intimate element to the animal watching experience. On the other hand, mountain biking through a game reserve adds a healthy active component that is rewarded by being close to nature.

WESTERN CAPE LODGES & RESERVES

Day visits are often encouraged, but it is always far more relaxing to stay overnight. These reserves are listed in order of proximity to Cape Town:

Clara Anna Fontein. Hike or mountain bike with free-roaming game, Only 30 minutes drive from the city. Tel: 021 975 1533, www.caflodge.co.za

Bartholomeus Klip. Blend gracious farm living with game viewing at this sophisticated country reserve 90 minutes drive from Cape Town. Tel: 022 448 1820, www.parksgroup.co.za

Aquila Game Reserve. Bushman paintings add an interesting element to game drives. 90 minutes into the mountains north-west of Cape Town. Tel: 023 358 2013, www.aquilasafari.com

Grootbos Nature Reserve. See spectacular whale sightings (June to November), from this stunning coastal nature reserve. Just past Hermanus, about 1½ hours drive. Tel: 028 384 0381, www.grootbos.co.za

Sadawa. Antelopes, wildebeest, zebra and ostrich graze amongst flowers after spring rains. Approximately 2 hours drive north-west of Cape Town. Tel: 023 312 2512, sadawa@iafrica.com.

Inverdoorn. A couple of rhino roam this reserve between mountain ranges, about 2½ hours by car. Tel: 021 464 4266, daytours@aecpt.co.za.

Sanbona Wildlife Reserve. Enjoy luxury in this extensive reserve, with lions and other big African game. About 3 hours from Cape Town on Route 66. Tel: 028 572 1365, www.sanbona.com.

Kagga Kamma. Bushmen encounters are the highlight of a stay at this lodge in the rocky Cederberg mountains, about 2-3 hours drive away. Tel: 021 863 8334, kagga@iafrica.com, www.geocities.com/tnetropics/6674

Bushmans Kloof Wilderness. Luxuriate in fabulous surroundings in wild and rocky Cederberg mountain. Drive 3 hours north of Cape Town. Tel: 021 797 0990, www.bushmanskloof.co.za

Garden Route Game Lodge. See Big 5 in restricted areas, while zebra, wildebeest and giraffe roam freely. They have a cheetah breeding programme and reptile centre. 3½ hours drive along the east coast road from Cape Town. Tel: 028 735 1200/1, www.grgamelodge.co.za

Botlierskop Game Farm. See rhino, buffalo, giraffe and rare black faced impala at this private farm just outside Mossel Bay, 4 hours drive along the Garden Route. Tel: 044 696 6055, www.greatbrakriver.co.za/botlierskop

Buffalo Hills Private Reserve. This friendly game lodge offers hikes through rhino, giraffe and buffalo country and there are plans for an elephant sanctuary. Tel: 044 535 9739, www.buffalohills.co.za.

Elephants

Elephants deposit around 150kg (330 pounds) of dung every day - approximately one deposit every 15 minutes! An elephants skin is up to 3cm (1 inch) thick, but is still quite sensitive. Their tusks are actually their upper incisors, and grow continuously until they die at around 60 years old.

Giraffe

Giraffes are the world's tallest animals, with males reaching 5.5metres (almost 18 feet). When a giraffe drinks it has to raise its head from around 2.1m below its heart, to 3.4m above its heart without getting dizzy! They live to about 25 years of age.

Buffalo

Buffalo

African Buffalo may look rather like large cows, but they are one of the most fearsome African animals - especially when wounded, when they will ceaselessly chase their attacker. An adult male buffalo weighs in the region of 600 kilos (1,320 pounds).

Aquila Game Lodge

AQUILA - CAPE TOWN'S AFFORDABLE SAFARI EXPERIENCE

The prestigious 4-star Aquila Private Game Reserve, offers 4 star luxury in eco-friendly cottages on 4,500 hectares of Southern Karoo highlands. Aquila has quickly established itself as the closest premier safari destination to Cape Town, with a good range of African game animals including lion and rhino. It is a mere two-hour drive from Cape Town.

Aquila is steeped in history with Khoi San rock art dating back 10,000 years, to Anglo Boer war stories from the late eighteen hundreds. This adds an interesting aspect to your Aquila visit, which can include game drives in open 4x4's, horseback and quad bike safaris - which are proving very popular. You can combine these safari options, in between a scrumptious buffet lunch.

Stay in Aquila's 4-star semi-luxury cottages or the spectacular honeymoon suite, that boasts a sunken rock jacuzzi. Every conceivable comfort has been thought of in the rooms such as romantic roaring log fires during winter months, wooden viewing decks, air conditioning, percale linen, mini bars, rock bathrooms & outdoor rock showers. Using only natural materials for the buildings Aquila has made a solid commitment and effort to the environment. Aquila is also set to become a unique wedding destination with unparalleled scenic backdrops.

Food is prepared by Aquila's renowned Executive Chef, with meals eaten in the atmospheric thatched Boma Restaurant. Lazy afternoons or pre and post dinner drinks are enjoyed in the new colonial Cigar Bar lounge, which is the ideal place to relax, read a book or view the majestic reserve unveiled before you. There is also a fully equipped 80-seater Conference Centre, for safari-based seminars with a difference.

The safari and outdoor experience at Aquila is its drawcard. The reserve is constantly expanding its African animal population, which will include three lion cubs, buffalo and several sleek cheetah. Aquila already boasts the closest lions to Cape Town, plus animals rarely seen in the Western Cape like rhino, hippo, crocodiles, giraffes, gemsbok and warthog. Grazing animals include black & blue wildebeest, Burchell's zebra, eland, red hartebeest, springbok, steenbok, klipspringer, blesbok and ostriches. Other carnivores include mountain leopard, caracal (lynx), bat-eared fox and black backed jackal, and baboon eat just about anything. Future plans are to introduce Elephant back safaris through the indigenous game, that have enjoyed the protection of this reserve since 1986.

Aquila is a year round destination as the rare renosterveld terrain of the Karoo takes on a different mood, shape and form throughout the seasons. The flower season from July through to September is most spectacular, when the reserve displays a splendid technicolour carpet of Karoo flowers.

Contact tel: 021 405 4513, email: res@aquilasafari.com,

website: www.aquilasafari.com

Lion Cubs

Finally! An
African Safari
less than 2 hours from Cape Town

AQUILA
PRIVATE GAME RESERVE
& SAFARIS

Game Drive Safaris

Horseback Safaris

Quad Bike Safaris

San Rock Art Safaris

Conference Facilities

Luxury ★★★★
Accommodation

4 of the Big 5

DAY TRIP SAFARI

* Morning pick-up from the doorstep of your hotel.
* Travel through the scenic Du Toitskloof Pass to Aquila.
* Enjoy a welcome cocktail and a light breakfast on arrival.
* Depart for a 2-3 hour game drive in 4X4 safari vehicles
  with experienced game rangers.
* Visit our renowned San Bushman rock art sites.
* Snacks and "champagne" will be served at lookout points.
* Return to the lodge for lunch in our restaurant or
  outdoor African Boma.
* Relax with a cocktail at the swimming pool in summer
  or enjoy a roaring log fire in our cigar bar in winter.
* Browse our African Curio Shop.
* Return to Cape Town.

RESERVATIONS
Tel: +27(21) 405 4513 (9am-9pm)
Mobile: 27 (0)82 295 4280

E-mail: res@aquilasafari.com
www.aquilasafari.com

INVERDOORN GAME RESERVE

In 1997 Inverdoorn Game Reserve was born. Our mission being to provide the warmest of welcomes, to offer traditional French cuisine, lovingly prepared using our own fresh produce, to provide comfortable accommodation in our rooms and chalets as well as to organise conferences to suit your needs.

Inverdoorn Game Reserve currently offers guests the advantage of more than 20 species of animals and 4X4 safaris while enjoying 4-star accommodation.

Each of our seven luxurious and beautifully appointed bungalows is specifically designed to offer you the very highest levels of comfort and is equipped with air-conditioning, bathrooms, and open fires.

Our two apartment buildings will enable you to discover Inverdoorn with your families. Apartment building 1 has four double bedrooms as well as a bathroom and lounge. Apartment building 2 has three double bedrooms, bathroom, and a family suite, as well as a kitchen and lounge area.

The Inverdoorn Game Reserve safaris are of the highest possible quality and diversity. All our guides are professionally qualified. Our 4X4 Land Rover Safari vehicles are ideal for getting you as close as possible to the animals.

On our daytime safaris you will be able to admire at extremely close quarters the herds of buffalo, giraffe, zebra, lechwe, and other rare antelopes, and of course, our splendid rhinoceroses.

On the evening safari, you will be served with an aperitif at the highest point on the reserve, at that special moment when the setting sun floods the sky before gently sinking behind the mountains, when the animals come to slake their thirst in the lake in the calm and quiet of the evening…

The pleasure of sharing a drink, meeting up, chatting and relaxing under the stars around our "BRAAÏ"……an unforgettable moment of happiness!

For seminars, our conference room (large enough for 30 guests) is fully equipped.

Take a stroll through our African treasure box and make your souvenir purchases to remind you of your stay as well as gift purchases that will be sure to delight your friends and family on your return.

Our quad bikes will offer you one and half hours of playing pleasure in the Karoo desert.

For more information Tel (021) 464 4266 (7 days a week – 07h00 – 23h00) or E-mail: daytours@aecpt.co.za or visit their web site www.daytours.co.za

Inverdoorn
Game Reserve

Ceres - Western Cape
South Africa

P.O. Box 327, Ceres
Tel: +27 23 316 1264 • Fax: +27 23 312 2187
Email: invdoorn@iafrica.com
www.inverdoorn

BARTHOLOMEUS KLIP FARMHOUSE

Bartholomeus Klip is unique. There are only five bedrooms in this small hotel, the original homestead on a large private estate which is both a working wheat and sheep farm and a nature reserve with a spectacular mountain backdrop.

Here, in this unexplored region only an hour by car from Cape Town's international airport, you can feel part of the peaceful life of rural South Africa and its clean crisp air and star-filled night skies. The 10 000 acre fynbos nature reserve is part of the Cape Floral Kingdom, the world's smallest, but the richest in species for its size. It has been declared a National Heritage Site in recognition of its importance as the last major habitat of the geometric tortoise, one of the world's rarest reptiles.

The Victorian homestead has been meticulously renovated, and the fine fabrics and family antiques make you feel as if you are a guest in someone's much-loved home. Rose-filled gardens and ancient oaks surround the house, with benches tucked away in quiet places perfect for absorbing the peace and relaxed atmosphere. Nearby, the deck of the salt-water swimming pool is ideal for sunbathing or sundowners, and the boathouse, where the wonderful brunches are served, has a spectacular view over the dam.

Comfort is the keynote in the bedrooms: specially made pure cotton bedding, luxurious toiletries, towelling gowns. No TVs to spoil the country feeling (although there are two in the main rooms for essential viewing).

The food, in the French tradition but with a local flavour, is one of the highlights of a stay at the farm. Tea is a serious affair, served daily and the selection changes daily. Brunch at the boathouse, with a bountifully laden table. Fill your plate and take it outside to the deck overlooking the dam, then drink in the view of the mountains opposite with your coffee.

The farm is surrounded by the famous winelands of the Western Cape, so the wine list reflects the achievements of our neighbours. We will be delighted to discuss your choice with you and give you our recommendations.

A stay at here is a wonderful opportunity for the energetic, who can walk or hike in the reserve, ride mountain bikes through the wheatfields, go windsurfing, birdwatching, boating on the dam or inspect the farming operations. For the more laid-back, there are loungers in the extensive gardens, at the edge of the dam or on the deck of the salt water swimming pool: read, relax, or even fall asleep.

Afternoon game drives end with sundowners in the veld: only an hour away from Cape Town, and you feel you are in Africa! The animals are easy to spot in the low-growing fynbos, especially since there are more than 500 head of game.

The reserve in the springtime: 'flower heaven', as one guest called it, with sheets of colour and a myriad of different bulbs, orchids and daisies to be discovered on closer inspection.

More than 160 species of birds have been identified at Bartholomeus Klip, among them the endangered blue crane and the African fish eagle as well as the ostrich, frequently seen in the reserve.

Among the animal species at Bartholomeus Klip are eland, springbuck, bontebok, wildebeest, both blue and black gemsbok, red hartebeest, baboon, bat-eared fox, jackal, lynx, Cape fox and leopard.

Bartholomeus Klip

F A R M H O U S E

Bartholomeus Klip   022-448 1820
Email: www.parksgroup.co.za

The Suite

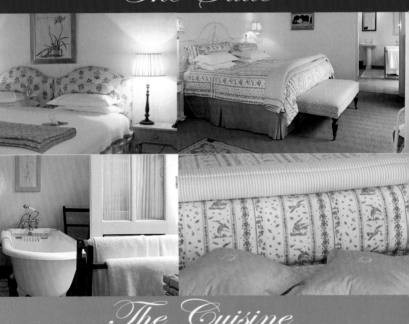

The Cuisine

The Farm

Speed-trap Camera Shoot Out

Cape Town Newspaper Extract...

Officers were stunned when at 3am on Sunday morning, a man in a double cab bakkie (pick up truck), drove up to a speed camera, stopped in front of it, took a rifle from his back seat and pumped three bullets in the camera.

Questions Overheard from Naive Visitors:

"Does the river always flow this way?"

"Do giraffes hunt in packs?"

"Are there lions in the streets?"

"Do you have many tigers?"

Giraffes

In the Mall

THINGS YOU SHOULD KNOW BUT NOBODY TOLD YOU

EATING & DRINKING

You are expected to tip waitrons 10-15% of your bill.

Waitrons do not wait until everyone has finished eating before clearing plates, they whip each one away as the diner takes his last bite.

If you are invited to a braai (barbecue,) you are expected to bring your own meat and drinks (and maybe a salad).

There are strict anti-smoking laws for public places, which most people respect.

Restaurants often close on Sunday and Monday nights.

Cape Town's tap water is fine to drink.

BANKS & MONEY

You can draw money from bank cash machine with overseas bank and credit cards, so don't forget your code.

You don't need to change money before arriving, you can do this at the airport Bureau de Change.

Banks are open weekdays from 9.30am to 3.30pm and on Saturday mornings until 11.30 am.

DRIVING

South African drivers are notoriously bad, especially the public taxi-bus drivers, so take good care.

Drinking and Driving is illegal but many people do it anyway.

You cannot pay for petrol with a credit card, you will need cash.

There are no taxi cabs driving the streets waiting for you to hail them, you should organise one in advance.

SHOPPING

Non residents can claim back VAT when leaving the country. Keep all receipts and be prepared to show some items at the airport before check-in.

By 1pm on Saturdays all high street shops are closed (except in larger malls and V&A Waterfront).

Shops are not allowed to sell alcohol on a Sunday.

SOUTHERN HEMISPHERE ODDITIES

If you are from the northern hemisphere, your sense of direction will probably be 180 degrees out (as the sun arcs in the opposite way and confuses your instinct).

If buying a property you want it to face north to catch the sun.

South of the equator the water goes down the plug hole clockwise.

At night look out for the Southern Cross pointing the way south.

In African custom the man enters a room first.

African Travel Quote

Visitor, *"What kind of fish is it"?*

Fisherman speaking little English, *"It is a nugget fish."*

Hout Bay Fisherman

When English is spoken by Africans, it is usually as a second language. This can result in some unusual and beautiful uses of English. The extract below is from a keen applicant requesting a job:

Dear Sir,

I am motivated and ambitious, and ability and stability has caused my pen to dance across this paper to ask for a job quite unexpectedly.

SOUTHERN TIP OF AFRICA

It is a common mistake to attribute Cape Point as the southern tip of Africa. This honour actually goes to Cape Agulhas, a couple of hours drive to the east. Both Capes are famous for their large and powerful lighthouses, but even these have not been able to prevent many ships from disaster. Dangerous submerged rocks and strong currents with swells whipped up by high winds, have claimed the lives of many unsuspecting passengers and crew. Cape Point is the most easily accessible and interesting of the two to visit, but the stark beauty and famous lighthouse museum of Cape Agulhas attract numerous visitors along the lonely road to L'Agulhas. For more information see our Lighthouse feature.

Sport

Province - Western Province Rugby Team based in Newlands

Bafana Bafana - SA's Football Team

Laduma - enthusiastic Xhosa expression when a goal is scored

Vuvuzela - long thin plastic horn blown by soccer supporters (making a terrible noise)

TALK LIKE A LOCAL

Capetonians have developed a style of English all of their own, much of which may baffle the visitor. The following words may help you decipher what the conversation is all about and might assist you in getting to your destination:

CONVERSATION

Howzit? -	hello how are you?
Lekker -	good, nice, great,
Jol -	have fun
Kief -	cool, good
Siff -	horrible, yuk
Skinnering -	gossiping
What's Your Pluck -	what gives?
Bliksem -	hit
Donner -	serious thump
Moer -	beat up
Oke or 'O' -	man, bloke
Broer -	brother, mate,
Lanie -	smart, posh
Braai -	barbecue
Takkie -	training shoes
Yes No -	standard answer usually meaning Yes

VAGARIES OF TIME

Just now - referring to some time later that day (if you are lucky)

Now - means soon but not at this exact moment

XHOSA GREETINGS

Injani -	Hello
Molo -	Hello Good Morning
Enkosi -	Thankyou
Goodbye -	Hamba kakuhle

TRAVEL

Uitgang -	exit
Stad -	city
Gevaarlik -	Danger
Lughawe -	Airport
Bakkie -	pick up truck
Robot -	traffic light

FOOD

Bobotie - curried mince topped with savoury egg custard, and coconut, banana & chutney sambals

Smoorsnoek - smoked snoek mush

Dom Pedro - a yummy mixture of ice cream blended with Kahlua or whisky, which is a cross between an after dinner drink and a desert

Rooibos Tea - locally grown caffeine-free herbal tea

Dop - drink

City Centre

Kopanong Restaurant

WOULD YOU REALLY WANT TO LEARN ENGLISH FROM A SOUTH AFRICAN?

Consider the following typical South African expressions (with thanks to Cape Town Tourism's Survival Guide for Visitors to South Africa)…

IZIT? Derived from the two words "is" and "it", it can be used when you have nothing to contribute. If someone tells you that, "The Russians will succeed in their bid for capitalism once they adopt a work ethic and respect for private ownership". It is appropriate to respond by saying: "Izit?"

JAWELLNOFINE Another conversation fallback word. Derived from the four words "yes", "well", "no" and "fine", it means roughly "how about that". If your bank manager tells you your account is overdrawn, you could confidently say, "jawellnofine"!

VROT (pron. Frott). A wonderful Afrikaans word meaning rotten or putrid. It is used by all language groups to describe anything they really don't like. Most commonly food, but a pair of smelly takkies (sneakers) can be termed vrot. So could a movie, as in this review headline: "Slick Flick, Vrot Plot". Needless to say, the headline was enjoyed more than the movie.

NO. No has many meanings in South Africa, other than the opposite of "yes." Your host at the braai (barbeque) is likely to say: "No, I see your plate is empty." Or in a shoestore you may reply to an offer of assistance with: "No, I'm looking for some tackies (running shoes) - effectively meaning "yes."

LEKKER. This word is used to describe virtually anything pleasant, be it food, the weather, people, a place, an activity or even to add weight to a description such as "lekker dronk". Lekker is scattered into the conversation at any opportunity.

The sentence will become clear after reading the rest of this page:

'Howzit broer' (how are you my friend) could be answered with 'Kief man' (fine thank you) or even 'Lekker jol' (very nice having fun), but if some oke threatens to donner you then I would take to your takkies (trainers), jump into your bakkie (pick up truck) and get the hell out of there. On the other hand you could just finish that last dop (drink), bliksem (thump) the troublemaker and carry on with your pluck (having fun), note several expressions for having fun!

V&A Waterfront

South African Sports Fans

Situated in Bellville, virtually on the N1 highway, this 24 hour pharmacy has a sister and pharmacist on duty through the night. Well known for its low prices and excellent service, M-Kem has it all, be it medicines, gifts, perfumes, sports supplements, homeopathic preparations etc. and each department is run by an expert in their field.

Tel: +27 (0) 21 948 5706
Durban Road, Bellville
www.gopassport.com

This world-class, state of the art business centre, providing business services to international guests, exhibitors and delegates at the Cape Town International Convention Centre. Services include printing, photocopying, faxing, binding, laminating, typing, email, self-service internet, laptop zone, international telephonic service, international courier service, short term mobile, phone rentals, sale of business accessories, forex service and travel desk.

Tel: +27 (0) 21 418 5881
Cape Town International Convention Centre,
1 Lower Long Street, Cape Town
www.gopassport.com

PARTHENON DRY CLEANERS

• Hand-finished dry cleaning • Specialist dry cleaning • Ball gown and silk finishing • Shirt service • Shoe repair • Laundry Service • Suede and leather • Invisible mending • Alterations • Curtain service • Rugs

Tel: +27 (0) 21 689 8313
A18 Station Road, Rondebosch
Tel: +27 (0) 21 465 2480
Gardens Centre, Buitenkant St, Gardens
Tel: +27 (0) 21 910 3006
Tyger Manor Shopping Centre, Willie van Shuur Road, Bellville
www.gopassport.com

Discover Blue Buyou, Cape Town's unique shopping experience and the only Tour Operator specializing in shopping. We tailor-make tour's around individual or group interests, introducing you to some of Cape Town's " hidden treasures" including Conference and Corporate Gifting.
Jewellery • Leather • Fashion • Décor • Textiles • Artworks • Antiques • Books • Wine AND MUCH MORE!

Tel: +27 (0) 21 671 1763
Mobile: +27 (0) 83 293 6555
www.gopassport.com

Land a gRAND total deal

- Highly competitive exchange rates
- We exchange all brands of travellers' cheques
- No commission charges when exchanging American Express Travellers Cheques
- We exchange cash in over 35 different currencies
- Major branches: Camps Bay - The Promenade, Canal Walk, Cape Town Tourism Centre, Cavendish Square, Fishhoek Town Square, Gardens Shopping Centre, Rheede Street Mall, Somerset Mall, Stellenbosch - Bird Street, Thibault Square, Tygervalley Centre, V&A Waterfront.

AMERICAN EXPRESS ®

Foreign Exchange

There's nothing foreign about us.

★ *Undertine* 2198

POLICE:..10111

HOSPITALS:

Cape Town Medi-Clinic.................................021-464-5500
Constantiaberg Medi-Clinic..........................021-799-2911
Durbanville Medi-Clinic...............................021-980-2100
Louis Leipoldt Medi-Clinic............................021-957-6000
Milnerton Medi-Clinic..................................021-529-9000
Panorama Medi-Clinic.................................021-938-2111

Travel Medicine:

Medi-Travel International..............................021-419-1888
City Park...021-480-6111
Kingsbury...021-670-4000
Red Cross Children....................................021-658-5111

LOST / STOLEN CREDIT CARDS:

American Express......................................0860-003-768
Diners Club...0800-112-017
Master...0800-020-600

LOST / STOLEN BANK CARDS:

ABSA...0800-111-155
First National...0800-110-132
Nedbank..0800-110-929
Permanent..0800-110-929
Standard..0800-020-600

TELEPHONE DIRECTORIES:

International Inquiries....................................0903
Domestic Inquiries......................................1023
Time..1026
Weather...082-162
Vodacom..021-440-8211
MTN..021-425-0500
Cell C..021-461-7306

CAPE TOWN INTERNATIONAL AIRPORT:

General Info...021-937-1200
Arrivals/Departures.....................................021-937-1200

Other airports:

Bloemfontein Int.......................................051-433-2901
Johannesburg Int.......................................011-921-6911
Durban Int'l...031-451-6666
East London Int...043-706-0306
George Airport..044-876-9310
Port Elizabeth Int.......................................041-507-7348
Windhoek Eros Airport (ERS...........................+264-61-996600

AIRLINES:

Air Canada..021-422-3232
Air France...011-770-1671
Air Mauritius...021-421-6294
Air Namibia...021-936-2755
BA Comair...021-936-9000
British Airways..021-936-9000
Civair...021-934-4488
Delta...021-425-7447
Egypt Air...021-421-7503
LTU Int Airways...021-936-1190
Lufthansa..0861-842-538
KLM..021-934-3495
Kulula.com...0861-585-852
Malaysia Airlines..021-419-7607
SAA..021-936-1111
Swiss..0860-040-506
Singapore Airlines......................................021-674-0601
United..021-422-3232
Virgin Atlantic...021-936-8000

FOREIGN CONSULATES:

Argentina	021-439-0527
Austria	021-421-1440/1
Chile	021-421-2344/6
Denmark	021-715-7019
France	021-423-1575
Germany	021-405-3000
Greece	021-424-8160
Italy	021-487-3900
Japan	021-425-1695
Netherlands	021-421-5660/1
New Zealand	021-696-8561
Norway	021-418-1276
Portugal	021-418-0081/1
Spain	021-422-2415
Sweden	021-418-1276
Switzerland	021-418-3665
United Kingdom	021-405-2400
USA	021-421-4351
Uruguay	021-425-1847

CINEMAS:

Grand West Casino	021-505-7777
Labia	021-424-5927
Ster Kinekor	082-16789

    Bayside Mall
    Blue Route Mall
    Cavendish Square
    Longbeach Mall
    Kenilworth Centre
    Somerset Mall
    Stellenbosch
    Tygervalley Centre
    Cavendish Square
    V&A Waterfront

Cinema Nouveau	083-16789
Nu Metro	0861-100-220

    V&A Waterfront
    N1 City
    Canal Walk

Cinema Prive	0861-100-220

TRANSPORT:

Airport Shuttle	021-934-0407
Magic Shuttle	021-934-5455
City Hopper	021-934-4440
Public Transport Inquiries	0800-656-463
Blue Train	021-449-2672
Greyhound	021-505-6363
Translux	021-449-3333
Inter Cape	021-380-4400

OTHER SERVICES:

Cape Film Office	021-483-9060
Cellurent	021-418-5656
Computicket	0861-100-220
Mr. Delivery	021-439-5647
Cape Town Events	021-487-4810
Louis Leipoldt Medi-Clinic	021-957-6000
Milnerton Medi-Clinic	021-529-9000
Panorama Medi-Clinic	021-938-2111

Travel Medicine:

Medi-Travel International	021-419-1888
City Park	021-480-6111
Kingsbury	021-670-4000
Red Cross Children	021-658-5111

CAPE TOWN VISITOR INFORMATION CENTRES:

Blaauwberg Tourism Bureau.............................021-557-860

Canal Walk...021-555-310

C'Town Int'l Convention Centre.......................021-483-941

C'Town Information Centre.............................021-422-461

CT Int'l Airport.....................................021-934-415

City Centre..021-426-426

Durbanville..021-970-317

Fish Hoek..021-782-453

Gugulethu..021-637-844

Hout Bay...021-790-126

Khayelitsha..021-364-966

Kraaifontein...021-980-611

Muizenberg...021-788-619

Noordhoek..021-789-281

Table View...021-557-8600

Tygerberg..021-914-178

Tyger Valley...021-914-182

Simon's Town...021-786-579

Southern Suburbs.....................................021-762-068

V & A Waterfront.....................................021-405-4500

REGIONAL TOURISM BUREAUS:

Helderberg...021-851-402

Stellenbosch...021-883-358

Franschoek...021-876-360

George...044-801-929

Knysna...044-382-696

Plettenberg..044-533-406

Mossel Bay...044-691-2202

Sun City Information.................................014-557-154

Kruger Park Reservations.............................012-428-9111

SOUTH AFRICAN TOURISM:

Head Office, South Africa............................011-895-3000

South Africa Hotline.................................083-123-2345

Australia..+61-292615000

France...+33-145610197

Germany..+49-699291290

Italy..+39-243911765

Japan..+81-334787601

Netherlands..+31-204714656

United Kingdom.......................................+44-2089719364

U.S.A..+91-2127302929

Other tourism authorities:

Johannesburg...011-327-2000

Namibian - in Cape Town..............................021-422-3298

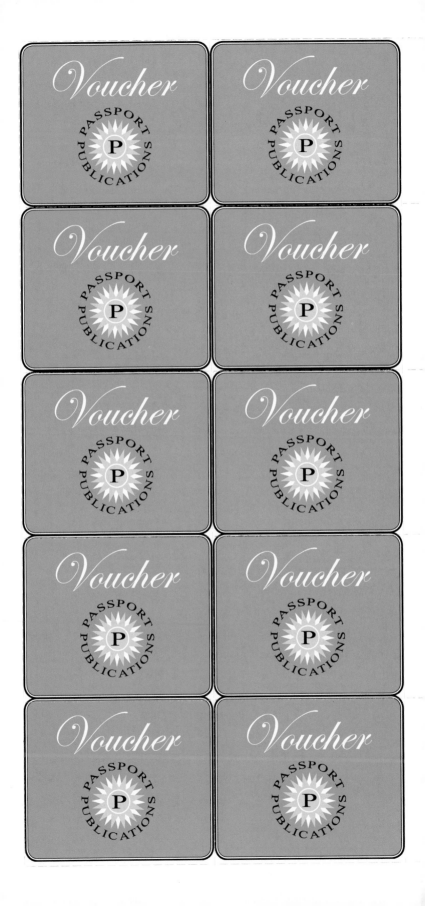

DIVA ITALIAN RESTAURANT

15% Discount on meals for groups of 4 or more excluding Fr & Sat nights

See our listing on page 172 of this guide

1. The voucher is valid until 28 February 2007
2. Only one voucher may be redeemed per booking / purchase
3. Vouchers are only redeemable on standard pricing and do not apply on any products or services that might be already discounted or on special
4. All vouchers must be handed to the vendor on redemption

www.gopassport.com

AFRICAN EAGLE

15% Discount all day tours booked

See our listing on page 113 of this guide

1. The voucher is valid until 28 February 2007
2. Only one voucher may be redeemed per booking / purchase
3. Vouchers are only redeemable on standard pricing and do not apply on any products or services that might be already discounted or on special
4. All vouchers must be handed to the vendor on redemption

www.gopassport.com

SCAR HAIR

15% Discount

See our listing on page 239 of this guide

1. The voucher is valid until 28 February 2007
2. Only one voucher may be redeemed per booking / purchase
3. Vouchers are only redeemable on standard pricing and do not apply on any products or services that might be already discounted or on special
4. All vouchers must be handed to the vendor on redemption

www.gopassport.com

PLACE ON THE BAY

15% Discount on accommodation

See our listing on page 143 of this guide

1. The voucher is valid until 28 February 2007
2. Only one voucher may be redeemed per booking / purchase
3. Vouchers are only redeemable on standard pricing and do not apply on any products or services that might be already discounted or on special
4. All vouchers must be handed to the vendor on redemption

www.gopassport.com

WHITE SHARK PROJECTS

15% Discount on dives

See our listing on page 231 of this guide

1. The voucher is valid until 28 February 2007
2. Only one voucher may be redeemed per booking / purchase
3. Vouchers are only redeemable on standard pricing and do not apply on any products or services that might be already discounted or on special
4. All vouchers must be handed to the vendor on redemption

www.gopassport.com

JUST MEN

15% Discount

See our listing on page 201 of this guide

1. The voucher is valid until 28 February 2007
2. Only one voucher may be redeemed per booking / purchase
3. Vouchers are only redeemable on standard pricing and do not apply on any products or services that might be already discounted or on special
4. All vouchers must be handed to the vendor on redemption

www.gopassport.com

NATURE DISCOVERY TOURS

15% Discount on all tours booked for 6 people weekdays

See our listing on page 231 of this guide

1. The voucher is valid until 28 February 2007
2. Only one voucher may be redeemed per booking / purchase
3. Vouchers are only redeemable on standard pricing and do not apply on any products or services that might be already discounted or on special
4. All vouchers must be handed to the vendor on redemption

www.gopassport.com

GLEN AVON

20% Discount on B&B accommodation between May & September

See our listing on page 138 of this guide

1. The voucher is valid until 28 February 2007
2. Only one voucher may be redeemed per booking / purchase
3. Vouchers are only redeemable on standard pricing and do not apply on any products or services that might be already discounted or on special
4. All vouchers must be handed to the vendor on redemption

www.gopassport.com

KIROV DESIGN STUDIO

R500 Discount on purchase over R4000

See our listing on page 214 of this guide

1. The voucher is valid until 28 February 2007
2. Only one voucher may be redeemed per booking / purchase
3. Vouchers are only redeemable on standard pricing and do not apply on any products or services that might be already discounted or on special
4. All vouchers must be handed to the vendor on redemption

www.gopassport.com

BUTTERFLY WORLD

30% Discount on entry + 10% on meals

See our listing on page 96 of this guide

1. The voucher is valid until 28 February 2007
2. Only one voucher may be redeemed per booking / purchase
3. Vouchers are only redeemable on standard pricing and do not apply on any products or services that might be already discounted or on special
4. All vouchers must be handed to the vendor on redemption

www.gopassport.com

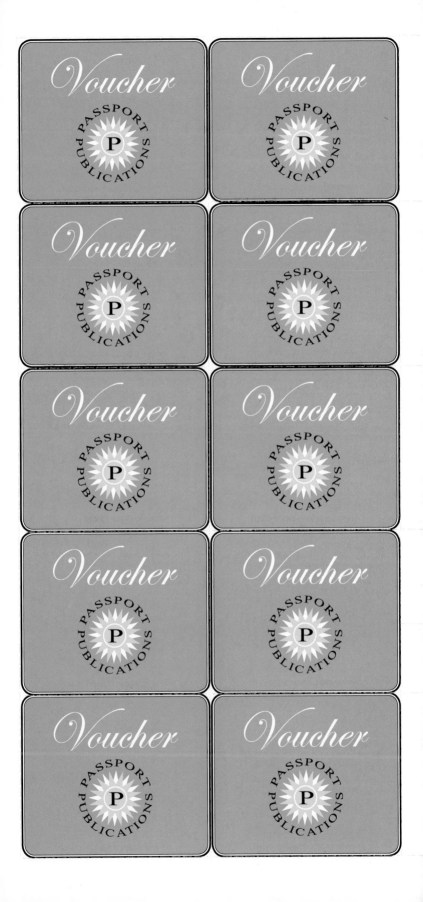

ACTIVE AFRICA

15% Discount all tours booked

See our listing on page 110 of this guide

1. The voucher is valid until 28 February 2007
2. Only one voucher may be redeemed per booking / purchase
3. Vouchers are only redeemable on standard pricing and do not apply on any products or services that might be already discounted or on special
4. All vouchers must be handed to the vendor on redemption

www.gopassport.com

TONG LOK

15% Discount on all meals

See our listing on page 167 of this guide

1. The voucher is valid until 28 February 2007
2. Only one voucher may be redeemed per booking / purchase
3. Vouchers are only redeemable on standard pricing and do not apply on any products or services that might be already discounted or on special
4. All vouchers must be handed to the vendor on redemption

www.gopassport.com

ROSSOUW ART GALLERY

10% - 15% Discount

See our listing on page 217 of this guide

1. The voucher is valid until 28 February 2007
2. Only one voucher may be redeemed per booking / purchase
3. Vouchers are only redeemable on standard pricing and do not apply on any products or services that might be already discounted or on special
4. All vouchers must be handed to the vendor on redemption

www.gopassport.com

ECHO BAY

20% Discount on accommodation bookings of 7 days or more

See our listing on page 143 of this guide

1. The voucher is valid until 28 February 2007
2. Only one voucher may be redeemed per booking / purchase
3. Vouchers are only redeemable on standard pricing and do not apply on any products or services that might be already discounted or on special
4. All vouchers must be handed to the vendor on redemption

www.gopassport.com

HOTEL LE VENDOME

25% Discount on B&B bookings

See our listing on page 154 of this guide

1. The voucher is valid until 28 February 2007
2. Only one voucher may be redeemed per booking / purchase
3. Vouchers are only redeemable on standard pricing and do not apply on any products or services that might be already discounted or on special
4. All vouchers must be handed to the vendor on redemption

www.gopassport.com

GRASS ROUTE TOWNSHIP TOURS

15% Discount on all tours booked

See our listing on page 110 of this guide

1. The voucher is valid until 28 February 2007
2. Only one voucher may be redeemed per booking / purchase
3. Vouchers are only redeemable on standard pricing and do not apply on any products or services that might be already discounted or on special
4. All vouchers must be handed to the vendor on redemption

www.gopassport.com

CARMANIA

15% Discount on car hire excluding insurance and other charges

See our listing on page 28 of this guide

1. The voucher is valid until 28 February 2007
2. Only one voucher may be redeemed per booking / purchase
3. Vouchers are only redeemable on standard pricing and do not apply on any products or services that might be already discounted or on special
4. All vouchers must be handed to the vendor on redemption

www.gopassport.com

METROPOLE HOTEL

FREE wine with any meal

See our listing on page 155 of this guide

1. The voucher is valid until 28 February 2007
2. Only one voucher may be redeemed per booking / purchase
3. Vouchers are only redeemable on standard pricing and do not apply on any products or services that might be already discounted or on special
4. All vouchers must be handed to the vendor on redemption

www.gopassport.com

ZERO 932

1 Cocktail in our monk bar

See our listing on page 171 of this guide

1. The voucher is valid until 28 February 2007
2. Only one voucher may be redeemed per booking / purchase
3. Vouchers are only redeemable on standard pricing and do not apply on any products or services that might be already discounted or on special
4. All vouchers must be handed to the vendor on redemption

www.gopassport.com

ALPHA DIVE

15% Discount on diving courses

See our listing on page 231 of this guide

1. The voucher is valid until 28 February 2007
2. Only one voucher may be redeemed per booking / purchase
3. Vouchers are only redeemable on standard pricing and do not apply on any products or services that might be already discounted or on special
4. All vouchers must be handed to the vendor on redemption

www.gopassport.com

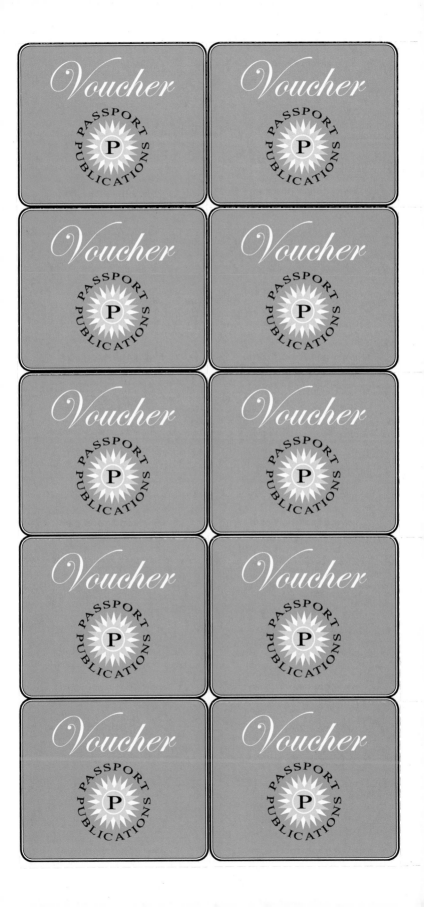

CAPE CAPERS TOWNSHIP TOURS

10% - 15% Discount all tours booked
See our listing on page 110 of this guide

1. The voucher is valid until 28 February 2007
2. Only one voucher may be redeemed per booking / purchase
3. Vouchers are only redeemable on standard pricing and do not apply on any products or services that might be already discounted or on special
4. All vouchers must be handed to the vendor on redemption

www.gopassport.com

BLOEMENDAL

15% Discount on meals for 10 or less people
See our listing on page 166 of this guide

1. The voucher is valid until 28 February 2007
2. Only one voucher may be redeemed per booking / purchase
3. Vouchers are only redeemable on standard pricing and do not apply on any products or services that might be already discounted or on special
4. All vouchers must be handed to the vendor on redemption

www.gopassport.com

CARCHELE SPA BEAUTY

15% Discount on treatments
See our listing on page 238 of this guide

1. The voucher is valid until 28 February 2007
2. Only one voucher may be redeemed per booking / purchase
3. Vouchers are only redeemable on standard pricing and do not apply on any products or services that might be already discounted or on special
4. All vouchers must be handed to the vendor on redemption

www.gopassport.com

AROKAN CAR HIRE

10% Discount on car hire
See our listing on page 111 of this guide

1. The voucher is valid until 28 February 2007
2. Only one voucher may be redeemed per booking / purchase
3. Vouchers are only redeemable on standard pricing and do not apply on any products or services that might be already discounted or on special
4. All vouchers must be handed to the vendor on redemption

www.gopassport.com

INVERDOORN

10% Discount
See our listing on page 291 of this guide

1. The voucher is valid until 28 February 2007
2. Only one voucher may be redeemed per booking / purchase
3. Vouchers are only redeemable on standard pricing and do not apply on any products or services that might be already discounted or on special
4. All vouchers must be handed to the vendor on redemption

www.gopassport.com

ROSEDENE

15% Between May & Sept incl. breakfast & Champagne, 2 movie tickets
See our listing on page 139 of this guide

1. The voucher is valid until 28 February 2007
2. Only one voucher may be redeemed per booking / purchase
3. Vouchers are only redeemable on standard pricing and do not apply on any products or services that might be already discounted or on special
4. All vouchers must be handed to the vendor on redemption

www.gopassport.com

MONKEY VALLEY

15% Discount on accommodation or meals
See our listing on page 138 of this guide

1. The voucher is valid until 28 February 2007
2. Only one voucher may be redeemed per booking / purchase
3. Vouchers are only redeemable on standard pricing and do not apply on any products or services that might be already discounted or on special
4. All vouchers must be handed to the vendor on redemption

www.gopassport.com

ECO TOURS SA

15% - 20% Discount all tours booked
See our listing on page 108 of this guide

1. The voucher is valid until 28 February 2007
2. Only one voucher may be redeemed per booking / purchase
3. Vouchers are only redeemable on standard pricing and do not apply on any products or services that might be already discounted or on special
4. All vouchers must be handed to the vendor on redemption

www.gopassport.com

WILDTHING ADVENTURES

15% Discount
See our listing on page 230 of this guide

1. The voucher is valid until 28 February 2007
2. Only one voucher may be redeemed per booking / purchase
3. Vouchers are only redeemable on standard pricing and do not apply on any products or services that might be already discounted or on special
4. All vouchers must be handed to the vendor on redemption

www.gopassport.com

GOLD DUST

15% Discount
See our listing on page 214 of this guide

1. The voucher is valid until 28 February 2007
2. Only one voucher may be redeemed per booking / purchase
3. Vouchers are only redeemable on standard pricing and do not apply on any products or services that might be already discounted or on special
4. All vouchers must be handed to the vendor on redemption

www.gopassport.com

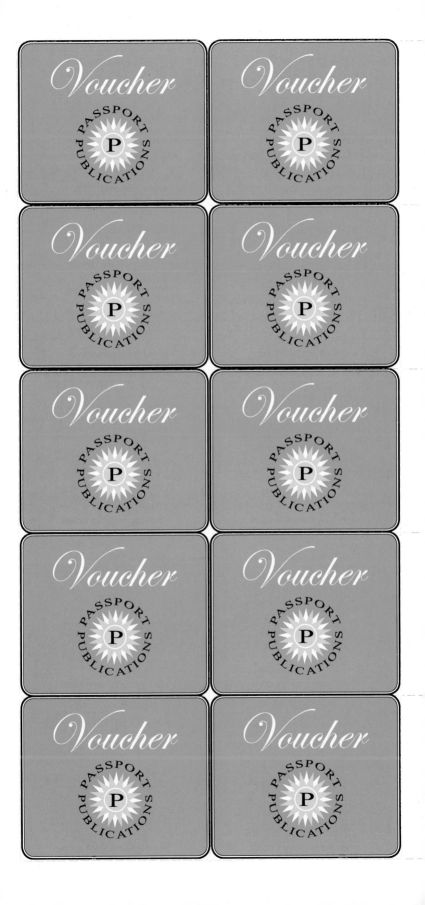

AQUILA

10% Discount on direct bookings

See our listing on page 289 of this guide

1. The voucher is valid until 28 February 2007
2. Only one voucher may be redeemed per booking / purchase
3. Vouchers are only redeemable on standard pricing and do not apply on any products or services that might be already discounted or on special
4. All vouchers must be handed to the vendor on redemption

www.gopassport.com

NAC MAKANA AIR CHART

10% Discount on trips

See our listing on page 110 of this guide

1. The voucher is valid until 28 February 2007
2. Only one voucher may be redeemed per booking / purchase
3. Vouchers are only redeemable on standard pricing and do not apply on any products or services that might be already discounted or on special
4. All vouchers must be handed to the vendor on redemption

www.gopassport.com

MARIMBA

15% Discount on food only

See our listing on page 179 of this guide

1. The voucher is valid until 28 February 2007
2. Only one voucher may be redeemed per booking / purchase
3. Vouchers are only redeemable on standard pricing and do not apply on any products or services that might be already discounted or on special
4. All vouchers must be handed to the vendor on redemption

www.gopassport.com

MONKEY TOWN

15% Discount on entry

See our listing on page 96 of this guide

1. The voucher is valid until 28 February 2007
2. Only one voucher may be redeemed per booking / purchase
3. Vouchers are only redeemable on standard pricing and do not apply on any products or services that might be already discounted or on special
4. All vouchers must be handed to the vendor on redemption

www.gopassport.com

QUINTESSENTIAL TOURS

15% Discount on direct bookings of 4 days +

See our listing on page 108 of this guide

1. The voucher is valid until 28 February 2007
2. Only one voucher may be redeemed per booking / purchase
3. Vouchers are only redeemable on standard pricing and do not apply on any products or services that might be already discounted or on special
4. All vouchers must be handed to the vendor on redemption

www.gopassport.com

CRUISE SUB AQUA

15% Discount on cruises and tours

See our listing on page 230 of this guide

1. The voucher is valid until 28 February 2007
2. Only one voucher may be redeemed per booking / purchase
3. Vouchers are only redeemable on standard pricing and do not apply on any products or services that might be already discounted or on special
4. All vouchers must be handed to the vendor on redemption

www.gopassport.com

AFTON GROVE

20% Discount on accommodation of 3 days+

See our listing on page 139 of this guide

1. The voucher is valid until 28 February 2007
2. Only one voucher may be redeemed per booking / purchase
3. Vouchers are only redeemable on standard pricing and do not apply on any products or services that might be already discounted or on special
4. All vouchers must be handed to the vendor on redemption

www.gopassport.com

SALON ANNIQUE

With each purchase of R500 receive R100 products FREE or a skin analysis

See our listing on page 235 of this guide

1. The voucher is valid until 28 February 2007
2. Only one voucher may be redeemed per booking / purchase
3. Vouchers are only redeemable on standard pricing and do not apply on any products or services that might be already discounted or on special
4. All vouchers must be handed to the vendor on redemption

www.gopassport.com

NICHE

10% Discount

See our listing on page 202 of this guide

1. The voucher is valid until 28 February 2007
2. Only one voucher may be redeemed per booking / purchase
3. Vouchers are only redeemable on standard pricing and do not apply on any products or services that might be already discounted or on special
4. All vouchers must be handed to the vendor on redemption

www.gopassport.com

SAVOY CABBAGE

1 Glass of Champagne with each 2 course meal

See our listing on page 169 of this guide

1. The voucher is valid until 28 February 2007
2. Only one voucher may be redeemed per booking / purchase
3. Vouchers are only redeemable on standard pricing and do not apply on any products or services that might be already discounted or on special
4. All vouchers must be handed to the vendor on redemption

www.gopassport.com

NOTES

NOTES

....

....

....

....

....

....

....

....

....

....

....

....

....

....

....

....

....

....

....

....

....

....

....

....

....

....

....

....